Mark Baker is one of Australia's most experienced journalists. He is a former Senior Editor of *The Age*, Editor of *The Canberra Times* and Managing Editor (National) of Fairfax Media. During 13 years as a foreign correspondent for Fairfax, News Corp and *The Financial Times* he had postings in China, Hong Kong, Thailand, Singapore and Papua New Guinea. He covered the wars in Iraq and Afghanistan and was wounded while covering the civil war in Bougainville in the early 1990s. He has also served as Political Editor and Canberra Bureau Chief of *The Age*. Mark Baker is now publisher of the independent online magazine *Inside Story* and author of several books.

Also by Mark Baker

Media Legends: Journalists Who Helped Shape Australia,
Co-editor

*Phillip Schuler: The Remarkable Life of One of Australia's
Greatest War Correspondents*

*The Emperor's Grace: Untold Stories of the Australians
Enslaved in Japan during World War II*

BUCKHAM'S BOMBERS

THE AUSTRALIAN AIRMEN WHO HUNTED HITLER'S DEADLIEST BATTLESHIP

MARK BAKER

ALLEN&UNWIN

SYDNEY·MELBOURNE·AUCKLAND·LONDON

Allen & Unwin
Cammeraygal Country
83 Alexander Street
Crows Nest NSW 2065
Australia
Phone: (61 2) 8425 0100
Email: info@allenandunwin.com
Web: www.allenandunwin.com

Allen & Unwin acknowledges the Traditional Owners of the Country on which we live and work. We pay our respects to all Aboriginal and Torres Strait Islander Elders, past and present.

 A catalogue record for this book is available from the National Library of Australia

NATIONAL LIBRARY OF AUSTRALIA

ISBN 978 1 76147 118 6

Map by Guy Holt
Index by Puddingburn Publishing Services Pty Ltd
Set in 12.5/18 pt Adobe Caslon Pro by Midland Typesetters, Australia
Printed and bound in Australia by the Opus Group

10 9 8 7 6 5 4 3 2

'With the flair of a writer and the skill of a journalist, Mark Baker has delivered a story alive in both colour and character. *Buckham's Bombers* not only brings to life a brilliant yet forgotten feat of arms of the World War II air war but also paints a picture of the complex and controversial organisation that was Bomber Command itself, as well as the often short lives of the men who flew and fought in her name with skill and unbelievable courage. A terrific read.'

Michael Veitch, author of *44 Days* and *Australia's Secret Army*

Contents

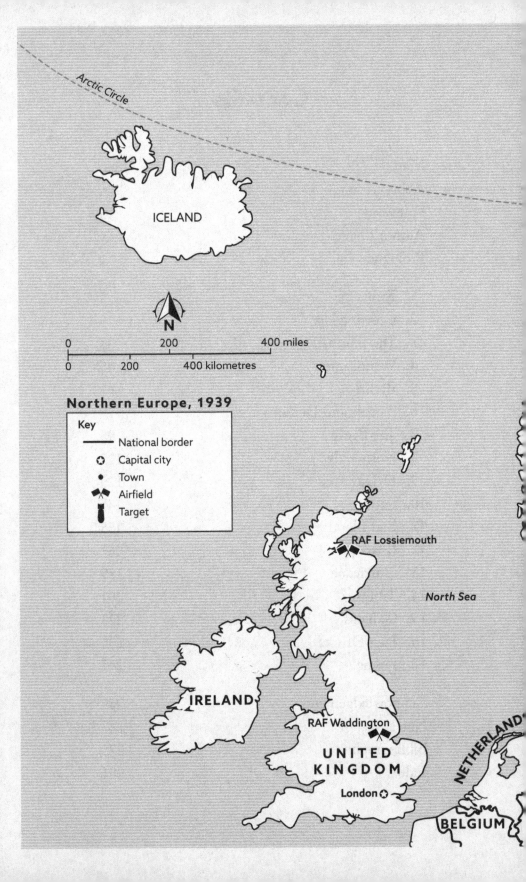

Arctic Circle

ICELAND

N

| 0 | | 200 | | 400 miles |
| 0 | 200 | 400 kilometres |

Northern Europe, 1939

Key
— National border
⊛ Capital city
• Town
✖ Airfield
▼ Target

RAF Lossiemouth

North Sea

IRELAND

RAF Waddington

UNITED
KINGDOM

London ⊛

NETHERLANDS

BELGIUM

Barents Sea

Kaa Fjord

Tromsø

Yagodnik

Norwegian
Sea

SWEDEN

FINLAND

NORWAY

Trondheim

Baltic Sea

Oslo

ESTONIA

RUSSIA
(USSR)

LATVIA

LITHUANIA

DENMARK

EAST
PRUSSIA
(GERMANY)

GERMANY

Brunswick

Berlin

POLAND

Abbreviations

AC2	Aircraftman Second Class	NCO	Non-Commissioned Officer
AFC	Air Force Cross	OTU	Operational Training Unit
AWOL	Absent without leave		
BBC	British Broadcasting Corporation	POW	prisoner of war
		RAAF	Royal Australian Air Force
BHP	Broken Hill Proprietary Company	RAF	Royal Air Force
CGM	Conspicuous Gallantry Medal	RANR	Royal Australian Naval Reserve
CO	Commanding Officer	RCAF	Royal Canadian Air Force
DFC	Distinguished Flying Cross	RN	Royal Navy
DFM	Distinguished Flying Medal	RNZAF	Royal New Zealand Air Force
DSC	Distinguished Service Cross	SS	Schutzstaffel, Nazi special police force
DSO	Distinguished Service Order	SS	Steamship
		USAAF	United States Army Air Forces
EFTS	Elementary Flying Training School	USS	United States Ship
FAA	Fleet Air Arm	VC	Victoria Cross
FPU	Film Production Unit	VE Day	Victory in Europe Day
GMT	Greenwich Mean Time	VJ Day	Victory over Japan Day
HMAS	Her/His Majesty's Australian Ship	WAAF	Women's Auxiliary Air Force
HMS	Her/His Majesty's Ship	WRNS	(Wrens) Women's Royal Navy Service
LMF	Lack of moral fibre		

Foreword

This book tells the story of an extraordinary RAAF crew who flew Lancaster heavy bombers over occupied Europe during World War II from March 1944 to January 1945.

The crew of five New South Welshmen, a Victorian and a Scot were led by the colourful and courageous Flight Lieutenant Bruce 'Buck' Buckham DSO DFC. Buck was an excellent pilot and a great leader of men. Under his inspirational, confident and enlightened leadership in the air, the crew bonded and worked well together to survive and achieve excellent results on two operational tours with Bomber Command.

They flew with No. 463 Squadron RAAF based at Waddington in Lincolnshire. In their first ten days on operations they flew four missions over Germany. The fourth mission was the ill-fated Nuremberg raid of 30–31 March 1944. This was the greatest disaster of the war for Bomber Command. Ninety five of the 608 aircraft from the bomber force were shot down and 545 Allied airmen were killed.

The beginning of April saw a major switch in Bomber Command's operations from targets in Germany to preparation for the Allied invasion of France. Buck and his crew were involved in the attacks that disrupted the German transportation system and the reinforcement and resupply of the German forces deployed to defend France. They also provided direct support to the D-Day Allied landings in Normandy on 6 June 1944, pounding the German coastal defences at Isigny-sur-Mer. This air campaign contributed substantially to the success of the D-Day landings and arguably saved many Allied lives.

A week after D-Day a new threat to London emerged in the form of the V-1 flying bomber. About 10,000 of the lethal unmanned weapons were fired at London. Buckham and his crew were one of many Lancasters that attacked the storage areas and the launch sites for this deadly capability.

On their second tour of duty with Bomber Command, Buckham and his crew took on the vital role of film reconnaissance to record the outcome of major bombing attacks. This was a high-risk endeavour, with the aircraft often descending to a low level after the departure of the mainstream of aircraft to record the results of the mission on film.

The author covers the crew's part in the three attacks on the battleship *Tirpitz* in northern Norway in magnificent detail. For their extraordinary role in recording most of the attacks at low altitude, Buckham was awarded the Distinguished Service Order (DSO) and each member of the crew a Distinguished Flying Cross (DFC).

The achievement of the 13,000 Australians who fought with Bomber Command as part of a large British Commonwealth Force was substantial. Four years before the D-Day operations, they helped open a second front against Germany. As Albert Speer, the German War Industry Minister, made clear, the bombing campaign was the most decisive element in reducing the German economy to the point of collapse and creating the conditions for eventual Allied victory.

The human cost of the campaign was enormous. The Australian airmen who flew with Bomber Command over Europe comprised only two per cent of those who enlisted in Australia's armed forces in World War II, yet they sustained twenty per cent, or one in five, of all Australian combat deaths.

This book is a tribute to the courage of Bruce Buckham and his brave crew who, against all the odds, not only survived but excelled in the most high-risk missions performed by Australians in World War II.

Lest we forget.

Air Chief Marshal Sir Angus Houston AK AFC (Ret'd)

Author's Note

All of the quotations, recalled conversations and other narrative details attributed to Bruce Buckham in this book are drawn from my extensive interviews with him and recollections he recorded in writing and gave to me between 2004 and his death in 2011, unless otherwise acknowledged.

Imperial measurements are used as they were in the context of World War II and the immediate post-war period in Australia.

Time references for all Bomber Command operations follow the military convention of the 24-hour clock, from 0000 hours (midnight) to 2359 hours.

The use of anglicised names for German and other European cities and towns accords with the names used by the Royal Air Force for operational targets (e.g., Brunswick for Braunschweig).

Bombing operations described as straddling two dates (e.g., 14–15 March 1944) reflects the fact that aircraft involved in most night raids took off late on one day and returned early the following morning.

Prologue

It is a day just like that final, fateful day.

A pure, cloudless sky bathes in brilliant light the snow-covered mountains that encircle the fjord. The clear waters that stretch far into the distance are dead calm, the mirror surface dappled by the sun that soon will shine right through the midnight hours of summer. There is an ethereal silence, broken only by the intermittent cries of a flock of seabirds further along the deserted rocky beach. Amid the stillness there is nothing to recall the horror that visited this shore almost 80 years ago; nothing to stir the ghosts of the thousand men who perished here.

I am standing where the long hunt finally ended. On this remote fjord, 350 kilometres north of the Arctic Circle and far from her home, the greatest battleship ever built—the pride of Adolf Hitler's fleet—met her inglorious end, blown apart and capsized in the shallows with her ochre red underbelly grotesquely upturned like the carapace of a giant dead turtle.

It had taken nearly five years and 24 perilous operations by Allied airmen and naval personnel, more than 200 of whom were killed or taken prisoner while trying. Many would be showered with honours for their heroic, ill-fated efforts—two receiving the Victoria Cross, the highest honour of all. But time and again the ship Winston Churchill branded 'The Beast' had evaded the hunters, sometimes seriously wounded but never vanquished.

Until that day.

Tromsø Fjord, Norway—12 November 1944

Flight Lieutenant Bruce Buckham, Royal Australian Air Force:

The day had dawned perfectly clear and still in the target area. It was a magnificent sight as we climbed to our planned height. There was Håkøya Island, a large snow-covered mound in the middle of Tromsø Fjord, and there, anchored in the tranquil waters, was the huge shape of the *Tirpitz*. We still had about fifteen minutes to fly and vast explosions were occurring in the middle of and all around our loose gaggle of aircraft. *Tirpitz* was firing her 15-inch main guns at us with short-delay fuses. As we got closer, we came under fire from the ship's secondary armaments, as well as fire from the shore batteries and two flak ships. Things were getting hot!

We went in at 6000 feet as Wing Commander Willie Tait and the others lined up to do their individual bombing runs, but this was too unhealthy, so we descended to about 2000 feet and isolated the guns lining the fjord. One of the flak ships became somewhat pestiferous so we shot her up a bit and she disappeared to the end of the fjord. The other one kept a respectable distance.

The bombers were right overhead now, doing a perfect run with bomb doors gaping wide open and the glistening wing of the huge 12,000-pound Tallboy bombs suspended. Now they were released.

PROLOGUE

To us they appeared to travel in an ever-so-graceful curve, like a high diver, heading with deadly accuracy towards one point, right amidships of the *Tirpitz*.

The first two bombs were very near misses. Then the third or fourth bomb went down into the main magazine beneath the bridge. Then a second hit straight after that. Suddenly there was a tremendous explosion on board the battleship and she appeared to heave right out of the water. It was awe-inspiring—a huge mushroom cloud of smoke rising thousands of feet. Two of the big 15-inch guns in the No. 1 turret were blown completely out of the vessel and into the water. We could see numerous fires and explosions on board and a huge gaping hole was visible on the port side, where a whole section of the hull had been blown out.

We descended to 200 feet and flew over it, around it, all about it, but still she sat there. After about 30 minutes we decided to call it a day and headed back out to the end of the fjord. Just then rear gunner Eric Giersch called out, 'Skipper, I think she's turning over.' I turned to port to take a look and sure enough she was listing over at an angle of 70 to 80 degrees. So back we went.

I swept in at about 50 feet above the water and we could see German ratings, 40 or 50 of them, jumping into the water. Then we watched with bated breath as the ship heeled over onto her side, ever so slowly and gracefully, leaving her red hull gleaming in the morning sunshine. It was the third time we'd knocked the *Tirpitz* about, but this time we had finished her.[1]

Within minutes of the first of the huge bombs landing on the ship, hundreds of mostly young German sailors were dead—drowned, incinerated or blown apart. Hundreds more would

3

suffer a slower death in the hours and days that followed, trapped within the thick steel hull and suffocating as the last oxygen was spent. The final toll would be 971 souls. And with them would perish Germany's last hope of supremacy in the bitter seas of the Arctic—a blow that would hasten Hitler's inexorable march to defeat.

The first of those to bear witness and to record confirmation of that moment—and the ones to bring home the first news of it—was a crew of young Australian airmen suddenly at the centre of an event that would trigger jubilation across the English-speaking world.

This is the story of Bruce Buckham, his crew, their fellow airmen and their remarkable war—and their many close encounters with disaster before the triumph of that day.

Chapter One

ENLISTING

The most enjoyable and wonderful experience of my
life . . . was to fly with a crew, to keep them together
and to bring them home.

Flight Lieutenant Bruce Buckham[1]

When World War II began, most young Australian men did not
think twice about enlisting. A threat to England was inseparable
from a threat to Australia in the minds of many Australians,
who took pride in their place in the British Commonwealth and
mostly still regarded England as the mother country. As Don
Charlwood wrote in his magnificent war memoir, 'Our generation never really emerged from the shadow of World War I, that
cataclysmic "war to end war". The rise of Nazism was a length-
ening of the same shadow over our youth. When this threat
was faced by Britain in 1939, the response in Australia was not
only that we, too, must face Nazism but that we must stand by
the threatened "Homeland".'[2] Charlwood believed most of the
Australians who flew with Bomber Command felt a powerful
sense of unity with the British people and 'laid claim to a subtler
level of citizenship than can be conferred by passport.'

5

The war of Bruce Alexander 'Buck' Buckham began with a false start and a white lie. Born in Goulburn, New South Wales, on 26 October 1918, just days before the end of World War I, Buckham was raised in Sydney. When his elder brother John was accepted to study medicine and the family knew it could not afford two sons in tertiary education, he joined Broken Hill Proprietary Limited as an accounts clerk. In May 1940 he was called up for national service and followed John into the army. After basic training, Buckham was attached to the 2/45th Battalion and sent to work in a Sydney enlistment office. Instead of being trained to fight he was assigned clerical duties—much the same tedious work he had been doing at BHP. In the end, the 2/45th would never serve overseas and was disbanded in 1944. Buckham's frustration became intolerable as the months passed, especially when John embarked for Malaya with the 8th Division in July 1941, an event that stirred much patriotic fervour in Sydney and throughout Australia.

Buckham hatched an audacious scheme to escape the stultifying clutches of the army. Pleading with his bosses at BHP and his father, who was a close friend of the chief of the army's Eastern Command in Sydney, Major General Albert Fewtrell, he managed to have his old job declared a reserved occupation. He was then discharged and excused from further military service ostensibly to enable him to return to BHP. Within a few days, the young man's real agenda was revealed when he came home to announce that he had enlisted in the air force. 'You should have seen the muck that hit the fan,' he would recall. 'My father was so angry. Of course, it had been my intention all along, but I couldn't tell anyone that.' BHP was similarly unimpressed with

Buckham's subterfuge. According to family folklore, Charlie Potts, BHP's Sydney manager, chased the young man around the company's boardroom table yelling that he would not release him to go to war, before he fled.

Buckham enlisted in the Royal Australian Air Force (RAAF) on 8 November 1941, twelve days after his 23rd birthday. The new recruit was given the service number 420437 and the rank of aircraftman second class, or AC2, more commonly known as an 'erk'—as Buckham would lament, 'the lowest form of human life, you can't get any lower than that.' His first posting was to No. 2 Initial Training School at Bradfield Park, in the northern suburbs of Sydney. Here the recruits received their basic induction to the air force and the process of screening began, to determine who had the potential to proceed with pilot training, who might have the skills to be a navigator and who would be marked for less coveted aircrew roles.

Under the Empire Air Training Scheme, the Australian Government had committed to provide Britain with 10,400 pilots, and 15,600 navigators and wireless operator/air gunners. By March 1940, 11,500 young Australian men had applied to become aircrew but only one in five were selected. Many of those who did make the cut, and the many more who would apply in the years that followed, would complete their training in Canada before reaching England. Others would be trained in Rhodesia. The RAAF was a glamorous, exciting and much more popular form of military service than the army and the navy— and far deadlier, for those who went to Europe. By the end of the war, 40 per cent of the Australians who served in Bomber Command—more than 4000 of the nation's most talented young men—were dead. The average age of those lost was 24, but from late 1943 they were more likely to be 22 or 23. As historian Hank Nelson would note, 'Late in the war, most of those men in bombers over Germany were at school when the war started.'[3]

Buckham passed the initial selection hurdles and in April 1942 moved to No. 4 Elementary Flying Training School (EFTS) at Kingsford Smith Aerodrome at Mascot, Sydney's civilian airport since 1920. Here he was introduced to the Tiger Moth, the staple aircraft of basic training for RAAF pilots. One of his first flights included an involuntary 'incident' that might well have ended his prospects of becoming a pilot, if not his life.

I did a loop-the-loop on the ground . . . and I wrecked the little Tiger Moth. It was a complete wreck. But the CO [commanding officer] thought it was a bloody good job. It was a grandstand job in front of masses of people at Mascot Aerodrome. He said, 'Okay Buckham, you can go solo tomorrow.' And they sent me off without even a test the next day. It didn't put me off flying. It made me keener not to do it again; a mistake I made that was never repeated.[4]

A fortnight later, when the Mascot school was shut down to accommodate some of the United States forces arriving in Australia, Buckham was transferred to No. 11 EFTS at Benalla in Victoria, where his training with the Tiger Moth continued. By late June, Buckham showed sufficient promise to be posted to No. 7 Service Flying Training School, which provided intermediate and advanced instruction of pilots at the new RAAF station at Deniliquin in southern New South Wales. Between June 1941 and August 1944 more than 2200 pilots would be trained at Deniliquin, flying the Australian-built, single-engine Wirraway trainer. In that time, at least 29 instructors and students were killed as a result of pilot error, mechanical faults and collisions in the air and on the ground. Bruce Buckham was lucky not to be another.

With his initial pilot training nearing completion and his posting to the United Kingdom imminent, Buckham decided to propose to Gwendolyn Pennell, the girl with whom he'd been smitten since their eyes first met across the pews at Penshurst Presbyterian Church in Sydney. Gwen would happily accept his unorthodox proposal.

He sent me a telegram: 'Wings leave. I suggest we get married if that's okay with you.' I thought it was a lovely proposal. We'd been going together since I was about 16, so long that we did feel that we would eventually be married. My mother told Harry the milkman. He asked her how old I was and when she told him I was 21, he said, 'My, she's getting on.' My father wanted me to wait to get married. His brother had been killed in the First World War in France and he didn't want me to be left a widow. But we were insistent, and he agreed. We were married on September the 2nd in the church where we had met, at night during the blackout. Dad was a very keen gardener and he brought 500 daffodils and they were gorgeous. It was a quiet wedding because we were living on coupons. We had the reception at Bruce's home and then went to Wentworth Falls for our honeymoon. We only had a few days then he had to go back.[5]

Soon after the honeymoon, Buckham would give his new father-in-law reason to believe he'd been right about the danger of his daughter marrying too soon. On 23 October, he crash-landed his Wirraway on a farm a few miles away from the Deniliquin station. The paperwork he had seen before taking off indicated that the plane had been fully refuelled but this was not the case. Luckily the pilot escaped with little more than a bruised ego, but the aircraft was a write-off.

I dropped the first bomb, then the second bomb and came up to seven or eight thousand feet and cough, cough, no motor. I switched over to the other tank and there was no petrol. I had nothing else to do but perform a forced landing. The Wirraway had a bad habit of flipping near the stalling speed. All these sheep were there—thousands of them. I landed okay but hit a fence, which cut the hydraulic lines, so I had no brakes. It went for miles and miles. They found me late in the afternoon.[6]

The air force was not amused. Leading Aircraftman Buckham was charged under Section 39A of the *Air Force Act 1923* with 'neglect likely to cause damage to His Majesty's aircraft in that he at Deniliquin at approximately 1045 hours on 23.10.42 whilst pilot of aircraft A20-362 neglected to switch from the starboard [right] to the port [left] fuel tank when the starboard gauge showed less than ten gallons.'[7] On 19 November, the accused was found guilty as charged and sentenced to seven days' confinement to barracks. The authorities can't have been too angry because on the same date his commission as a probationary pilot officer was confirmed, but the convict still had to do his time, to the shock and amusement of his new bride when she eventually found out what had happened. Gwen had arranged to travel down to Deniliquin to share some of the little time that remained before her husband departed for Europe. Only after she arrived did she discover what he had neglected to tell her.

The day I moved down there he was in jail for pranging one of their planes. I got the shock of my life. He was in the clink! But he worked around it. A friend of Bruce's would sleep the night in his bed in the clink and Bruce would sneak out and ride over on his bicycle and spend the night with me. And in the morning, he would ride back, and the other guy would leave. Boys will be boys. They are all the same. That was quite a lot of fun.[8]

Their time together would be short. Within weeks Pilot Officer Buckham was on his way to Europe and to war. On 16 January 1943, Buckham embarked from Port Melbourne for San Francisco aboard USS *West Point*. Formerly the ocean liner SS *America*, flagship of the United States Lines, *West Point* had been requisitioned by the US Navy and converted into a troop transport in June 1941. On her voyage from Melbourne, she carried 600 Australian airmen, most bound for training courses in Canada, and 2400 wounded men from the US 1st Marine Division who had been evacuated from Solomon Islands after the Battle of Guadalcanal. Buckham would share a cabin with four others, including a young West Australian pilot, Ken Lyon. After choosing their bunks and stowing their gear, it was time to relax.

Ken Lyon: What I wouldn't do for a real good Scotch!

Bruce Buckham: Would someone please get five glasses from the bathroom.

Lyon: You wouldn't be kidding would you, Buck?

Buckham: And what brand would you like?

Lyon: If you're kidding, you'll get a black eye, but I would like a drop of King George IV whisky.

Buckham: Sit down gentlemen, and I shall pour.

The large bottle of King George IV that Buckham pulled from his haversack had been a farewell gift from his father-in-law, Pop Pennell. It was demolished in short order by the occupants of cabin 615, who slept well that night, inured to the wild weather that beset USS *West Point* as she traversed Bass Strait and headed into the Tasman Sea. The ship called briefly at Auckland before crossing the Pacific to San Francisco. After farewelling their compatriots who were headed north to Canada, Buckham and Lyon took a six-day train journey across the United States. Their destination was Camp Myles Standish in Taunton, Massachusetts. The big United States Army camp was the main staging area for the port of Boston and hundreds of thousands of US and Allied servicemen passed through there during the war on their way to Europe. After a month at the camp, Buckham and Ken Lyon were ordered to escort a party of a dozen non-commissioned officers (NCOs), airmen who were facing disciplinary action for misconduct while they were in the US—'breaking camp, being AWOL [absent without leave], not attending lectures, not turning up for parades, etc.'—on the final leg of their journey to Britain.

They sailed from New York in early February aboard the 14,000-ton troop transport *Highland Princess*. Unusually, because of its slower maximum speed of 18 knots, the ship travelled alone and not as part of one of the big merchant ship convoys protected by British and American warships on the perilous Atlantic crossing. They were very lucky to make it across unscathed. Within days of their voyage, convoys HX 229 and SC 122, with 90 merchant ships and 16 escorts, were targeted by three wolfpacks of 38 German U-boats. In what German radio would boast to have been 'the greatest convoy battle of all time', 22 merchant ships were sunk and more than 300 merchant seamen killed, compared with the Germans' loss of just one U-boat.

The three-week voyage of *Highland Princess* was not without incident as they evaded German U-boat packs and were constantly on alert for torpedo attack. All the passengers, including the airmen facing misconduct charges and their escorts, had to share watch duties. Buckham and Lyon were impressed with the contribution of their 'prisoners'.

Their behaviour, as far as I was concerned, was exemplary. They really put in a good job for gunnery and submarine watch on the way over. Ken and I elected to see what we could do about getting their charges withdrawn, which we did, with the exception of two boys who later went missing in London and didn't turn up until a week or so later. They copped it in the neck.

They reached Bristol's Avonmouth Docks on 13 March. Soon after *Highland Princess* had docked, the Australians were given an immediate taste of war when several German bombers swept in over the harbour, as Buckham recounted.

The bombs were falling all around the docks and certainly very close to the ship. We went up on deck to watch all the excitement, which was made greater because also joining in the party were six or eight of our Hurricane fighters. They came tearing over the hills and made short work of the Germans. There might have been one or two that were lucky enough to make it back to France.

The new arrivals spent their first night in London, where they experienced another brief air raid. The next day they were transferred to Royal Air Force (RAF) Bournemouth, the home of No. 11 (RAAF) Personnel Despatch and Receiving Centre, which screened thousands of newly arrived airmen before they were sent on to advanced flight training stations across Britain. Shortly after their arrival, the young Australian airmen were introduced to an English family. Lady Frances Ryder, daughter of the Earl of Harrowby, had founded the Dominion and Allied Services and Hospitality Scheme to provide a homely welcome and wholesome entertainments for the boys from overseas joining the war effort. Bruce Buckham and Ken Lyon were invited to spend a few days at the home of Colonel Guy Townsend-Rose, of the Hampshire Regiment, and his wife Margaret, in the village of Brockenhurst in Hampshire. It proved to be the perfect antidote to any homesickness they might have been feeling, but perhaps not quite as Lady Ryder might have wished, as Buckham would recount.

We went down there and were made very welcome although the colonel, who was a very pukka fellow and veteran of the North-West Frontier campaigns, didn't seem too impressed with young bloods like us. So dinner that night was a very formal affair. We behaved impeccably but thought he was a pain the arse all the time, although she was a most gracious woman. Anyway, we got up in the morning and went in for breakfast. Before I sat down, I said, 'Where's the colonel?' Margaret said, 'Oh, he's gone off to the club in London. He had some business to do.' I think we were there for four or five days, and we didn't see the colonel again. Clearly, he wasn't going to muck around with fledglings like us who hadn't seen anything. Not a bit like the Khyber Pass!

Buckham's first posting would be to RAF Grove in Oxfordshire, a Bomber Command training station that within a few months would be taken over by the US Ninth Air Force as a staging centre for the Normandy landings the following year. At Grove, the Australians were trained to fly their first twin-engine aircraft, the Airspeed Oxford. Airspeed Limited had been founded in 1931 by engineer Nevil Shute Norway and aircraft designer Hessell Tiltman. The development and mass production of the Oxford, a key training aircraft, was an important contribution to the war effort. Norway was subsequently awarded Fellowship of the Royal Aeronautical Society for his pioneering work in adding retractable undercarriages to aircraft. (Later, writing as Nevil Shute, Norway would become one of Australia's most celebrated novelists, his 24 books including the classics *A Town Like Alice* and *On the Beach*.)

During his time at Grove, Buckham was sent briefly to nearby RAF Watchfield, one of the first airfields that taught beam approach landing techniques. Here pilots were instructed on how to use signals from ground radio beacons to undertake emergency landings with little or zero visibility. Initially formed as the Blind Approach School, it was later renamed, perhaps less alarmingly, as the Beam Approach School. When no other aircraft were flying due to poor weather, aircraft from Watchfield still flew constantly, as pilots learned how to land in dangerous conditions. It would prove a vital skill that would save Buckham and his crew from potential disaster 18 months later. During the course, he was required to fly in very thick fog, doing figure-eight circuits, and taking off and landing with just the runway radio beacons to guide him. If that was hair-raising, an incident just before he completed the training at Grove would be even more so. One of the final exercises was a night cross-country flight to Scotland. All went well until Buckham turned to start the journey home and discovered that his rudder controls were jammed. He only had use of the ailerons—the horizontal flaps on the outer ends of the wings used to bank the aircraft—to facilitate a turn.

All I could do was use the turn and bank on the ailerons for direction, but the rudder pedals were jammed, they wouldn't move. Anyway, I managed to get all the way back and land with no rudder. I asked the ground crew chiefie to take a look, and they found a big torch jammed in the connection between the rudder bars. The pilot before me had dropped it and hadn't said anything. I wasn't too pleased about that.

At breakfast the next morning, Buckham encountered the pilot in question.

Buckham: Do you want your torch back?

Pilot: Waddaya mean?

Buckham: You left it in the aircraft last night.

Pilot: Oh, did I?

Buckham: You should bloody well know, it was jammed in the rudder bars. I had no rudders to fly by.

Pilot: Oh, you want to watch those things in future.

Once he had completed training at Grove, the next step would be the biggest so far in Bruce Buckham's already long journey from rookie pilot to bomber captain. His new posting was to RAF Lichfield, north of Birmingham. Lichfield was the home of No. 27 Operational Training Unit (OTU), which was established in April 1941 to form and train aircrew before, finally, they were posted to the squadrons with which they would go to war. This was where friendships would be formed that would be tested to the limit in battle and that often would last a lifetime—at least for those with the skill and good fortune to survive the required minimum 'tour' of 30 bombing operations over German-occupied Europe.

But first the crew had to find each other.

Chapter Two

CREWING UP

> You were seven men brought together by conflict
> and you came to know each other's every mood and
> reaction, ability, humility, and likes and dislikes ...
> seven men who not only flew together but ate, drank,
> slept, and played together. You were one and gener-
> ally inseparable. Rank meant little between you,
> yet you knew the dividing lines between respect,
> authority, and familiarity.
>
> Flight Lieutenant Eddie Tickler CGM,
> Lancaster pilot 57 Squadron RAF[1]

Given the exhaustive planning that went into Bomber Command tactics and operations, it is remarkable how little science was applied to the formation of aircraft crews. In fact, it was left almost entirely to the men themselves to work out who would fly with whom. Yet these choices involved matters of life and death. The odds of survival on operations were already slim at the outset, but they were even worse for poor crews or crews with weak links. Bruce Buckham, by his own account and that of many who got to know him well during the war, was captain of one of the finest crews in Bomber Command. And that crew, who would fly with great distinction through two tours of operations, came together by chance and a series of improbable circumstances.

For Buckham, the process of 'crewing up' began soon after he arrived at RAF Lichfield in late July 1943. One day he was waiting on a station platform in Birmingham to catch a train back to the airfield with his friend Arthur Probert, another pilot from Sydney. There they bumped into Eric Giersch, an air gunner. Giersch was already something of a celebrity among the Australian flyers. In March 1942, while serving with 215 Squadron RAF, he and his crew were dispatched to fly a new Wellington bomber to India via Gibraltar. As they flew south off the coast of Portugal, one of the Wellington's two engines failed. Four minutes later, the second engine also failed, forcing the pilot, Sergeant Maurice Smithson, to ditch about fifteen miles off Cape Espichel. The aircraft sank within seconds, killing two of the crew. The four survivors who managed to escape from the wreckage, including Giersch, were rescued an hour later by Portuguese fishermen. The Australian then spent a week in Lisbon before being repatriated to England. On his return, Giersch told RAF intelligence staff: 'We were very well treated by the Portuguese.'[2] Indeed he was. Billeted at a comfortable hotel, he had enjoyed an even more comfortable relationship with the hotelier's daughter. ('Oh Buck, she was a bit of alright. I didn't want to come back.') Having been repatriated from a neutral country, Giersch was not permitted to fly on operations for twelve months. He was assigned as a gunnery instructor at RAF Manby in Lincolnshire, where he was commissioned as an officer. Once cleared to resume operations, he was posted to Lichfield. A few nights after their train trip together from Birmingham, Giersch and Buckham were playing snooker in the mess.

Buckham: You will enjoy flying with Mr Probert.
Giersch: What do you mean?
Buckham: Well, he seems to be pretty pally with you, and you seem to be getting on pretty well with him. You will find him a pretty good pilot.
Giersch: I am not flying with him.
Buckham: Are you crewed up?
Giersch: Yes, I am.
Buckham: Who are you going with?
Giersch: You, you stupid bastard. I'm not flying with anyone else.
Buckham: You might be sorry.
Giersch: I don't think so.

And so began a great partnership between pilot and rear gunner and an enduring bond of friendship.

Eric Heinrich Giersch was born into a farming family at Henty in New South Wales and had turned 30 in February 1944—the oldest member of the crew with whom he was about to spend the most intense year of his life. Giersch had enlisted in the RAAF in September 1940 and trained in Montreal, Canada, before arriving in England and starting his first tour of operations. Giersch's grandfather had migrated to Australia from Germany, but Eric had never visited the country of his ancestry and, mercifully, never would through the course of the war—except through the sights of his Browning machine guns.

Whether or not he had ever contemplated joining Arthur Probert's crew, teaming up with Bruce Buckham would prove to be a fortuitous alternative. In early April 1944, Probert and his entire crew were killed when their Lancaster crashed during a raid on the railway marshalling yards at Aulnoye in northern France. Giersch would rate his decision to team up with Buckham as the best choice he made during the war.

The chances that I feel may have altered the course of my war duties were the crash off the coast of Portugal and being fortunate enough to be rescued by a Portuguese fishing boat, not a Spanish one. Also, since I was not able to operate for twelve months, by good luck I met Bruce Buckham and joined what was later known as 'Buckham's Circus'. Bruce and I have remained firm friends ever since.[3]

Asked, years after the war, why he had chosen to fly with Buckham, Giersch's response was succinct: 'He was the only one I thought had any future.'[4]

After shaking hands at Lichfield to confirm their new partnership, the pilot and the gunner went in search of a dedicated wireless operator, using somewhat unorthodox methods. One night they broke into the office of the chief wireless instructor at Lichfield and sifted through the test result papers of all the airmen who had completed the most recent course. Suddenly, Giersch held up one of the papers and said, 'I think this bloke's got it. He looks to me as though he's the best of the Australian wireless operators.' So, they put everything back as they had found it, tucked the papers back in the drawer and went in search of 22-year-old Edwin John Holden, as Buckham would recount.

He was a big, tall fellow, a bit gruff, but Eric had a talk to him, and he gave me the nod. I said, 'Would you like to fly with us, John?' And he said, 'Yeah, what crew have you got?' When I said we had just the two of us, he said, 'Well, you will need a good navigator, but I think most of them are taken.'

Holden was born in Melbourne, the son of an English migrant from Lancashire who had served with the First Australian Imperial Force during World War I. His mother was from Mortlake in Victoria's Western District and had been a nurse during the first war. After completing secondary school in 1938 at Melbourne's Scotch College, where he excelled in mathematics but struggled with English, Holden worked as a clerk with the Wheat Board in Melbourne. He was determined to join the air force once the war started, but his enlistment was delayed after he was forced to spend months recuperating from a bout of pneumonia. He then had to spend another six months in the air force reserve before he was finally accepted for full time service on 8 December 1941—the day after Pearl Harbor. After completing preliminary training in Australia, he arrived in England soon after his 21st birthday. His only reservation in accepting the invitation to join Buckham's crew was that he would be outnumbered by New South Welshmen. 'I was the only Viccy-ike amongst the other four, so you can imagine the trials and tribulations of Melbourne-versus-Sydney,' he later recalled.[5]

Soon after signing up Johnny Holden, Buckham, Giersch and Holden went off to attend a lecture in the Lichfield assembly room. The room was full of crew, including gunners, wireless operators and navigators. One navigator in particular caught Buckham's eye.

There was one fellow there who was wheeling around, swaying in his seat. He looked a bit tousled after a night out on the herbs. He was two or three rows from us, but I could smell that he'd been on the beer. Then Eric said to me, 'He's our man.' I said, 'You've got to be joking.' Then he said, 'No, I don't like people who don't have a drink.'

Once everyone moved outside, Buckham approached the navigator, who was still swaying on his feet. He said he had not yet crewed up and ventured the view that he was unlikely to receive an invitation. Asked his name, he replied, 'Board, they call me Doc Board.'

I asked him why they called him Doc and he replied, 'For operating on women with a blunt tool.' He was a shocker! I said, 'Would you like to fly with us?' He said, 'Alright, what's your name?' That was the beginning of a wonderful friendship, an understanding between pilot and navigator which was probably the keenest of the cooperative efforts of the team. We didn't know then, but we had picked up probably the best navigator in the whole of the air force. Nobody could touch that boy. He was a marvel. His logs were immaculate. During operations he was a precise perfectionist.

Robert William Board, who was also from Sydney, had the dashing looks of an Errol Flynn clone with his dark hair and clipped moustache. And, at 26, he had the swagger to match. Board had an exceptional talent for hitching up with the prettiest woman at the dance or in the pub, and for regularly consummating his new-found friendships. 'Every time we went out with Doc, he picked up a sheila or they picked him up,' Buckham would recall. 'But he was very fussy, he always picked up the most beautiful one.' Board also had a habit of bending the rules. When he enlisted in the RAAF in December 1940, the form would declare a six-shilling fine for 'a minor traffic offence' in 1936. During initial training in Melbourne, he would be confined to barracks for seven days for 'neglecting' to obey an officer. And during a stopover in Panama on his voyage to flight-crew training in Canada, his excessive revelry earned him a night in a police cell. But while a larrikin on the ground, Board was a meticulous professional in the air. His exceptional navigational skills would save his crewmates many times, getting them safely home on operations when many other crews were lost.

Board, in turn, introduced the man who would become their mid-upper gunner and, between operations, Doc's enduring partner in carousing crime. John William Muddle had already done a tour of operations and had spent a year as gunnery leader at RAF Church Broughton, a satellite airfield for No. 27 OTU Lichfield. Buckham was puzzled why Muddle would volunteer to do a second tour, particularly one with a 'sprog' crew like his. After being sent to get an explanation, Board reported back: 'He said to tell Buck that it was twelve months since he'd been on operations and that he had to do a second tour before he can finish. He said yours is the only crew so far, out of the hundreds who have passed through Lichfield, that he can see has got any bloody possible future at all.' Johnny Muddle was from the town of Gloucester in the beef and dairy cattle country north of

Newcastle, New South Wales. Tall and gangly, he had enlisted in the RAAF in January 1941, a few weeks before Singapore fell to the Japanese. Then just 21, he had been a clerk with the Bank of New South Wales. Like many Australian aircrew, most of his training had been done in Canada before he finally reached England.

The search for a bomb aimer took time. One day, Buckham and Giersch came across a group of bomb aimers huddled in a corner of a lounge room at Lichfield. One by one, Buckham approached individuals in the group only to be told that they all had already joined other crews. Increasingly desperate, they noticed a small man sitting alone reading a comic book. Asked his name, the man looked Buckham straight in the eye and replied curtly, 'Manning, what's it to you?'—then went back to reading his comic. Eventually, it was established that Lionel James Manning was available.

Buckham: Are you crewed up?

Manning: No one's asked me.

Buckham: Well, if you're not spoken for, we've got everyone but a bomb aimer.

Manning: Oh, so you come to me last do you?

Buckham: No, but you can be last if you want to be. If you keep on sitting there, no one will ask you.

Once again, Bruce Buckham would soon discover that he had struck gold.

We drew the best bloke I could have chosen. He had the most wonderful eyesight. He was an absolute purist in bombing technique.

He only ever sent me around twice—when we couldn't drop the bombs, either because we were disturbed by a fighter, or we weren't strictly where we should have been and his instruments weren't lined up. It was extraordinary. He wasn't just going to drop them, like many did, and get out of the place. At the end of two tours, we saw the extraordinary photographic record of all the targets we had hit, all the places where he had been accorded an A/P [aiming point] because our bombs had hit the target right where they were meant to.

Jimmy ('Don't call me Lionel') Manning, from Murrurundi in the Hunter Valley of New South Wales, was a 23-year-old clerk with the New South Wales Railways when he enlisted in December 1941, having previously served in the army militia. Like Muddle and Board, he had been sent to Canada for training. When he embarked for Ontario in late 1942, he left behind his wife Ethel. Their son, James, who Manning would not see until he returned to Australia four years later at the end of the war, was born in April 1943.

The final task for Buckham and his new partners was to find a flight engineer. With the widespread introduction to service of the heavy bombers by 1942, this position had become necessary to manage the more complex mechanical, hydraulic, electrical and fuel systems of the aircraft. Seated beside the pilot, the engineer, many of whom were former ground crew, had to monitor the heavy bombers' four engines via about twenty gauges, propeller and throttle controls as well as overseeing the fuel and electrical systems. In an emergency, if the pilot were killed or incapacitated, they might be called on to take over flying the plane. Finding one was a particular challenge, because relatively few Australians had been trained as flight engineers and most crews, including those in the Australian squadrons, needed to find an RAF airman to fill the role.

Buckham chanced upon the perfect candidate during a long-distance training flight. As they were flying 600 miles up over the North Sea, a group of trainee flight engineers aboard were unable to come up with an answer to an emerging fuel crisis.

We got up close to the turning point and I asked for a fuel position. On the way up I'd made a number of changes to the petrol loading from the outside tanks. There were about ten or a dozen of these blokes on board and no one could give me a straight answer. Then a Scots voice from the back said, 'Well skipper, I think I can give you a fairly accurate fuel situation.' Even though there were seven tanks in each wing, he worked it out so accurately that we only just made it back. That was the day that all the props stopped at the end of the runway after we landed. We were out of juice!

William Sinclair—thereafter 'Jock' to his adopted Australian family—was offered and accepted the flight engineer's position in Buckham's crew. Sinclair, aged 22, was from Dundee and had enlisted in the RAF Volunteer Reserve in 1942. He had completed the engineers' training course in Rolls-Royce engines with flying colours. In their first weeks together, Buckham's crew were sent on a test flight to Scotland and organised to drop off Jock and his mate, Tim, a ground-crew technician, to begin a short leave in Dundee. Six days later, the crew returned on another test flight and picked up the two men. As they flew south back to RAF Waddington, Sinclair's mother, forewarned, stood near the entrance to the family residence at 16 Ogilvie Street, Dundee. As the plane swept low above the rooftops of the rows of tenements, Sinclair called out, 'Oh, there's me wee mother!' As she stood waving jubilantly, Bruce Buckham rocked his wings to return the greeting.

Buckham was delighted with the talented men that had fallen together as his crew. In one of his many letters home to Gwen, he would write: 'I know I possess an A1 team and feel sure we shall give a good account of ourselves.' Chance and good fortune had brought together a group of men who were very skilled in their individual roles. The challenge now was to form them into a single cohesive crew that could withstand the intense strain of bombing operations, hit the assigned targets and get home safely. That task would draw heavily on Bruce Buckham's abilities as a leader as well as his talents as a pilot. The man himself would credit their success to the intense concentration and discipline that each member of the crew brought to their roles and their sense of duty to their fellow crew members.

The crew worked and combined like a well-oiled machine. Their timing was excellent. There was complete silence in the aircraft through an operation. There was no stupid talk. There was no panic. It was just an atmosphere of quiet confidence. They used to be as worried, and probably as terrified, as anybody else before take-off. But as soon as they got into the plane, I would speak to them and say, 'Look, forget it. Let's just get up there and do our jobs.' As soon as the motors started, everything was right, it was go. We didn't follow the textbook patter they required between crew in the air, or between the aircraft and the ground. Ours was well known as an aircraft that just got on with it.

~

With crews now formed, a new round of intensive training began, to familiarise those crews with the bombers they would take to war and to build their skill in operating as teams.

From Lichfield, Buckham's crew were sent to RAF Church Broughton, the No. 27 OTU satellite station, where they were trained to fly the twin-engine Vickers Wellington bomber. Designed in the mid-1930s, the Wellington had become the mainstay of medium-range bombing operations in the early years of the war. One of its most significant innovations compared with the underwhelming aircraft that it superseded was that it had a geodetic airframe fuselage structure designed by the legendary engineer Barnes Wallis (who later developed a series of new bombs that would transform the performance of Bomber Command). The new airframe was formed from a spirally-crossing weave of load-bearing parts that could withstand much greater combat damage than earlier, more fragile aircraft structures. The innovation, and later advances in airframe structures, would save the lives of hundreds of aircrew whose planes, though badly shot up during operations over Europe, were still able to fly home— including the Buckham crew, on multiple occasions.

During their training on Wellingtons, the crew were given their first taste of operations over Europe when they were sent on a 'nickel' run over the city of Rennes in north-western France. From the earliest days of the war, the RAF had been ordered by the government to fly hundreds of sorties over Germany and occupied Europe, dropping thousands of tons of propaganda leaflets intended, with great optimism, to undermine the morale of Nazi forces and encourage civilian resistance. Many regarded the exercise as futile and a waste of time and resources. As Bomber Command chief Arthur Harris would famously remark: 'The only thing achieved was largely to supply the continent's requirements of toilet paper for the five long years of the war.'[6] While the official view was that dropping leaflets was safer than dropping bombs for 'sprog' crews getting their first taste of action, the German fighters and anti-aircraft gunners failed to discriminate and there were many casualties on nickel runs.

The Bomber Command War Diaries would record the eleven sorties flown by OTU crews on the night of 25–26 September 1943 as 'minor operations', but for Buckham's crew there was nothing minor about their experience. Soon after dropping their load of pamphlets over Rennes, they came under intense anti-aircraft fire from German ground batteries, as Buckham would recall.

We got hit by a heavy shell and there was a hell of an explosion but everything still seemed to be functioning alright and so we headed home and landed. At the briefing they asked me if there was any damage to the aircraft and I said, 'Oh, yes, we collected some heavy flak coming away from Rennes.' The next morning, I got a call up and they told me to go and take a look at the aircraft. Half the jolly fuselage was missing! The geodetic airframe had saved us—it could take a hell of a lot of punishment. But most of the left side of the fuselage had been blown away. It was torn ragged like someone had gone along one side with a giant can-opener. That plane never flew again. It was incredible that none of the vital components had been damaged. I had full control of the rudders, the ailerons. It became a much heavier aircraft to fly after we were hit but it still flew. We didn't feel scared by it. I didn't, anyway. We were too young and inexperienced to worry. We just took it for granted that that was what happened when you went on ops.

Before their training at Lichfield was completed, and after 80 hours flying time on the aircraft, the RAF decided to phase out the Wellington from Bomber Command frontline operations. The Buckham crew was then transferred to RAF Swinderby in Lincolnshire to retrain on the Short Stirling, the first four-engine heavy bomber to see service with the RAF. And after almost 40 hours of training on the Stirling, there would be yet another change. This time, it would be a marriage made in heaven between Buckham's crew and the plane that many would credit with turning the tide in the air war over Europe.

Chapter Three

THE LANCASTER

I would say this to those who placed the shining
sword in our hands . . . without your genius and
efforts we could not have prevailed, for I believed
that the Lancaster was the greatest single factor in
winning the war.

Air Chief Marshal Sir Arthur Harris[1]

Despite the ominous resurgence of German militarism through
the 1930s, the outbreak of war had seen the RAF woefully
ill-prepared to meet the challenge. In late 1939, Britain had 608
fighter aircraft—just half Germany's total of 1215. The disparity
in bombers was far worse—Britain had 536 while Germany had
2130. More serious still was the gap between the two countries
in the quality of most aircraft. While the Supermarine Spitfire
fighter would brilliantly prove its worth in the Battle of Britain,
many of Britain's other aircraft had advanced little since World
War I. Most were simply not up to the challenge of taking
the air war into the heart of Nazi Germany. As historian Max
Hastings would write: 'It was the Whitleys, the Wellingtons and
the Hampdens, blundering blindly through the nights skies over

Germany in 1940 and 1941, who were the pathfinders for all that followed, for good or ill.'[2]

But the ability of British engineers and British industry to adapt quickly and rise to the existential challenge would be a key element in the ultimate Allied victory. In particular, the genius of one man would transform the fortunes of RAF Bomber Command. As a boy growing up in Lancashire, Roy Chadwick had been obsessed with making and flying model aeroplanes. At the age of 14 he got a job as a trainee draughtsman with British Westinghouse in Manchester. On turning 18, in 1911, Chadwick boldly called at the headquarters of fledgling aircraft manufacturer A.V. Roe and Company and asked for a job. Edwin Alliott Verdon Roe's brother Humphrey suggested that the smartly dressed young man come back the following Wednesday for an interview. A.V. Roe was so impressed with Chadwick's models and drawings that he hired him as his assistant. Soon appointed the company's chief draughtsman, Chadwick would, over the next three decades, design 30 aircraft under the 'Avro' marque.

In the late 1930s, Chadwick began work on the Avro Manchester, under Air Ministry specifications for the supply of a medium bomber to replace the RAF's inventory of Whitleys, Hampdens and Wellingtons. The first Manchesters were completed in July 1939 and the aircraft began squadron service in November 1940. Hopes that the new bomber would solve the RAF's problems were soon dashed. The Manchester was a dud, primarily because its twin Rolls-Royce Vulture engines were unreliable and under-powered. Production was stopped in 1941.

The failure of the Manchester did not discourage Chadwick. Instead, he set to work immediately to create something bigger and much better. It would become his masterpiece, the Avro Lancaster heavy bomber. With a length of 70 feet and a wingspan of 102 feet, it was simply the most formidable fighting aircraft ever built. Its four Rolls-Royce Merlin engines, more reliable but less powerful than the Vulcan engines, gave the Lanc a cruising speed of 282 miles per hour and enabled it to carry a crew of seven and a 14,000-pound bomb load to a range of 1660 miles—more than enough to attack Berlin and beyond. Its range and bomb load capacity were three times that of the Wellington. It was also substantially superior in speed, range and load capacity to the Handley Page Halifax, which shared the bulk of the workload of Bomber Command in the final years of the war.

The first Lancaster flew in 1941 and the aircraft went into full-scale production the following year. By the end of the war, 7377 had been built—and more than 3000 were lost in the skies over Europe and in accidents in British airspace. It became the most heavily used of the World War II night bombers, delivering a staggering total payload of more than 600,000 tons of bombs in 156,000 sorties. Just as the Spitfire had answered spectacularly the Luftwaffe threat in the Battle of Britain, the Lancaster would turn the tide in the air war over Europe—and enable Britain to take the fight back to the Germans at a time when there were no other effective options to do so. It also had the best defensive weapons of any bomber ever built. A rear turret was mounted with four .303 Browning machine guns, another pair were housed in a turret on the upper rear fuselage and there were two more in the nose of the aircraft. Together, the three positions could encircle the Lancaster with machine gun fire to a range of 400 feet and strike any enemy aircraft that came within that distance.

In August 1942, Alf King, the London editor of *The Sydney Morning Herald*, was one of the first civilians to be shown the new aircraft. During a visit to an A.V. Roe test aerodrome, King had stood in awe on the tarmac: 'I saw six bombers fresh from the production lines capable of carrying about 50 tons of death and destruction in one journey over Germany.'[3] King would get the opportunity to witness that death and destruction firsthand sixteen months later, joining a raid to Berlin with the crew of Squadron Leader Bill Forbes from 467 Squadron RAAF. He would be lucky to live and write his tale. Three journalists who flew on another aircraft that night were killed, including Norman Stockton of the *Sydney Sun*.

Wing Commander Rollo Kingsford-Smith, nephew of Australian aviation pioneer Charles Kingsford-Smith, was one of the first pilots to fly the Lancaster in action. 'There was no doubt that the Lancaster was the best four-engine heavy bomber in the European war, used either by the British or the Americans,' he would later declare. 'It was highly manoeuvrable for such a big aircraft and could carry the largest bomb load and fly higher than any other English heavy bomber. Most important, if handled carefully, it could hold height even with two engines out of action on the one side.'[4]

Many pilots would wax lyrical about their relationship with the extraordinary aircraft, which embodied the breathtaking advances in aviation technology that were now under way. Flight Lieutenant Russell 'Rusty' Waughman, a pilot with 101 Squadron RAF, would declare: 'It was a living thing. There were times almost when she spoke to you, or you felt that she did.'⁵ Don Charlwood would write, 'We saw them coming like relief to a hard-pressed army. They were unconquerable. The days of heavy losses were over.'⁶ For Bruce Buckham, meeting the Lancaster would be love at first flight.

At the very beginning, when I first stepped into the Lancaster, I felt I was getting into a very, very special flying machine. It looked as though it had plenty of character on the ground and I was soon to discover that applied equally well in the air. Climbing up through the aircraft I felt at home and when the instructor told me to hop into the pilot's seat, I had the most wonderful feeling I had ever had in any plane in my life. I was egotistical enough to feel that the Lancaster had been specially built for me to fly. I never lost that feeling. I've still got it today. I think I could go out onto the tarmac now, hop into the cockpit, get Jock to start the motors up and we could take off just as nicely as we did then. It was just a home away from home.

Buckham's first encounter with the plane that he would go on to fly on two tours of operations took place at RAF Syerston in Nottinghamshire on 21 February 1944. His instructor was a veteran New Zealand pilot, Flying Officer Bernard Gumbley from 617 Squadron, which had mounted the fabled 'Dambusters' Raid in May 1943. Earlier in his career Gumbley had won the Distinguished Flying Medal (DFM) on his first tour of operations as a sergeant pilot with 49 Squadron RAF. Nine months after they met at Syerston, he and Buckham would both be flying Lancasters on the final *Tirpitz* raid. And four months after that, Gumbley would be shot down and killed during an attack on a German oil refinery near Bremen. On the day Gumbley was assigned to begin instructing Buckham, weather conditions were poor with strong winds. The commanders at Syerston ordered that there was to be no solo flying by the converting pilots.

We went up and he put me through the paces, all the things you needed to know all the way down to flying on just one engine. After doing the various manoeuvres and whatnot with me flying and him sitting in the right-hand instructor's seat, he said, 'Well, let's go back to the aerodrome.' I landed and when I had finished pulling up at the end of the runway, he got up out of his seat and I said, 'Where are you going?' He said, 'I'm going out for a smoke. You can go out and do a couple of circuits and then pick me up here after you've done that.' But I said, 'There's no solo flying. You heard the instruction.' He said, 'That's alright. Off you go, but don't bend it!' So I did two or three circuits, went back to meet him and we went back in together.

That night at dinner an announcement came over the tannoy speaker in the mess calling Gumbley to come immediately to the station commander's office. A little later, the instructor rejoined his dinner companions, who were drinking at the bar.

Buckham: So what was that all about?
Gumbley: You'd have a guess, wouldn't you?
Buckham: Well, I didn't dob you in.
Gumbley: No, but it showed up on the records.
Buckham: What did you say to him?
Gumbley: I told him you fly the bloody thing better than I do, so there was no point in me staying in the cockpit anymore!

After several more days of training, flying alone and with his crew, Bruce Buckham was ready to take his new love out on operations—and there he found the aircraft performed flawlessly, even when flying in extreme conditions.

The Lancaster was never found wanting, even in the most rigorous manoeuvres that might be necessary because of the circumstances we found ourselves in. They performed like no other aircraft I had flown. It was magnificent. You could do almost anything with it. The Merlin engines! As soon as you started them up there was a certain deep throb, a hum about them that pulled at your heart strings. Oh God, I used to love the sound of them. Once you heard that, all feelings that might have been there, I won't say fear, but trepidation, it all disappeared once you started the motors up. You were in business.

While the Lancaster was a brilliant fighting machine, the comfort of its crew had not been a design priority. Conditions were cramped and the heating was rudimentary.

There was heating but we couldn't use it. When the flight engineer turned the heater on at altitude you would get a heavy mist and then a snowstorm. It fogged up the windscreen and you couldn't see the instruments. So, we left it turned off. The only ones who had heating were the gunners whose flying suits were plugged into the circuitry. They were exposed and had a pretty rigorous time with the elements. At altitude, it was mostly minus 30 or 35 degrees. Eric got frostbite on one occasion because there was something wrong with his flying suit. He nearly lost his fingers. Once my hands got stuck to the control column. When I landed, they had to come and prize them off. My hands were just frozen stiff.

The crew had to dress for polar conditions. Long johns were mandatory beneath their service uniforms—which they had to wear in case they were shot down and taken prisoner—and their battledress. On his feet Buckham wore silk stockings, wool stockings and chamois overstockings inside sheepskin-lined boots. The discomfort was compounded by the cramped conditions, in which all the crew had little or no space for movement, as John Holden would explain.

Most of the targets we went to were up above 12,000 feet, which meant you were on oxygen. Freedom of movement in the aircraft was [only] in a particular area. You could move from your seat and stand up in the astrodome. Well, in my case, I could sit alongside the navigator. The navigator could get up and move and stand behind the pilot . . . he'd come out of his curtain because we were in a blacked-out area and, if we had a light on, we didn't want to have that showing out in the darkness. The pilot was fixed there all the time. He could stand up, with difficulty, but that was about the only movement he had. The rear gunner was fixed in his turret. He had no chance of moving about. The mid-upper gunner could get out of his turret and move around, in a limited circle, according to the length of his oxygen tube. The same with the bomb aimer.[7]

For all its strengths, the Lancaster, while faster, more manoeuvrable, and much better armed than any of the older bombers it replaced, was still easy prey for the much faster and more agile German fighter aircraft, as Buckham would acknowledge.

The aircraft was very vulnerable because we were such a big target and we didn't have the speed or manoeuvrability that the fighters had. But I don't think there is any other bomber that is as manoeuvrable as the Lancaster if you know how to fly it properly. You need to be able to know what it will do and what it won't do. I could spin it around in the air on one wingtip for that matter and not get into strife. We did an accidental loop one night and that was quite stunning. It was caused by a massive blast of anti-aircraft fire. I'm up there doing a corkscrew and this massive explosion occurs—it may have been a bomb load for all I know—but the next thing we were over on our back and going down. So, I just completed the loop and carried on. You should never worry about the unusual. You should just deal with the situation as it looks to you in the moment.

Once they had graduated from 5 Lancaster Finishing School at Syerston, Buckham and his crew were ready to be posted to a squadron—and, after being trained on three different bombers, they were exceptionally well qualified. Buckham by then had flown an extraordinary 849 hours in training in Australia and England—more than the total hours he eventually would fly during two tours of combat operations.

An impromptu visit in late 1943 would be Bruce Buckham's first contact with the station that would soon become home for the rest of his time in Bomber Command. While completing his training on Wellington bombers at Church Broughton, Buckham had been instructed to ferry a Percival Proctor, a single-engine light plane, across to RAF Waddington on the outskirts of the city of Lincoln. He took Eric Giersch with him. The Proctor was the personal aircraft of Air Vice-Marshal Ralph Cochrane, the Air Officer Commanding 5 Group. Cochrane had sealed his reputation as one of Britain's most formidable air force commanders after mounting the spectacular Dambusters Raid a few months earlier. The son of an aristocratic Scottish family, Cochrane had joined the Royal Navy (RN) in 1912, flew airships during World War I and took a commission with the RAF in 1920. In the mid-1930s he was seconded to help establish the Royal New Zealand Air Force (RNZAF) and became its first Chief of Air Staff in 1937. Brilliant but reserved and sometimes imperious, Cochrane was intolerant of insubordination, as Bruce Buckham was about to discover.

The Proctor was Cochrane's private plane. He always insisted on being flown. It was beneath his dignity to drive. When we met him after bringing the plane over to Waddington, he said, 'I'll get you to take me back to Silverstone.' RAF Silverstone was a station down south, near Northampton. I said, 'No, I'm sorry, sir, I can't. I'm on roster tonight. I've got cross-country night flying and I don't want to miss my training.' He said, 'You'll do as you're told.' I said, 'Look I'm awfully sorry sir, but I only brought this thing up here as a gesture to help you and, if you don't mind, we have to get back to Church Broughton.' So he said, 'Alright, I'll come back with you.' But we then had to wait until he was good and ready. He never forgot that. It was so funny to meet up with him again months later—and he wanted to come on ops with us!

The visit to Waddington was also Buckham's first meeting with Air Commodore Allan Hesketh, the base commander. Hesketh had begun his career as a navigator with the Royal Flying Corps (the air component of the British Army before the formation of the RAF) late in World War I. He was wounded in action over the Western Front a fortnight before the Armistice. In 1919 he was sent to south Russia with 47 Squadron to support General Anton Denikin's White Russian forces in their fight against the Bolsheviks and was awarded the Distinguished Flying Cross (DFC) for gallantry. Hesketh later retrained as a pilot and narrowly survived a training crash in which his instructor was killed. At the end of World War II he would crown his adventurous career by being sent as air attaché to Nanking (Nanjing) at the height of the Chinese communist revolution. Bruce Buckham was immediately impressed with the man who would become a mentor and important ally.

Hesketh was there at Waddo, so we went up to the mess and made ourselves known. He was a very big man and used to be the heavyweight boxing champion of the services. He looked like an old bruiser, but he had a heart of gold and he loved Aussies. He'd had quite a bit to do with them in World War I. We were his favourites. Apparently, Eric and I appealed to him with just that one visit. He asked us where we were bound for and I said, 'Hopefully we'll go to Pathfinders.' He said, 'What do you want to do that for?' And I said, 'Well, we've done exceptionally well as a team in navigation tests.' Then he said, 'No, you won't be going there.' I think he had decided right then to put in a bid for us.

In October 1943, Buckham and his crew were formally advised that they had been posted to the newly formed 463 Squadron RAAF at Waddington. But they were still determined to join one of the glamorous new Pathfinder squadrons, which had been set up under the leadership of Australian Don Bennett to mark targets and improve the accuracy of Bomber Command operations. Buckham dug in his heels until an order came from the very top that put an abrupt end to the argument.

When the posting came through, I said, 'That's no good to me. You have spent all this money on me, and time and care, I want to go to Pathfinders where I can make a difference.' They said, 'No, you can't.' This went on for a week or so, and then a message came through to me at Syerston, the last one. It was from the boss, signed by the Commander-in-Chief, Bomber Command, Arthur Harris: 'Tell Buckham and crew to go to 463 Squadron or go home.'

Air Commodore Allan Hesketh had got his way.

Chapter Four

WADDINGTON

This pretty patch of Lincolnshire countryside . . .
should in reality be as indelible a part of Australia's
military heritage as Lone Pine, Fromelles or Kokoda.

Michael Veitch, *Heroes of the Skies*[1]

The airfield straddles the old Roman road from York to London on a limestone escarpment that stretches through the heart of Lincolnshire, separating the marshlands of the Trent River valley to the west from the wolds and plains that run 60 kilometres east to the North Sea. They call it the Lincoln Cliff, a rather grand appellation for a formation that is more molehill than mountain. But the south-westerly winds that often sweep the high ground were a bonus for the first warplanes struggling to lift off after RAF Waddington opened in 1916 at the height of World War I.

At the outbreak of World War II, Waddington was one of five RAF stations operating across Lincolnshire. By the war's end, there would be 49, some located so close to each other that their flight circuits intersected. While there were many more stations spread across eastern England, the concentration of squadrons from Groups 1 and 5 of Bomber Command earned

Lincolnshire the title of 'Bomber County'. A light on top of the central tower of the grand Gothic Lincoln Cathedral would guide the bombers on their way to war and provide a welcoming beacon for weary crews heading home from battle.

Four principal Australian combat squadrons would operate in Bomber Command—one, 466 Squadron, flew Halifaxes from RAF Driffield in Yorkshire, and the other three all flew Avro Lancasters from Lincolnshire. Perhaps the most famous was 460 Squadron, thanks to its association with the 'G for George' Lancaster, now a star of the Australian War Memorial collection. It was based at Binbrook, north of Lincoln, where the station commander throughout 1943 and 1944 was Group Captain Hughie Edwards, one of the two Australians in Bomber Command to win the Victoria Cross (VC) and the only one who would survive to wear it. The twin Australian squadrons—467 and 463—flew from Waddington.

No. 467 Squadron was originally based north-west of Lincoln at Scampton. It was formed on 7 November 1942. Under the articles of the Empire Air Training Scheme it was created as an Australian squadron, but at the outset its crews were predominantly British. It would not be until late in the war that they were mostly replaced with Australians. The squadron was moved to Bottesford in November 1942 and then to Waddington from November 1943. No. 463 Squadron was formed from C Flight of 467 Squadron on 25 November 1943. While it was the last of the Australian squadrons to be established, it only had two flights (tactical subunits) rather than its parent's complement of three and it flew combat operations for less than eighteen months, earning the sad distinction of having one of the highest casualty rates of any of the Australian squadrons. It lost 546 aircrew on operations and 78 aircraft during a total of more than 2500 sorties flown.

The inaugural commanding officer (CO) of 463 Squadron was Wing Commander Rollo Kingsford-Smith, who had been a flight commander with 467 Squadron. On arrival at Waddington, he liked what he found: 'Large solid hangars, but not sufficient to take our aircraft, which were dispersed permanently, right around the airfield, well established engineering and maintenance buildings, a splendid, almost lavish, peacetime officers' mess and good, comfortable NCOs and other ranks' messes. Being a permanent base, it was well provided with married quarters. Pre-war officers and NCOs did not suffer much hardship.'[2] The arrival of the new fighting squadrons would transform Waddington, which had ceased flying operations for several months while its old grass runways were rebuilt to handle the new heavy bombers. It was a shock for the longer-term residents of the station, as Kingsford-Smith would recount.

During this time a handful of elderly administrative officers (they must have been in their late thirties to the early fifties) stayed on to look after the general housekeeping of this place. They had the beautiful, large and comfortable officers' mess all to themselves and nice nine-to-five working hours. They thought they were in clover. Then overnight the tranquil lifestyle was destroyed by the intrusion of large numbers of boisterous aircrew, flying around the clock, wanting meals at the most audacious hours, sharing the mess with their betters and, what was worse, they were Colonials. The old chaps thought that because they had been there first they had priority to the best chairs, especially those close to the fireplace, so important in the winter, and to the best table in the dining room. I remember, I think, on our second night there, when a group of aircrew came into the mess at about 8 p.m. tired and thirsty and cold after flying all day and the old men would not give up their chairs drawn up around the fire. One of our young men went outside for a minute or two, came back, stood in front of them all, and displayed in his hand a handful of live .303 rounds. All he said was, 'Look! Live bullets!' then tossed them into the fire. There was a mad scramble, and all the chairs were empty. Unworldly people will think that a live round thrown into a fire will explode violently and the bullet whiz out as from the barrel of a gun. All I have ever seen, on many occasions, is that the brass cartridge splits down the side, the gas comes out with a little 'phhhhht' and some ash flies up for about 30 cm. Nevertheless, it was effective. It did not take long after that before the real workers assumed their rightful place in what was to be their home, maybe for the remainder of their short lives.

While the vast majority of aircrew assigned to 463 Squadron were Australians, there were also New Zealanders and Canadians and, towards the end of the war, members of the Royal Indian Air Force. Almost all of the flight engineers, including William 'Jock' Sinclair in Buckham's crew, were British because none had been trained by the RAAF. There were some Australian flight engineers in Bomber Command, but they had been trained within the RAF. The ground crews also were predominantly British, but there were hundreds of Australians among those working at bomber and fighter stations scattered across England.

Bruce Buckham and his crew arrived at Waddington in mid-March 1944 after graduating from their two weeks of training at 5 Lancaster Finishing School, RAF Syerston. Their new squadron had already logged a grim toll of casualties in the first few months of its existence. In January alone 463 Squadron lost eight aircraft and 53 aircrew killed in action. Two surviving aircrew became prisoners of war and another gunner died when his oxygen system failed while flying above 20,000 feet. On the night of 30–31 January four out of a total of fourteen Lancasters sent from the squadron to Berlin were shot down. The losses—almost a third of his men—were a devastating blow to Kingsford-Smith, who would write a personal letter of condolence to the families of each of the lost men. The arrival of Bruce Buckham, a fresh and talented pilot, with his smart crew would be a welcome relief for the CO, but the two strong-willed men would have a difficult relationship before becoming lifelong friends. Kingsford-Smith conceded that his tough and uncompromising leadership style made him 'a right bastard' in the view of many of his men but, he argued, it was better that they complained about him than about their aircraft or their operational duties. And Buckham accepted the tough love of his boss: 'I think he knew I was a bit of a reprobate, a brigand.'

By March Kingsford-Smith had become increasingly alarmed at the slow pace at which the RAF authorities were replenishing his seriously depleted crews. His suspicions that the Australian squadrons were not being given priority by Bomber Command leaders were soon vindicated. On 13 April he visited the 5 Group headquarters at Grantham, about eighteen miles south of Waddington, and met with Wing Commander Keith Sinclair, the Group Staff Operations Officer. Sinclair had been one of the original flight commanders with 467 Squadron and had won the DFC after nursing his bomber home over the Alps on three engines after a raid on Friedrichshafen. He was notable among aircrew in that he had met Adolf Hitler—as a journalist covering a Nuremberg rally in the 1930s for Australian Associated Press. After the war, Sinclair would become editor of the Melbourne *Age* newspaper. At Grantham he showed Kingsford-Smith a confidential document that made his visitor's blood boil. It was a letter, written by a senior member of the British Government, complaining about Australia's recent insistence that RAAF airmen who had completed a tour of duty with Bomber Command should be allowed to return to Australia to crew the new American Liberator bombers being acquired for operations against the Japanese. The letter argued that any shortfall in Australian crew reinforcements should not affect RAF squadrons but should be at the expense of 463 and 467 squadrons. 'I was furious, with my own Government as well as the English,' Kingsford-Smith would later write, 'I could understand Churchill's motives. He had to deal with the English voters and would do everything possible to minimise English losses even if it meant making the Australians suffer. It was my own Government, which handed over the power of life and death of Australians to another country, that upset me.'

By the time of his arrival at Waddington, Bruce Buckham had logged more than 800 flying hours as a pilot in the two years and four months since he first enlisted in the RAAF. This was an astonishingly long apprenticeship given many pilots began flying ops after 100 hours' training, but it was a record that would help Buckham to better handle the immense challenges he was soon to face. Before he and his crew could begin their full operational careers, they were required to fly a sortie with an experienced combat pilot in command of their aircraft and Buckham as the 'second dickie' pilot. That senior pilot would be one of the legendary Australians in Bomber Command, a man who would become both a close friend and a mentor to Buckham.

Among the larrikins who commandeered the officers' mess at Waddington in late 1943 was a large and larger-than-life character named William Lloyd Brill. One of seven children from a farming family in the Riverina district of southern New South Wales, Bill Brill had joined the RAAF in 1940. His first tour of operations had been with 460 Squadron RAAF at Binbrook where he won the DFC in May 1942 for pressing on to attack a target despite his Wellington bomber being badly damaged by flak. His persistent courage and heroism would see him go on to win the Distinguished Service Order (DSO) and a second-award bar to his DFC. On the formation of 463 Squadron, Brill was appointed commander of one of the squadron's two flights. An inspiration to others in the perilous skies over Europe, he was also a challenging drinking partner in the often rowdy downtimes between operations. Historian Hank Nelson recounted Brill's famous party trick, often performed in the mess at Binbrook and then Waddington:

'There was a cry, "Clear the runway! Bill Brill will do the impossible." Airmen shifted furniture and bodies to clear a strip, a sofa was set across the far end and beyond it a leather officer's chair was laid on its back. Brill in his socks ran flat out down the runway, grabbed the back of the sofa with his hands, somersaulted, landed in the chair, and his momentum turned the chair upright, leaving Squadron Leader Brill sitting at ease in an armchair.'[3]

As Nelson noted, many drunken rivals would seek to replicate the feat, but few would succeed, leaving the end of the runway 'littered with pranged airmen.' In May 1944 Brill would be appointed CO of 467 Squadron. He would go on to have the grim distinction of being the only one of the five wartime holders of that position who was not killed in action.

On the night of 20–21 March 1944, Squadron Leader Brill took Buckham and crew on their first combat operation over Europe. A total of 25 Mosquitoes and 20 Lancasters from 5 Group—14 of them from 617 'Dambusters' Squadron—attacked five targets across Germany, including the city of Munich. It would be a relatively quiet night with no aircraft lost. Brill and Buckham's target was the city of Stuttgart, home of Mercedes-Benz and Porsche. The weather was cloudy and the target was obscured but marked by flares hung from parachutes. Brill thought it was way too quiet an introduction to night bombing operations and insisted that the crew come out with him again two nights later. This time, there was plenty of action—both inside and outside the aircraft, as Buckham would recount.

On March 23 we went out again with Brill, to Frankfurt, and this time we saw everything—the flak barrages at the coast and across France and into Germany. From the ground, we had attacks by fighters. I saw all the manoeuvres that the experienced pilots used to get away from the fighters, including the corkscrew. This involved a series of steep diving and climbing turns in alternate directions to make it harder for the attacking fighter to fix the bomber in his gun sights.

The operation that night was a 'maximum effort' for Bomber Command, which meant as many aircraft as were available were required to fly. More than 800 aircraft were deployed, flying a diversionary route crossing the Dutch coast north of the Zuiderzee before turning almost due south to attack Frankfurt. The defenders were not fooled for long and the anti-aircraft barrages and German night fighter squadrons were ready when the main bomber stream reached the city. A total of 34 aircraft were lost—and more than 200 crew. But the target marking was accurate and the bombing effective. Almost 1000 people were killed on the ground and another 350 seriously wounded. Massive damage was done to the city, including to the main industrial areas and to many Nazi Party buildings. The target of the Buckham crew was an ammunition factory on the outskirts of the city. But many historical buildings also were ruined. The city records would describe the impact of the raid, along with other attacks in the days just before and after 22 March: 'Their combined effect was to deal the worst and most fateful blow of the war to Frankfurt, a blow which simply ended the existence of the Frankfurt which had been built up since the Middle Ages.'⁴ The understandable fury of the residents of Frankfurt meant that captured Allied airmen had to be protected by their guards from being attacked as they were transported through the city to the nearby interrogation and transit camp at Oberursel.

It was a challenging night for the new Australian pilot, particularly as Bill Brill was indisposed, as Buckham would recount.

He had diarrhoea. After we got well into France, he handed over to me and that was when the fun started. The crew said, 'Oh no, skipper, stay there.' But Brill said, 'No, I can't. I'm crook.' So I had to do most of the flying while he was down the back stuck on the Elsan toilet—literally stuck! He forgot to lift up the dual lids of the Elsan and got burned on the bum by sitting on the bare metal of the crew toilet. We were up at about 20,000 feet and it was minus-40 odd. He was a big bloke—17 stone—and he gave this bull roar and screamed out, 'Oh, my God—I've burnt my arse!' When he got free, he had this great red ring all around his bum. Later in the mess, the boys embarrassed him in front of the WAAF [Women's Auxiliary Air Force] officers by asking him how his picture framing was going. The girls were quite intrigued to hear that Billy might have taken up the arts. They started asking if they could see the frames and his work. The boys were laughing their heads off.

In their first weeks at Waddington, Buckham and his crew were allocated their own Lancaster, or at least the one aboard which they would fly most of their combat operations. Its serial number was ME701 and it carried the code JO-F to designate that it was from 463 Squadron. All she needed was a name and an identity. While it was never officially condoned, the custom of giving aircraft nicknames and 'nose art' figureheads flourished during World War II. Most commonly, caricatures of naked or semi-naked women would adorn the forward fuselage and nearby rows of small bomb emblems would count the number of successful sorties flown. In the event the crew succeeded in shooting down an enemy aircraft, a small iron cross or swastika would also be added. Lancasters of the RAAF squadrons often competed to assert national pride. Kangaroos were a common theme and one of the Waddington Lancs used small boomerang emblems to denote completed operations. It was a design challenge that had Buckham's crew stumped until one day, during a visit to Lincoln, they stumbled on an idea in an unlikely place, as Buckham would recall.

You might find this hard to believe from one of the drinkiest crews in the air force, but this day we dropped in to a milk bar. The subject of a logo for the plane came up. Right opposite the bar where we were waiting for our malted milks we looked up and saw this massive painting of a rampant cow with fire coming out of its nostrils and between the legs was the biggest udder you ever did see. We all thought this was terrific and someone said, 'Let's use this and every time we do an operation, we can put a bottle of milk up there with her.' Then Jock said, 'Whoa Bessie!' And that was it. The ground crew went in and took a look at it and they thought it was wonderful. So that was it. From then on, we were flying Whoa Bessie.

Bessie would become one of the most famous aircraft at Waddington, particularly after some of the more dramatic adventures of Buckham and crew unfolded. She would survive a remarkable 33 combat operations, including some with alternating crews, and several near-death experiences before finally being brought down—on home ground. Soon after his arrival at Waddington in June 1944, Flying Officer Freddy Rush, a new pilot from Bondi in New South Wales, was required to do a night cross-country training flight and Bessie was the allocated aircraft, as Buckham would explain.

I'd given Freddy 12,000 pounds of lead weights to let him fly with a virtual bomb load and he had to perform fighter affiliation and that sort of thing in the air and then bring the 'bombs' back in at the end. He dropped the aircraft too fast and strained the wings, so they had to take her into the hangars and go over the wing structure to strengthen it. The job had been finished and I was at lunch when I heard the fire bells go and the first thing I thought of was my aircraft. I was due to do an air test that afternoon and I said, 'Bessie!' just like that. I got up and tore down to the maintenance hangar and there was the poor old thing up in flames. They had allowed an erk, a junior ground staff fellow, up into the cockpit seat and apparently, he'd got excited and pulled the red toggle down the side of my seat. It was the fuel jettison toggle and there was petrol in the tanks, which went everywhere. There was a spark and the whole thing went up.

Despite her premature demise, Bessie had achieved what relatively few other Lancasters would achieve—she had brought every crew member home alive, every time. Whoa Bessie!

∽

Within weeks of the Japanese attack on Pearl Harbor, the United States Army Air Forces (USAAF) had been mobilised to join the air war in Europe. In February 1942, General Ira C. Eaker, second in command of the US Eighth Air Force, arrived in

London and soon after set up a base at High Wycombe, Bucking-hamshire, where RAF Bomber Command had its headquarters under the newly appointed Commander-in-Chief, Air Marshal Arthur Harris.

The arrival of the Americans had been a turning point in the war. In a very short time they took over from the RAF or built from scratch 67 bomber stations and more than 200 airfields, mostly in the eastern English counties of Essex, Suffolk, Norfolk and Cambridgeshire. The influx of tens of thousands of American personnel—including many black servicemen—transformed life in the cities and villages of rural England. But relations between established British and Commonwealth squadrons and the new arrivals were not always cordial. The Americans were often resented by the men of the RAF because they were much better paid, had better facilities and perks and were allowed more generous leave entitlements. And the style and swagger of some of the Yankee airmen—whose numbers included Clark Gable and Jimmy Stewart—could rankle. Sometimes those resent-ments would boil over into violence.

Bruce Buckham recalled one dramatic incident when he and his crew were still with their OTU before being posted to Waddington, but the circumstances were far more serious than petty jealousy and rivalry.

One of our boys, Bluey Freeman, was coming home from a local hostelry on his bike one night when he suddenly saw a flash of silver ahead of him and another Aussie being stabbed by an American serviceman. As he swung off the bike, Blue hit the attacker square in the jaw, and he hit him so hard that it took them two days to revive him.

The American had certainly tangled with the wrong man. Edward Roy Freeman—known among his fellow Australians as Blue or Bluey on account of his 'blaze' of red hair—had form with his fists. According to Don Charlwood, who trained as a navigator with Freeman in Canada and was posted with him to 103 Squadron, he was 'a wild Irishman who got into some dreadful fights.'[5] Once, Charlwood recalled, 'Blue had taken on the local police and was under close arrest but fortunately he got out of it.' In April 1943, Freeman was court-martialled for misconduct at a hearing presided over by the legendary Australian airman Hughie Edwards VC, but he was acquitted on all charges. Freeman was a brave and talented navigator who would go on to do a second tour in the crew of Wing Commander Bill Brill at 463 Squadron and win a DFC. His encounter with the American attacker would have an explosive sequel, as Buckham recounted.

A few nights later there was another incident. Nobody said anything but we got ourselves prettied up and we went to the local village and beat up every Yank that we could find. We really went to town on them, and we told them why. The guy who'd been stabbed was an absolute gentleman, a navigator. He would have got himself killed that night if Bluey hadn't turned up at the right time.

Once at Waddington, Buckham himself was involved in an ugly confrontation with some American airmen. On this occasion, several American bombers had been diverted to Waddington. Before getting clearance to return to their home bases, some of the Americans made their way to the officers' mess for a drink.

A group of them came into the mess and one, a captain in his great leather and wool bomber jacket, went up to the bar and demanded a drink. One of the stewardesses, Georgie Tothill, a lass from the Isle of Wight, served him the drink and asked for payment. He then said to her, 'You have one too.' She said, 'No, I don't drink sir.' He then said, 'You heard what I said, you'll have one.' And she said, 'No, I can't drink in the officers' mess.' Then he grabbed her around the back of the neck and picked up the glass. Well, that's as far as he got. A bunch of us were standing just a few feet away and we just turned around and got him by the scruff of the neck and dragged him into the centre of the room and pounded him. We flattened the bastard. Then we dragged him outside, kicked him in the bum and told him to get. When we came back inside, nobody said anything to us, but then someone said to the other Americans, 'Take heed, if anyone steps out of line the same thing will happen to you. We don't behave like you bastards.' There was no love lost between the Yanks and the Aussies. It got so bad that the high command had to do something about fraternisation between the various services. We had to go and visit Yank stations and occasionally they would come to Waddington and other bases.

Chapter Five

BERLIN

It was a cauldron of hell, magnificent, awesome,
and we had to fly into and through it. It scared
the self-confidence out of me. I remembered how
to pray.

Wing Commander Rollo Kingsford-Smith[1]

In late 1940, Air Marshal Arthur Harris stood on the roof of
the Air Ministry in London as one of the worst nights of the
Blitz unfolded. 'I watched the old city in flames,' he recalled,
'St Paul's standing out in the midst of an ocean of fire—an
incredible sight. One could hear the German bombers arriving
in a stream and the swish of the incendiaries falling into the fire
below.'[2] Later accused of ruthlessly driving the counterattacks
that laid waste to dozens of German cities, Harris would insist
that this was 'the one occasion and the only one' when he was
stirred by vengeful feelings. But the moment steeled his long-
held conviction that a full-scale strategic bombing campaign
against Germany was not just the way to bring the Nazi regime
to its knees, it was the *only* way, at least in the early years of
the war. Evoking the Old Testament, he would that night
declare to Sir Charles Portal, the Chief of Air Staff: 'Well, they

61

are sowing the wind.' In later broadcast remarks he would add the rejoinder, 'and now they are going to reap the whirlwind.' The death of 43,000 British people in the Blitz—most of them civilians— would be seen by Harris as ample justification for the retribution that followed.

Harris was a tough, uncompromising but widely respected commander who, like most of the RAF leadership, had cut his teeth as a Sopwith Camel fighter pilot in World War I, claiming five enemy 'kills' and winning the Air Force Cross (AFC). Known to his friends as Bert, to the world as 'Bomber' and to some of his impudent but mostly admiring subordinates as 'Butch' (short for butcher), Harris drove Bomber Command with a relentless determination from the moment of his appointment. He would famously write in a minute to Winston Churchill in November 1943: 'We can wreck Berlin from end to end if the USAAF will come in on it. It will cost between 400–500 aircraft. It will cost Germany the war.'[3] If anyone could deliver on that promise, it was Arthur Harris. As historian Max Hastings would write: 'The C-in-C of Bomber Command was an elemental force, single minded in his conviction that he, and he alone, could contrive the defeat of Nazism through the systematic, progressive destruction of Germany's cities.'[4] It was Harris's belief, historian Martin Middlebrook would write, 'that strategic bombing on a large enough scale and relentlessly pressed home would cause the collapse both of German industrial production and the spirit of the German people. If this was successful, the war would end.'[5] The culmination of the strategy, once Britain had assembled sufficient and sufficiently capable bomber aircraft, was what became known as the Battle of Berlin.

Between November 1943 and March 1944, a total of nineteen massed raids were mounted by the RAF against the German capital and other large cities. The raids involved more than 10,000 bomber sorties, and more than 30,000 tons of bombs were dropped on or near Berlin. The crews faced a formidable opponent. By 1943, the great city was defended by a vast array of anti-aircraft guns and searchlights that stretched 40 miles from the city centre, not to mention the scores of Luftwaffe fighter squadrons based in the area. As the incoming crews diced with death at every moment, they would marvel at the spectacular sound and light show that unfolded beneath and around them. Bursts of German flak and dazzling searchlight beams were soon augmented with multicoloured showers of target-marking flares. The maelstrom reached its crescendo with the explosion of scores of bombs and the ensuing inferno on the ground. As Hank Nelson would write, 'For aircrew, the spectacle was an immediate measure of what they had to do and what they did. It was gratifying, seductive and terrifying.'[6] A total of 1047 RAF bombers were lost in the few months of the Battle of Berlin and more than 7000 aircrew were killed or captured. The campaign would be far from the knock-out blow that Harris had envisioned, and the loss of the equivalent of Bomber Command's entire frontline strength was a very high price to pay, but the effort, as Middlebrook would argue, 'reduced Germany's war effort and made a contribution to victory.'[7]

One of the last big raids of the Battle of Berlin was the first solo operation for Bruce Buckham and his crew. It almost claimed their lives but it launched their reputation as one of the most tenacious young crews in Bomber Command. On the night of

24–25 March 1944, a 'maximum effort' operation was declared, requiring all available crews to join the attack on Berlin. Despite very strong winds that night, the operation was not scrubbed and, in the end, more than 800 aircraft took off from dozens of airfields across eastern England. When the time came for Buckham's crew to depart, they could not start any of the four Rolls-Royce Merlin engines of their Lancaster. It took ground crew 45 minutes to replace the faulty starter motors, by which time the rest of the bombers were already tracking into German-occupied Europe. Buckham was convinced that they would not be expected to chase the main force and follow them into the holocaust that the raid would ignite, especially given that they were a novice crew on their first solo combat operation. But they were about to learn a sobering lesson about the ruthless, even callous, determination of some of their commanders.

As soon as the ground crew completed their work, Buckham peered down from his cockpit to witness an animated conversation beside the tarmac between the Waddington station commander, Air Commodore Allan Hesketh, and the Air Officer Commanding 5 Group Bomber Command, Air Vice-Marshal Ralph Cochrane. While he could not hear a word of the conversation, its conclusion was soon made very clear when Cochrane lifted his arm and pointed firmly down the runway. Moments later, an Aldis signal lamp turned green—the order to go.

After the Lancaster, weighed down with full tanks of fuel and a full bomb load, lumbered into the air, Buckham set course as briefed across the North Sea to Denmark then over the Baltic Sea to the German coastal city of Rostock before turning southeast towards Berlin. Despite the foreboding that gripped every heart, the tension was leavened by some black humour. As they crossed into German air space for the first time, Eric Giersch chimed in from his rear gun turret, 'I feel at home now!' According to Buckham, another of the crew shot back immediately, 'Yeah, bail out you rotten German bastard!'

During the long flight, the winds intensified and by the time they reached the German capital it was an hour since the raid had ended—and long after the bomber stream had turned for home. The lone crew arrived to find a sea of fire on the ground from the recent incendiary bombings and the skies alight with searchlight beams and anti-aircraft fire, as Buckham recounted:

We had the whole show to ourselves—ground defences, searchlights, heavy ack-ack and fighters galore—particularly through the bombing range. We had to get right through the lot on our own. Everything was being thrown at us and we were the only plane up there. And it was the same thing coming out and home. After we dropped the bombs, I looked out the front of us and there were three German fighters almost in formation going round in a perpetual turn. They must have been going off their heads because the people on the ground would have been in touch with them and yelling out, 'We know he's there, he must be right there with you, we can see him on the screen'—the giant Würzburg and Freya radar units would have been tracking us. And here I was following them. After about ten seconds following them in a gentle starboard turn, I dived away to the left, down into the darkest part of the sky, and came around behind Magdeburg and got home.

By the time they reached Waddington, having endured an eight-hour flight and dodged flak and marauding German night fighters all the way back to the Dutch coast, they were greeted by a distraught base commander. Allan Hesketh had stayed up late in the vain hope that they would survive what he had concluded was a suicide mission.

He had waited and waited and when we strolled into the interrogation room there were tears streaming down his cheeks and he bellowed out, 'Oh God, I tried to stop it. You weren't expected to make it back tonight and I am so glad to see you boys back.' And we said, 'Not half as glad as we are to see you!' He had tried to keep us on the ground, but Cochrane had insisted that we must go. Hesketh didn't want to see a young crew go out and not come back and he was convinced we would be killed.

The remarkable good fortune of Buckham and his crew was soon put in sharper focus when they discovered the fate of the others who had flown ahead of them that night. The severe weather had scattered the bomber stream and those who reached Berlin had bombed well to the south-west of the targets in the city centre. A total of 72 aircraft were lost, 8.9 per cent of the force—more than 500 crew killed or captured. 'I was too young and probably too silly to know in those days how great the danger had been,' Buckham would remark, 'but I learned a hell of a lot on that first trip with my own crew and that knowledge helped us to survive what was ahead of us.' While it would not be confirmed until months later, Bruce Buckham's gallant leadership that night would be a key element in his award of the DFC—a rare achievement for a pilot on his first solo mission with Bomber Command. The citation would note: 'Crossing the enemy defences alone, he completed a determined and successful attack. This officer's resource, fine fighting spirit and devotion to duty have been most praiseworthy.'[8]

Rollo Kingsford-Smith would later lament the lack of recognition for the great courage and sacrifice of the many Australian aircrew who took part in the Berlin raids: 'Despite the involvement of so many Australians, the Battle of Berlin seems unrecognised in Australia as a major battle involving many of our men. I believe it was the bloodiest and costliest four-month campaign involving Australians in World War Two.'[9]

The night after their lone mission to Berlin, Buckham's target would be a far easier task—if any flight over German-occupied Europe could be deemed less risky than another, given the vagaries of weather, anti-aircraft fire and German fighters. The attack was on the railway marshalling yards at Aulnoye, near the Belgian border, 50 miles south-east of Lille. It was one of a series of raids against transportation infrastructure across France designed to disrupt German logistics and reinforcements ahead of D-Day, then just over two months away. After the bloodbath of the Battle of Berlin, it was a remarkable success. A force of 192 aircraft took part in the raid and none was lost. The following night, 26–27 March, would be another successful operation for Bomber Command but not for Buckham's crew. It very nearly was their last.

Essen, the second largest city in the Ruhr, had been the target of more than twenty massed bombing raids over the previous two years. The main focus of the attacks had been the giant Krupp steelworks and shipyards. The Krupp factories supplied tanks, artillery, naval guns, armour plate, munitions and other armaments for the German military. Krupp's Germaniawerft shipyard had launched the cruiser *Prinz Eugen* and built more than 130 U-boats. The company's fabled 88 mm anti-aircraft cannon had proved to be ruthlessly effective against tanks and aircraft. A total of 705 aircraft, including 476 Lancasters, were sent into action on the evening of 26 March. The sudden switch to target Essen caught the German fighter controllers by surprise and only nine of the attacking aircraft—six Lancasters and three Halifaxes—were lost. Despite extensive cloud cover, the RAF Mosquitoes marked the targets well and 48 industrial buildings were seriously damaged or destroyed.

For the Buckham crew it was a special night—their first flying ME701 JO-F, 'Whoa Bessie'. They reached the target and completed their bombing run without incident. Minutes later, as they headed out of the Ruhr towards the Dutch border and home, they suffered a fate that all aircrew feared. They were 'coned' by the German air defence searchlights. First caught in the intense pale blue light of the master beam, a clutch of surrounding search-lights then homed in and also fixed their beams on Bessie. As night turned instantly to dazzling day, they were like the prover-bial deer in the headlights—a primary target for the dozens of German night fighters darting among the fleeing flock of British bombers. Momentarily blinded by the intense light, Buckham turned all his cockpit lights to full strength so that he could still read his instruments. Then they were 'smacked hard'—a burst of flak hit the starboard wing, which instantly caught fire. Buckham immediately ordered Jock Sinclair to activate the fire extinguishers and 'feather' both the starboard engines—turning their blades to minimise drag and allow shutdown.

I was weaving around madly trying to avoid a fatal hit. It was plain hell. The fighters stood outside the cone—far enough not to get hit themselves—but trying hard to shoot us down. And the fire was still burning fiercely on the wing. I then sang out to the crew, 'Hang on, we're going down.' After one more violent evasive manoeuvre, I was virtually on my back and I just turned us straight down, straight down towards the big blue beacon.

As Buckham threw the plane into a vertical dive, he also threw out the rule book, the lessons of which had been drummed into him during pilot training. The Lancaster was rated to a maximum diving speed of 395 miles per hour. Beyond that, the airframe could not be guaranteed to withstand the intense gravitational pressures. And neither could the crew.

As we dived, we went way past the safe diving speed. I saw the needle go past 395, 400, 405 and still we were accelerating. About halfway down, Jock yelled, 'We've lost the fire, skipper.' Sure enough, it wasn't attached to the aircraft anymore, but the fuel vapour was still burning in the air—this great long flame trailing behind us. The people on the ground put the lights out. They thought they had shot us down. And the fighters had disappeared. Nobody was shooting at us anymore.

The bold tactic to extinguish the fire had worked. But the relief was short-lived as the aircraft continued to plummet towards the ground and Buckham struggled desperately to regain control.

We were now hurtling at close to 500 miles per hour—over 100 miles per hour faster than the rated maximum—and we must have been up to six or seven times the force of gravity. I had been pressing down hard on the stick and I couldn't get it back. I had my feet up on the instrument panel and I was heaving but nothing was happening.

Buckham then decided to try adjusting the trim of the aircraft's tail planes in the hope that might turn them out of the dive. He had never been taught such a technique to recover from a terminal dive and had no idea whether or not it would work. It was a gamble but their only hope to survive.

I rotated the wheel for the trimming tabs very carefully and soon I could feel the attitude of the plane changing ever so slowly. At one point I thought, I won't take it any further, but we finished up levelling up pretty close to the ground. When I pulled it out, we were no more than a few hundred feet up. It was very, very close.

In those final moments, Buckham and most of his crew passed out from the immense gravitational pressure.

I blacked out but I knew we were levelling out by the time we got to the bottom of the dive. I was out for quite a few seconds. It might have been five, might have been ten. But I still had all my senses. I made sure I didn't do anything bloody stupid with the stick. I held it firmly and kept my feet on the rudders. I couldn't see anything. The others were also out for a few seconds. I heard them coming to: 'What happened to us? Where are we? Are we in heaven or what?' I said, 'You're doing alright. I am pleased to see you back on the job.' They told me what they thought of my flying. They told me to be more careful next time. Doc said, 'I wish you'd be more careful. You're doing this all the time. All my charts and pencils, everything's been scattered all over the place.'

As the plane finally levelled off, Jock Sinclair managed to restart one of the two starboard engines—which gave them enough power to limp home on three engines. But the extent of the damage was confirmation, had any been needed, of how close they had come to disaster. The entire wing was charred and there was a large hole and multiple punctures near the dead engine. By the time they reached Waddington, they were one of the last crews back from the Essen raid, and the last to be interrogated.

When we got in, I had a cup of coffee and sat down in the interrogation office. We hadn't said a thing about being hit or the fire. The intelligence officer looked at us and said, 'Did you see the aircraft on fire that was reported just north of Duisburg?' I said, 'Yeah, we know about that.' He said, 'What did it look like?' One of the crew then said, 'It didn't look too good to us as a matter of fact.' It went on for a few more questions and then he asked whether there was any damage to our aircraft. Then Jock, who used to give the damage report, said, 'Yeah, we had a bloody fire on the starboard wing, we got smacked with heavy flak and we burst into flames.'

But humour had its limits. All of the crew were sobered by the realisation of how narrowly they had escaped death, not least the pilot who had saved the day.

It was absolutely miraculous that we came through an ordeal like that. I think it was possibly one of the worst events we experienced, although I didn't measure these things from one operation to another as time went on. We were just so pleased to be able to move on and look forward all the time. I never worried about whether or not we were going to make it or even queried in my own mind whether we would. Very early in the piece I saw how quickly you can be here and, a split second later, you no longer are. So why worry about it? You signed up. You put your mark on the line. That was all there was to it.

In early 1944, the pace of operations was relentless and there was no respite even for crews that had endured such terrifying ordeals as the Essen raid had been for Buckham's men. Four nights later they were sent on what would go down in history as perhaps the most disastrous mission of the air war over Europe. On the night of 30–31 March, a force of 795 aircraft was dispatched to attack Nuremberg. It was said that Arthur Harris had prioritised the targeting of the grand mediaeval city because of its indelible association with the rise of Nazism. The second national convention of the Nazi Party was held in this Bavarian city in September 1923. Soon after, it became the backdrop for the annual mass rallies that had fixed the rise of Adolf Hitler in the world's consciousness, with their blaring Wagnerian overtures, swastika banners, goose-step marches and the demonic oratory of the Führer. It was also the place where the Nazi Party in September 1935 approved the infamous Nuremberg Laws, which stripped Jews of German citizenship and forbade marriage or sexual relations between Jews and 'citizens of German or kindred blood'—another step on the path to the horrors of the Holocaust.

The maximum effort raid on Nuremberg was to be the last operation of the Battle of Berlin and Harris was looking for a grand crescendo after a month of relatively poor bombing results, aside from the success of the Essen raid. As with most operations, the plans were based on unpredictable meteorological factors. The bombers were to take off late and follow an expected line of high cloud associated with a cold front over Norway before attempting a fast passage into southern Germany using the tail wind. Another key factor that night was the moon. A half-moon would be at its maximum elevation an hour before sunset and would not set until early the following morning. The threats of icing and moonlight could prove a dangerous mix for the bomber stream. Not everyone was happy with Harris's call. His deputy, Air Marshal Robert Saundby, thought it was too late in the lunar cycle for an attack on a target so deep into Germany—and everyone was aware that the cloud that was expected to give cover to advancing bombers could not be relied upon.[10]

No sooner had the first bombers crossed the coast over Belgium than the protective cloud disappeared, leaving the leaders of the stream bathed in bright moonlight. Simultaneously, German intelligence identified the path of the attack and night fighters were scrambled from as far away as Berlin. With more than 400 miles still to fly to Nuremberg, the force was exposed and in great peril. As the first Allied aircraft reached the German frontier moments after midnight, a swarm of more than 200 German fighters converged on the area. The first of their victims was an Australian 467 Squadron Lancaster piloted by Flight Lieutenant Bruce Simpson, which was hit by a burst of cannon fire from a Messerschmitt 109. Simpson and his entire crew managed to bail out before their aircraft crashed and exploded. Few of the following casualties would be so fortunate. Over the next hour another 58 bombers—40 Lancasters and 18 Halifaxes—were shot down. As Martin Middlebrook would write: 'It is unlikely that a single hour, before or since, has seen a greater rate of aerial destruction.'[11]

Bruce Buckham and his crew were in trouble from the moment they began to approach the Belgian coast. Twice, severe icing forced Buckham into a dive after his engines stalled.

At the operation briefing they had warned us that there was a very high icing index and we had to get up and over it into the dry air. But I never managed to get up through that section of the sky that night. We piled on ice in next to no time and I think I got to 14,000 feet at one point and we still weren't over it. Then all the motors coughed, the whole lot of them. We plummeted down, I reckon a good six or eight thousand feet. We weren't too high when I came out of the dive. All the way down I was pumping the throttle backwards and forwards making sure the movement was still there and there was work being done in the carburettors. As soon as we got back down low into the warmer air, one motor coughed back into full life and then the next one and the next one. I had them all going in about ten seconds. We were very lucky to get out of that.

Just moments after Buckham had regained control of the Lancaster, they were attacked by multiple German fighters, which forced him to quickly regain altitude as his rear and mid-upper gunners fought off the attackers. After climbing back into the protective cloud, severe icing again stalled all four engines. This time they plunged about 6000 feet before Buckham could restart the engines.

I was then meat for the German fighters. Every time we got up into the clouds we iced up. Every time we came out of the clouds we ran into a whole heap of German fighters and ground defences, but we pressed on. It was only when the gunners told me they had no more ammunition that I said, 'Okay Jimmy, get rid of the bombs, we are going back.' By that stage, we were somewhere out north of Nuremberg. As soon as I gave the order there was silence in the plane, absolute silence. You always feel it's a bit of a slur to abandon an operation even though it is regarded as legitimate, but this time we had no choice.

That was not the view of some of those on the ground back at Waddington, despite the heroic effort of Buckham and his crew to escape the fate of so many other crews who perished that night. Soon after they landed back at the station, Buckham was called in and 'carpeted' by the 463 Squadron commander Rollo Kingsford-Smith: 'He went lousy on me.' Buckham argued that he had been flying for five or six hours before he turned for home, by which time the main force attack had finished and there was no point in continuing with no ammunition left to defend the aircraft on the run home. Kingsford-Smith was unmoved. As he continued to angrily abuse Buckham, Air Commodore Allan Hesketh, the Waddington base commander, intervened. 'Forget it,' he told Kingsford-Smith, who had also flown as part of the raid, 'That laddie went to Berlin and bombed it alone. You had the protection of hundreds and hundreds of bombers tonight.'

Kingsford-Smith, a tough and gallant squadron commander, was perhaps suffering temporary memory loss when he upbraided Buckham for abandoning the Nuremberg raid. Just three months earlier, on 23 December 1943, Kingsford-Smith had flown to Berlin on his first operational sortie since taking command of 463 Squadron. About an hour out, flying over France at 20,000 feet with the outside air temperature at below minus 40 degrees Celsius, gunner Darrell Procter reported that the electrics to his rear turret and his electrically heated boots and gloves were not working. The pilot later described his dilemma: 'Either he abandoned the turret leaving us with no chance at all if we were attacked or he stayed there and would have been severely frostbitten with almost certain loss of fingers and toes.'[12] Kingsford-Smith reluctantly decided to return to base. While he would remember it as a 'shameful episode', Procter would have fonder recollections. He kept his life and limbs and would go on to finish his tour of operations with Bruce Buckham's crew.

As the reckoning of the cost of the Nuremberg raid unfolded in the hours after Buckham's return to Waddington, it was clear how lucky those who did survive had been. Historian Alfred Price would describe it as 'the greatest air battle of all time.'[13]

If so, it was the greatest disaster of all time for the RAF and perhaps the most triumphant hour for the Luftwaffe, which lost just 10 aircraft. At least 82 British aircraft were shot down before reaching the target and another 13 were shot down leaving the area—a staggering 11.9 per cent loss rate. Another 10 aircraft either crashed on return to their bases or were written off due to battle damage. At total of 545 aircrew were killed and a further 152 men, many of them badly injured, were taken prisoner after bailing out of their stricken bombers. Among the dead were 47 Australians but, astonishingly, there were no casualties from the 18 Lancasters dispatched from 463 Squadron and all, apart from Buckham's crew, completed their bombing runs.

Most of the crews that got home from Nuremberg reported that they had succeeded in bombing the target, but later intelligence indicated about 120 aircraft had bombed the town of Schweinfurt, 50 miles north-west of the city, due to strong winds causing havoc for navigators. Two of the Pathfinder aircraft actually dropped their markers at Schweinfurt, yet even then, most of the bombing thus directed fell outside the town. The attack on Nuremberg itself was also a failure. Thick cloud and a fierce crosswind that sprang up during the final main force approach to the target resulted in many of the Pathfinders marking too far to the east. A 10-mile-long creepback (where bombs that were released too early landed) also developed into the countryside north of Nuremberg. Little damage was caused in Nuremberg and civilian casualties were relatively light. And so, the costliest Bomber Command mission of the war in men and matériel—arms, ammunition and equipment—was also one of the most useless. Its one clear outcome was to spell the end of the Battle of Berlin—and the end of Arthur Harris's dream of bombing Germany into surrender. There was still another target that remained a high priority for the British Government, but the focus of Bomber Command would now turn sharply to the preparations for D-Day.

Chapter Six

ANGELS AND DEMONS

> You knew you were facing death all the time, night
> after night after night, but it's just a thing you
> accepted.
>
> Flight Lieutenant Peter Kelsey, 186 Squadron[1]

Every raid was dangerous and many for Bruce Buckham and his
crew would see dramatic incidents that brought home how fine
was the line between life and death. One operation in particular,
early in their first tour, would test to the limit the nerves of the
crew, and the sanity of one. As they headed towards their target
over Germany, the bomber stream was caught in an intense
barrage of flak that claimed multiple aircraft—including one
that was flying just above and behind Whoa Bessie, as Buckham
would recount.

The plane blew up right on our tail just above Eric Giersch in the rear
gunner's turret and bits and pieces of bodies were flying past him—
arms, legs and torsos. It was right on top of him and the turret was
covered in blood and he had blood spattered all over him. He just lost
his nerve. He was screaming and screaming. I didn't know what had
happened and I couldn't hear what Jimmy was saying to me and the

other boys were all worried. They didn't panic but I knew Eric must have seen something terrible. He was still screaming, and I just spoke to him quietly until I got my voice through. I had to stop him. It took a good five minutes, but I just spoke quietly to him, and he said, 'Oh Buck, you should have seen it. Oh God, I can't talk about it.' I said, 'Well, just calm yourself down if you can Eric because it is terribly important for you. We can talk about it as soon as we get down.'

It was only after they had landed back at Waddington that Giersch, still severely shaken by the experience, was able to explain exactly what had happened.

After we got out of the plane he turned around to all of us and spoke so nicely and quietly and he said, 'You've no idea what it was like. I was absolutely shocked, but I am so sorry for what I did, it must have unsettled you all.' And the lads, without exception said, 'Look Eric, you've done well, you're a bit of alright. Now you'd better go and get cleaned up.' And that was it. It was never mentioned again, not anywhere, not even at reunions after the war. That was something that happened within the family, and it stayed within the family.

While Eric Giersch was able to recover from his trauma and continue normal flying duties, many other airmen were not so fortunate. Much has been written celebrating the quiet heroism of the men of Bomber Command, and rightly so, but much less has been heard about those who failed to meet the exacting standards demanded of them through their tours of duty. In April 1945, the Director General of Medical Services of the RAF, Air Marshal Sir Harold Whittingham, reported:

'Each year there are about 3000 cases of nervous breakdown in aircrew and about 300 cases of lack of confidence. A third of the neurosis cases occur in Bomber Command.'[2] A large proportion of those cases were in training units where the men had not yet been exposed to the perils of combat operations but were still tested in extreme flying conditions. More than 8000 airmen were killed in training accidents or other non-operational flying during the war.

Lack of moral fibre (LMF) was the term coined by the RAF leadership early in the war to shame aircrew who refused to fly on operations, avoided operations or did a 'boomerang'—flew home early from a sortie without a persuasive excuse. In early 1940, senior officers had become increasingly concerned that medical staff were allowing too many men to avoid flying. A memorandum issued by the Air Ministry to all Commands in April sought to limit the definition of mental incapacity by promoting the alternative, if unspoken, diagnosis of cowardice. A revised version in September 1941 declared that those who 'come to forfeit the confidence of their Commanding Officers'[3] and who were proven medically fit would be classified LMF and their service records stamped with a large red 'W' for 'waverer'. All would be stripped of their flying badges, sometimes publicly in front of their peers. Officers would lose their commissions and be refused ground jobs in the RAF. Non-commissioned officers would be demoted to aircraftmen second class and assigned menial tasks for at least three months. From 1944, LMF cases could be sent to work in coal mines or drafted into the army. Many RAF psychiatrists, while accepting the policy's deterrent effect, thought it was wrong not to take account of individual conditions and mitigating circumstances. Their disquiet was ignored. Senior commanders, including Arthur Harris, regarded it as an essential measure to maintain discipline and aircrew numbers.

Historian Christopher Kingdon of the University of Chicago would write: 'RAF Command had an obsessive predilection, based upon Freudian concepts, that rises in neurotic rates were attributable to the character deficiencies of its wartime recruits, and not to the combined effects of prolonged exposure to combat stress and high attrition rates.'[4] In a report to Air Command in July 1943, Dr Edward Jewesbury, an RAF psychiatric specialist, demonstrated the force's intolerance and lack of sympathy for those airmen who suffered severe combat stress: 'The airman thereafter developed symptoms of an anxiety state and was treated in sick quarters for a month without improvement. In previous wars he would probably have been shot for cowardice. Today he is a "medical case", albeit a medical nuisance.'[5]

The rules were often ruthlessly applied. The authorities actively sought to ignore the reality that the mental trauma that made some airmen unwilling or incapable of flying was often due to factors well beyond their control. Historian Richard Overy describes the official embrace of the notion of LMF as 'a stigma designed as an emasculating deterrent to any sign of weakness.'[6] As with the victims of 'shell shock' in World War I, LMF often became a cover for the reality of a mental condition yet to find a name, post-traumatic stress disorder.

While relatively few of the tens of thousands of men who flew with Bomber Command were sidelined or disabled by trauma, there is little doubt that many of them were deeply affected by the terrible things they were required to do and experience night after night, day after day in the skies over German-occupied Europe. Not to be afraid was not to be human—and not to be afraid could expose crews to even greater levels of danger than were part of their basic job description. It could sap the confidence and focus of men whose survival often depended on that concentration.

Many aircrew would simply sublimate the stress or become fatalistic, according to Bruce Buckham:

There was no counselling. If the boys felt the need to talk to someone then sometimes they might go along to the padre and have a bit of a chat with him and a cup of tea. But I don't think I saw too many people looking for relief that way. It's an unfortunate thing that so many had reached the point where they said, 'Okay. It will be up any time now.' But others would say, 'Bugger that. Let's have another beer. We'll forget about it and let it stay forgotten.' But it was hard for some.

Buckham's way of dealing with the issue with his crew was to be inscrutable about his own feelings.

Some nights they felt a bit toey, a bit nervous after being briefed about a tough raid. They were intrigued with me. They didn't know how I felt inside. They used to say to me, 'Aren't you worried? You must be bloody frightened!' I would say, 'Oh no, I'm alright. It'll be alright. We're out there to do a job, you know, we've got to look after things. Do it right.'

I didn't want the crew to be affected by any change in me and how I reacted. I think I was able to be constant and maintain, at least to them, the same mental attitude that would not undermine their own confidence in being able to get through. But that was the hardest thing to do, not to let them know at all how I felt inside. To be perfectly honest, there were a few times when we listened to the details of the pre-flight briefing and realised it was going to be the most dangerous bloody affair, but you couldn't reveal any doubt that we would not come through. If I'd shown any inkling at all of trepidation it would have gone through the whole crew. But as soon as those motors started up, any concerns we might have had about tough operations were quickly forgotten. All of us would be concentrating on what we had to do. And it was just a plain wonderful feeling to be on operations with those fellers.

Buckham's reserve about revealing his feelings was not false bravado but rather a protective mechanism to ensure, as best he could, that the crew banished their own fears and remained focused on their mission. He was often 'bloody worried' about the challenges they faced on some operations but was driven by a pragmatic fatalism: fate would deal you the hand it had in store for you. The best you could do was to confront the risks that were within your power to mitigate: maintain discipline during operations, stay united as a team dealing with the tasks at hand and avoid the simple mistakes that had often been fatal for other crews.

I never really worried about whether we were going to make it or even queried in my own mind whether or not we would. Very early in the piece I saw how quickly you can be here and, a split second later, you are not here. The thing that benefited me was that the people back home had no idea what we were going through. If they'd known, and I knew they knew, I wouldn't have been able to do it. I'd done 43 trips before Gwennie even found out that I had been operational. It changed the tone of her letters then!

While claiming not to be a religious person, more than once after narrowly escaping a mid-air crisis, Buckham sensed 'a presence' that he felt had guided his reflexes to save him and his crew from likely disaster.

Sometimes we were in serious trouble and I did something without even thinking that kept us alive. And I can't quite grasp the peculiar feeling I had immediately afterwards. Why did I do that thing? What made me do it? Now that happened to me a few times. It wasn't an impulsive reaction on my part because I had no idea what was coming. I was aware of a presence, a most peculiar feeling I had on two or three occasions. I did something that was so precipitous, so quick, I can't tell you why I did it, but it made the difference between life and death. I didn't think too much about it at the time because we were still living, weren't we? But I was certainly aware of a presence being there. I am not a religious guy. I do believe that the only God is that of love, companionship, of goodness, of one being to another and the rest of it. But I felt I had a guardian angel.

The moment of reckoning with lurking demons would come at the end of his final tour.

For those who were not part of it, it is hard to comprehend how thousands of young men in Bomber Command willingly flew off into the heart of the war knowing full well how short the odds of survival were, how any moment over enemy-controlled territory they might be shot down or blown apart, or miraculously survive the jump from a crippled or burning aircraft only to spend years in a prisoner of war (POW) camp. A total of 125,000 aircrew served with Bomber Command during the war. More than 44 per cent of them were killed—the highest rate of attrition of any Allied unit. The average age of those killed was just 23. Many more aircrew were seriously injured or became POWs.

Life at the Bomber Command stations was deliberately structured to condition airmen to the almost daily death toll, or at least to avoid as much as possible contemplation of the losses by those who might be next to fall. Early each morning the names of those crews that had failed to return from operations were quietly scrubbed from the blackboard where they had been listed for operations the night before. Funerals and memorial services were never held for those known to have been killed over Europe. Often the slender hope that missing crew might have survived crashing or bailing out of a stricken aircraft, and been taken prisoner, was embraced to avoid confronting the probability that they were dead. For those known to have perished, a glass raised quietly in the mess or at the pub would be their farewell. When an airman failed to return, a group of officers known as a 'Standing Committee of Adjustment' would gather the missing man's personal effects and forward them to a central RAF depository, eventually to be returned to the family. Frequently the empty bed would be filled by a new crew member within a day or two. While these rituals could seem callous, many airmen who already were too aware of their own mortality appreciated not being required to dwell on the fate of those whose luck had run out. Bruce Buckham was one: 'We honoured them silently in our own minds. We'd have a drink the next night and the equanimity of life was restored straight away. You wouldn't dwell on it. You couldn't, because you had to keep going.'

Part of the answer as to why these men were able to stare death in the face and carry on lies in who they were and why they enlisted. All aircrew were volunteers—from Britain and throughout the Commonwealth—who signed on as patriots determined to fight an enemy that threatened the freedom of the mother country and therefore the freedom of all their nations. Training bonded them and, not least for the Australians, the mateship that infused their national identity was strengthened by the sense of mutual responsibility that flourished in the squadrons. But that spirit was severely tested at times when the airmen thought the commanders were indifferent to the losses of their comrades, according to Bruce Buckham.

There was no evidence, any sign at all, of sympathy when things went wrong and a lot of crews were lost. The attitude seemed to be, 'Oh well, too bad, we won't do that again,' or it was, 'Well, let's try something else.' The force was only a number of bodies who were sent out to do a job. That's the way they looked at it. We had bigger and bigger forces going out. They built up a thousand-odd planes for Hamburg. They burnt that out. There were a couple of thousand-bomber raids on Cologne. There were many other raids of 800 and 900 aircraft. To the commanders it was just bodies and numbers of bodies that were involved.

Early in his operational career, Buckham had kept a diary noting the losses of other aircraft after each mission. He soon concluded that this was not a constructive exercise.

After about half a dozen trips I stopped. I realised this was crazy. All I was doing was taking a note of the 'birds' that were not coming back. And I tell you what, it was a bit heart-rending when you have to go down to the flight next morning and wipe out half the names on the board where the crew were listed. The board had three lines for each crew and not many were able to fill those three lines— 30 trips. I didn't like it. There was no time differential between life and death. I worked out that I was worrying about something that wasn't manageable. And so I stopped keeping a count. I never thought about luck and I never thought about the lack of luck. I couldn't. Every split second of life out there had to be dealt with at the time as you saw fit.

Many airmen were convinced they had no hope of survival. Don Charlwood would write, 'We even became accustomed to the idea that to reach 30 ops was no longer possible, that home was a place for which we could afford no longings.'[7] Phil Eyles, who was Don Bennett's navigator when they were shot down over Norway in early 1942, was another fatalist. 'Everybody seemed to have the impression that they were going to cop it,' Eyles would recall. 'That is why, right from the start when I joined up, I wanted twelve shillings and sixpence a day [as a sergeant] instead of being an AC2 [aircraftman second class] on a shilling a day, and that was all I wanted. There was going to be a pension for my wife and child.'[8]

The exhilaration of battle and dicing with death would drive a lot of airmen to perform superhuman feats, night after night. In fact, Rollo Kingsford-Smith found that the intensity of battle could supplant other drives. After a few weeks at RAF Bottesford, before moving to Waddington, Rollo met Jane: 'She was a vivacious and petite WAAF sergeant on the station. She was fun to be with and I really enjoyed her company. But my marriage vows were not challenged. It seems that war was better than sex or should I say war was stronger than sex. The fear before combat, then the excitement followed by the fatigue put sex right out of my mind and possibly my ability.'[9]

But even the toughest and most stoic of airmen could be brought undone by dramatic events. Jamaican Billy Strachan flew a tour as a wireless operator/air gunner before retraining as a pilot and joining 576 Squadron, based at RAF Fiskerton near Lincoln, in the final months of the war. His flying career came to an abrupt end one night soon after his Lancaster took off carrying a 12,000-pound bomb to attack German shipping, as Strachan would recount.

Our flight path was over Lincoln Cathedral. It was a foggy night, with visibility about 100 yards. I asked my engineer, who stood beside me, to make sure we were on course to get over the top of the cathedral tower. He replied: 'We've just passed it.' I looked out and suddenly realised that it was just beyond our wingtips, to the side. This was the last straw. It was sheer luck. I hadn't seen it at all—and I was the pilot! There and then my nerve went. I knew I simply couldn't go on—that this was the end of me as a pilot. I flew to a special 'hole' we had in the North Sea, which no Allied shipping ever went near, and dropped my 'big one'. Then I flew back to the airfield.[10]

Strachan's navigator that night was Flight Lieutenant Len Dorricott, who had earlier won the DFM on operations with 460 Squadron RAAF aboard the celebrated 'G for George' Lancaster. In his flying logbook, Dorricott would note with great understatement, 'Skipper sick.' Following the incident, Strachan was sent to a large country house in Coventry where he stayed for 48 hours. A psychiatrist who interviewed him attributed his breakdown to 'war weariness'. Billy Strachan never flew again but also was never awarded the DFC that undoubtedly was his due after such long and brave service with Bomber Command. After the war he became a famous communist and leader of the black rights movement in Britain.

Many airmen relieved the intense stress of operations by drinking hard and playing hard in their free time. The Australians were notable for their excess on both counts. Rollo Kingsford-Smith liked to drink and found that teetotallers, who were often alone when not flying, did not cope as well with the stress of operations as those who drank. 'Drinking (draught beer only—spirits were nearly unprocurable), the company at the bar and forgetting about the war was important therapy,' Kingsford-Smith would write. 'Many misinformed English people did not really warm to Australian aircrews' hijinks when not on duty. My enduring memory of most of my aircrew is of young men who, between fighting and dying, lived wildly, played exuberantly, and loved sometimes imprudently.'[11]

Bruce Buckham's crew was famous for their exploits in the air and infamous for their escapades on the ground. Doc Board and Johnny Muddle were repeat offenders who often pushed their luck to the limits on nights of heavy drinking and carousing. One night on leave they went to Leeds to watch *Target for Tonight*, the award-winning film that recreated a bombing attack on Germany. While waiting outside the cinema, after a long session at the pub, they saw a raft leaning against the cinema wall. The raft was promptly removed, placed in the middle of the street, and they jumped in and started paddling. A policeman confronted the pair who told him they had just bailed out and were rowing to safety—before they fled the scene, as Buckham recounted.

They disappeared around the corner into a pub. Two sheilas who saw this took them in charge and said, 'They'll find you here and you'll be in hot water. You'd better come with us.' So they took them home to their flat and looked after them. They fed them and then it was bedtime and these lasses said, 'We'll go and get changed now if you don't mind.' And those two rascals looked at each other. Next thing, the girls came out wearing practically nothing. They had on these flimsy night things and down below they had cut two of these advertisements from the newspaper with the caption, 'Target For Tonight.' So the girls wheeled them off to bed and made them perform.

Another time, Board and Muddle went to London with mates from Bill Brill's crew. The next morning Brill and Buckham were having breakfast in the Waddington mess when a news report came over the radio about an incident in Trafalgar Square the night before. There had been a substantial fire when bales of hay being used in a display for a recruitment promotion to encourage women to join the Land Army caught fire. It was reported that several men in the distinctive blue uniforms of the RAAF had pitched in heroically to help put the fire out. Brill turned to Buckham and declared: 'I'll bet those bastards were responsible for that. I can see them there! They weren't trying to put it out. They were fanning the bloody flames.' Subsequent investigations confirmed Brill's suspicions. Board and friends had wandered into the square 'a bit blotto' after a long lunch and had decided to have a little fun setting alight one of the hay bales, before things got out of hand. A disciplinary charge was prepared but later dropped. 'They got off, yet again. But only because of the vigilance of those who had their best interests at heart,' Buckham explained. 'They had to let off steam. You were aware of having to live for six weeks before you got six days off and that was a pretty trying experience sometimes. You would ask yourself, "Will I last from one leave to another?" It was hard.'

Other crew members had more conventional ways of entertaining themselves while on leave. Buckham and Giersch bought a car together while they were still in training at RAF Swinderby. It was a Standard which they acquired from a scrap yard in Nottingham for fourteen pounds. Their first journey was almost their last. While heading back to the station in a severe rainstorm with 'five or six' mates crammed into the dilapidated car, they almost drove over a 30-foot drop into the Trent River. Back at Swinderby, Buckham handed over the vehicle to Johnny Ball, who ran a garage not far from the perimeter track at Swinderby.

I said to Johnny, 'We'd appreciate it if you would turn this into a car.' He did it up and charged us a whole nine pounds. He told us we would have to get it properly shod, and we told him we only had coupons to get two tyres. He said, 'There's nothing wrong with you selling the car to Mr Giersch and he will get two and then you'll have all good tyres.' So that's what we did, and we would sell the car to each other from time to time as necessary. When we went on leave, if we hadn't been too extravagant using up our petrol ration, we would be right. But there were other times we wouldn't have been able to get much further than Lincoln, four miles away. Sometimes it just happened by accident that, when we left the car at the airfield dispersal point when we went on operations, which we shouldn't have done but we did, the tank would be full when we got back.

Chapter Seven

THE BEAST

The destruction or even crippling of this ship is the greatest event at sea at this present time. No other target is comparable to it.

British Prime Minister Winston Churchill,
January 1942[1]

In late 1936, at the Wilhelmshaven dockyards on the North Sea coast, Nazi Germany began constructing the biggest battleship ever built by a European navy. Under the Second London Naval Treaty signed on 25 March 1936—the revised arms control convention first ratified after World War I—new German and Allied capital ships were restricted to 35,000 tons with a maximum armament of 14-inch guns. But less than a week after that agreement was struck, the ship that Winston Churchill would call 'The Beast' was laid down with a planned displacement of 42,200 tons and a bristling arsenal crowned by eight 15-inch guns. If there had been any lingering doubts about Hitler's belligerent intentions, they were extinguished with the launch on 1 April 1939 of Kriegsmarine Schiff (KMS) *Admiral von Tirpitz*. She would be known simply as *Tirpitz*. Indeed, Churchill would insist on this short form in all official communications, to save the time of typists, cipher staff and signallers, much of whose work would be consumed with the battleship's fortunes and fate. 'Surely *Tirpitz* is good enough for the beast,'[2] he would gripe to Albert Alexander, the First Lord of the Admiralty. Her destruction would become a strategic imperative of the first five years of the war that began soon after her launch. And by January 1942 Churchill made plain the price he was prepared to pay for this—in matériel and men's lives: 'The crippling of this ship would alter the entire fact of the naval war and . . . the loss of 100 machines or 500 men would be well compensated for.'[3]

Tirpitz and her slightly smaller sister ship *Bismarck*, launched two months earlier, were juggernauts: more than 275 yards long with beams 44 yards wide. Their steel hulls were 12.5 inches thick below the waterline and 5.6 inches above, encasing double and traverse internal bulkheads to guard against torpedoes, mines and bombs falling nearby. The upper decks were covered with strengthened plate between 2 and 5 inches thick. The layers of protective steel would account for about 40 per cent of the weight of *Tirpitz*. Her huge, 15-inch main guns were set in four twin-gun turrets—forward, Anton and Bruno, and aft, Caesar and Dora—and had a range of more than 23 miles. In addition, she had twelve 6-inch guns, fourteen 4-inch heavy flak guns, sixteen light flak guns and two quadruple 21-inch torpedo batteries. As the RN and the RAF were soon to discover, she was virtually unsinkable. Virtually.

The *Bismarck* would prove the relatively easier quarry. In May 1941, as she attempted to break into the Atlantic with the heavy cruiser *Prinz Eugen*, the battleship was engaged by a fleet of British warships including the battlecruiser HMS *Hood* and the battleship HMS *Prince of Wales* in what became the Battle of the Denmark Strait. *Hood* was destroyed by combined fire from the two German warships, sinking within three minutes with the loss of all but three of her crew of 1418. *Prince of Wales* was damaged and forced to retreat after scoring three hits against *Bismarck*, which consequently was forced to abandon her raiding mission. Stung by the shocking loss of *Hood*, the RN returned in force two days later and intercepted *Bismarck* as she headed to the dockyards of Saint-Nazaire on the Bay of Biscay in occupied France to undergo repairs. A squadron of torpedo bombers launched from the aircraft carrier HMS *Ark Royal* attacked, one scoring a direct hit that wrecked the battleship's steering gear. The following morning, the crippled *Bismarck* was engaged by two British battleships and two heavy cruisers, suffering severe damage and heavy loss of life before she was scuttled to avoid being boarded by the British. Winston Churchill was in Church House, temporary home of the House of Commons, when the news broke. 'A slip of paper was passed to me,' he later recalled. 'I asked the indulgence of the House and said, "I have just received news that the *Bismarck* is sunk." They seemed content.'[4] Hitler was furious at the loss of one of his most prized battleships and ordered that none of Germany's capital ships were to be again put at risk by engaging the British in major battles. He was determined that *Tirpitz* would not suffer the same fate as *Bismarck*. His caution would blunt the impact of Germany's naval forces for the rest of the war but helped give *Tirpitz* a few more years of life.

Britain's first concerted attempt to sink *Tirpitz* was made on the night of 9-10 July 1940. Eleven Hampden bombers from

RAF 5 Group in Bomber Command targeted the battleship at her berth in Wilhelmshaven. It would be recorded that 'owing to searchlight activity, darkness and haze, results of the attacks were not observed.'[5] In fact, all of the bombers missed their target—as did most of Bomber Command's operations in the early stages of the war. That operation would be the first of no less than 24 mostly fruitless raids mounted by the RAF and the Royal Navy against *Tirpitz* over the next three years, involving submarines, torpedoes, mines and every incarnation of bomber and fighter in the British inventory. Many of the raids were spectacular if unsuccessful and many involved great daring on the part of pilots, aircrew and naval personnel, including many Australians serving with the RAF and the RN.

In January 1942 *Tirpitz* and her crew of 2608—108 officers and 2500 men—were relocated to German-occupied Norway, where it was thought she would be safer from British attacks and could be deployed against Allied shipping in the North Atlantic and the vital Arctic convoys supplying Russia. The decision is also believed to have been influenced by Hitler's fears that Britain might be contemplating an invasion to liberate Norway. The move, in turn, intensified British fears of the threat posed by the battleship as German U-boats wrought havoc on vital trans-Atlantic shipping convoys and the Arctic convoys resupplying the embattled Russian forces. Churchill railed: 'The whole strategy of the war turns at this period on this ship, which is holding four times the number of British capital ships paralysed, to say nothing of the two new American battleships retained in the Atlantic. I regard the matter as of the highest urgency and importance.'[6]

The first Norwegian refuge of *Tirpitz* was in Faetten Fjord (Fættenfjord), near Trondheim, about 300 miles north of Oslo. Here she was anchored 40 miles from the open sea and protected from most forms of attack, surrounded by hills and moored close to cliffs on one side and hemmed by torpedo nets on all others. On the rare fine day that made air attacks possible, she had only to request a rapid smokescreen from generators positioned around the shore to become invisible.

Despite these defences, RAF Bomber Command mounted a series of attacks in the early hours of 31 March and 28 and 29 April 1942—the Halifax raids. The weather conditions during the first of these operations were so bad that only one of the 33 aircraft succeeded in finding *Tirpitz* at all. The usual smokescreen was deployed, and the attack was aborted. During the second and third attacks, most of the aircraft dispatched, 40 and 34 respectively, managed to find the ship but again the smokescreens prevented useful results from being achieved. The damage suffered by the attackers was greater than that inflicted on their enemy.

The raid on 28 April would help make the name of perhaps the most famous Australian to serve in Bomber Command. Wing Commander Don Bennett—who would later become an air vice-marshal and founder of the legendary Pathfinder Force—was one of the leaders of the five squadrons that took part, as officer commanding 10 Squadron. As he crossed the North Sea, Bennett dropped flame floats to guide his pilots towards the Norwegian coast. As the attack commenced, soon after midnight, the bombers faced a heavy smokescreen that quickly obscured sight of the ship and they were harassed by heavy flak that brought down four aircraft and inflicted serious damage on others. The Halifax bomber piloted by RAAF Flight Lieutenant George 'Dusty' Miller was hit by a barrage from one of the German ships guarding *Tirpitz* and he was forced to make a crash landing on an adjoining fjord with his starboard wing trailing 300 yards of fire. His air gunner and flight engineer were killed instantly. He and the other crew had to dive beneath 'a sea of flames' streaming from their aircraft's ruptured fuel tanks.

When I surfaced, I looked around for the tail gunner at the rear of the aircraft. I could not see him, so I started to swim slowly back in my Mae West lifejacket. I couldn't find the others so concluded they must have drifted away . . . I was already feeling numb from the cold and realised I would soon lose consciousness so I fixed my inflated collar to ensure my head stayed out of the water and I wouldn't drown. I must have passed out for the next thing I recall is that I was on the table in a small minesweeper surrounded by sailors with the word *Kriegsmarine* on their hats and they were holding a mug of rum to my mouth.[7]

Along with his New Zealand navigator, Flight Sergeant Keith Gregory, Miller was transferred from the minesweeper to the German cruiser *Prinz Eugen*. After being treated by medical orderlies and plied with more rum and cigarettes, he was escorted by two sailors with sub-machine guns to meet the admiral.

I went with two sailors along passages and up stairways to the top of the ship just behind the bridge . . . I went into a beautifully set up large cabin with, I recall quite clearly, a coal fire burning in a fireplace, and a most distinguished-looking, gold-braided, grey-haired, fairly large gentleman sitting at a table with a bottle of Dewars Scotch Whisky.[8]

Miller was told that he had been very foolish to attack *Tirpitz*, that he would now be sent to Germany as a POW and—in answer to Dusty's question—that the Dewars had come from the naval officers' stores at Narvik when the northern town was captured by the Germans in 1940. Miller would spend the rest of the war in various POW camps, including the infamous Stalag Luft III during the time of the Great Escape. After the war, he would return to Papua, the land of his birth, where he would partner the buccaneering actor Errol Flynn in an ill-fated business recruiting native labourers and running a coastal shipping service before settling down as a copra planter on an idyllic island in the Louisiade Archipelago. When Flynn contracted a dose of venereal disease and was 'broke', Miller stumped up a loan of 100 pounds to pay for his passage back to Sydney and medical treatment—a true measure of Australian mateship.[9]

Another of those shot down on 28 April was Don Bennett, Dusty Miller's squadron commander. As Bennett's Halifax crossed the coast into Norway, it was hit repeatedly by anti-aircraft fire from the shore batteries, and the rear gunner, Flight Lieutenant Herbert How, was wounded. When Bennett reached Faetten Fjord, he found 'fog filling the whole of the fjord' with only the masts of *Tirpitz* visible through the thickening blanket of smoke. As he approached the great ship, the flak intensified, and his starboard wing caught fire. After dropping his load of mines close to the hidden ship, Bennett banked sharply to the east with the fire on his wing spreading, his starboard undercarriage down and the starboard flap beginning to trail. Struggling to keep control, he ordered the crew to abandon the aircraft.

Things were getting fairly hot in the cockpit and the flames were very extensive and fierce on the starboard wing. We were losing height rapidly ... the ground was getting very close. Finally, as I was holding the wheel hard over to port, I eased myself out of my seat preparatory to jumping and just at that moment the starboard wing folded up. I jumped through the hatch below me like a shot, and pulled the rip cord the moment I was clear. It was only just in time; my parachute opened just as I was striking the snow.[10]

The abandoned aircraft flew on for another half mile before crashing and exploding. What happened next would be the subject of two florid and totally contradictory accounts given by Don Bennett—one in his post-war memoirs and the other in the secret records of MI9, the British Directorate of Military Intelligence.

According to Bennett's memoirs and a post-war interview with the Imperial War Museum, after shedding his parachute and Mae West life vest, the pilot found his wireless operator, Sergeant Clive Forbes, and the two men climbed through the night and the next two days over the frozen mountain range, narrowly avoiding German border ski patrols with barking tracker dogs. As they approached the sanctuary of neutral Sweden, they stumbled on a remote farmhouse. Tired, hungry and 'in a pretty bad state', the two men decided to risk the possibility of a hostile reception that would deliver them into the hands of the Germans. Instead, they were warmly welcomed by the farmer and his wife. 'He was able to speak English,' Bennett recalled. 'He'd lived in Australia and generally was wonderful. They gave us some of the very little food they had, laid us on the floor in front of a wood stove and gave us two hours' sleep, the only sleep we got in three days.'[11]

As well as Bennett and Forbes, two other members of the crew managed to evade capture and cross independently into Sweden—second pilot Sergeant Harry Walmsley and engineer Flight Sergeant John Colgan. Interned for a month, all four airmen were eventually repatriated to England. The remaining members of the crew, who had been captured soon after bailing out, would spend the rest of the war in German POW camps.

On 26 May 1942, two days after his return from Sweden, Don Bennett gave a dramatically different account of his escape from Norway in a formal record of interview with MI9 that would be classified 'Most Secret'.

I landed in snow among sparse trees near Elvran at 0115 hours and gave a shout in the hope that some of my crew would hear. I got an immediately reply from Sergeant Forbes who had been the last to jump before myself. Just as I met him, a German soldier on skis, armed with a rifle, appeared and indicated we were to accompany him. After that we heard other calls and, after signing to us to stay where we were, our captor dashed off to round up the rest. When he had gone 200 yards, we ran. We ran for about five hours through deep snow.[12]

Harry Walmsley gave an even more exotic account to the MI9 interrogators on the same day as Bennett. He described having met up with Colgan soon after they had bailed out of the Halifax.

We found a cart track and followed it for about three minutes but were suddenly faced by three Germans who covered us with revolvers. They had just patted us over in search of weapons when other shouts were heard and two of them went off leaving the other to watch us. When the two had disappeared, I tackled our guard and Sergeant Colgan kicked the revolver out of his hand. We then rendered him unconscious and ran off into the woods.[13]

It would not be until October 1942, after Clive Forbes was belatedly repatriated from Sweden, that the true story would be acknowledged. In his intelligence debriefing, Forbes would make no mention of escaping from German soldiers with Don Bennett. He said that after landing in the snow he had buried his parachute and begun hiking east towards the Swedish border. He said he had later met up with Bennett while trying to cross a river and they had then continued on together before reaching Sweden without being detected. A note added to the record of interview would say: 'This statement contradicts that given in paragraph 2 of Wing Commander Bennett's statement telling of capture by a German soldier on skis. The story of capture was invented and agreed upon in order to avoid internment.'[14] The method in the subterfuge orchestrated by Don Bennett was simple. The convention was that airmen who *evaded* capture and reached neutral territories would be interned in those countries for the duration of the war, but airmen who *escaped* after being captured were entitled to seek repatriation. Without his fictitious capture by a German soldier, Bennett would likely have been stuck in Sweden for the rest of the war and have missed his date with destiny.

Despite the heroic persistence of the 40 RAF crews that had reached the target on the final April raid, *Tirpitz* was unscathed. The cost to the RAF had been substantial. Six aircraft had been brought down and fifteen airmen killed.

After further damaging but not fatal attacks from air and sea over the following months, the German high command resolved in March 1943 to relocate *Tirpitz* 200 miles further north to Kaa Fjord (Kåfjorden)—well north of the Arctic Circle and well beyond the range of Allied bombers in Britain. Her new berth, about 40 miles from the northern city of Tromsø, also lay beside the route of the Arctic convoys carrying vital cargo to the northern Russian port of Archangel. It was a threat that the Allies could not allow to continue unchallenged. But to the protective tyranny of distance was added a formidable defensive shield for the great warship. Kaa Fjord was located 80 miles from the main entrance to Alten Fjord (Altafjord), which was guarded by a boom. *Tirpitz* was further shielded by mines and anti-submarine nets. In addition, there were eight batteries of flak guns positioned ashore around the fjord as well as generators that could within minutes envelop the area in a thick defensive smokescreen.

In late 1943 the most daring—and damaging—attack on the *Tirpitz* so far was mounted by the RN. It would be described by the operation's commander, Rear Admiral Claud Barry, as 'undoubtedly one of the most hazardous enterprises undertaken in the war.'[15] Six purpose-built midget submarines crept into Kaa Fjord around 1900 hours on the evening of 22 September 1943. Two of the three-man subs—the X6 and the X7—managed to breach the battleship's underwater defences and place two-ton mines on the sea floor near the hull before being spotted and attacked. The six crewmen were captured and brought aboard *Tirpitz*. While they were being interrogated the mines exploded, causing extensive damage to the ship. The eruptions caused her to heave more than a metre out of the water. As more than 1400 tons of water surged through the damaged hull, the ship listed two degrees. A ruptured oil tank disabled most of the generators and spilled oil across the fjord for several miles from the vessel. There was further serious damage to the ship's electrical and mechanical systems, two float planes were thrown from the deck and destroyed, and Dora, one of the four 15-inch gun turrets, was torn from its mountings and would never be fired again. The raid would put *Tirpitz* out of action for six months before the extensive repairs could be completed.

For their heroic efforts, the commanders of the two successful subs, Lieutenant Donald Cameron and Sub-Lieutenant Godfrey Place, were both awarded the VC. But they would have to await the end of the war to receive their medals, biding their time in Marlag 'O', the German POW camp for naval officers near Bremen. Controversy would develop in the years after the war over the fate of the third midget submarine—the X5—captained by Lieutenant Henty Henty-Creer, a 22-year-old officer of the Royal Australian Naval Reserve (RANR) from Sydney who had been seconded to the RN. The dashing and gregarious son of a naval officer, Henty-Creer had worked in the film industry before enlisting in 1940—most recently in Canada as a cameraman on the film *49th Parallel*, starring Laurence Olivier and Leslie Howard.

As Cameron and Place were being interrogated aboard *Tirpitz*, just before the explosions, they saw what was later confirmed to be the X5 surface outside the triple netting around the ship and come under fire before disappearing. The later naval report concluded that the submarine had been sunk by a depth charge about half a mile from *Tirpitz*, after failing to penetrate the nets. Lieutenant Henty-Creer and his crew were presumed to have been killed in action. To the disgust of his family, Henty-Creer's undoubted bravery was rewarded not with a gallantry medal but merely a 'Mentioned in Despatches' certificate. The family argued that no evidence had been offered to support the conclusion that the X5 had not completed its mission. They believed that, having placed its mines, the submarine had got back out through the nets and was escaping when it surfaced and was sunk. The family's case was strengthened by evidence gathered from Norwegian seamen who reported seeing *Tirpitz*'s stern rise out of the water during the explosion. Godfrey Place confirmed after the war that neither he nor Donald Cameron had placed their charges directly under the stern. Admiral of the Fleet Sir George Creasy, who was the RN's Commander of Submarines from 1944 to 1946, conceded the possibility that Henty-Creer had already succeeded in placing his charges when X5 was attacked. When the wreckage of the submarine was located by amateur divers in the 1970s, there was no sign of the two big saddle mines that it had carried into the operation. But the hopes of Henty-Creer's family were again dashed in 2011 when the British Government rejected a formal petition that he be posthumously awarded a VC.

At least the role of another Australian naval officer involved in the daring midget submarine operation would be rightly honoured. At the same time the four submarines were sent to attack *Tirpitz*, two more—the X9 and the X10—were tasked with attacking her support ship, *Scharnhorst*, which had been berthed nearby. The X9 sank with loss of all crew while under tow across the North Sea. That left the X10—commanded by Lieutenant Ken Hudspeth of the RANR—to continue alone into the fjord, unaware that *Scharnhorst* had shifted berth and was now in nearby Alten Fjord. As they headed towards the target zone, one of the side-cargoes flooded. Hudspeth, who was born in Echuca in Victoria before moving to Tasmania with his family and training as a teacher, then asked each of his crew whether they still wanted to proceed with the attack. All agreed, but their problems soon began to multiply.

Within four miles of where they still thought *Scharnhorst* was located, the periscope motor burned out and the submarine filled with fumes. Then the gyro compass and the magnetic compass light both failed. Soon after that, the boat started to leak, all of the switchboard fuses blew and one of the two side-cargo explosive saddles began to leak. Hudspeth then took X10 down onto the sea floor to try to make repairs. When those efforts failed, he was left with no choice but to abandon the attack. By that stage, they had been submerged in the fjord for nearly 24 hours and their oxygen supply was almost exhausted. Hudspeth took the X10 out of the fjord to rendezvous with their escort submarines. For his gallant and determined leadership, Ken Hudspeth was awarded the Distinguished Service Cross (DSC) 'for outstanding courage and devotion to duty.'

Over the following year he would twice more be awarded the DSC for his bravery captaining the mini-subs, earning a first bar for landing special forces personnel along enemy-held coastlines in early 1944 and a second for his work guiding the D-Day landings.

While the Germans were licking their many wounds from the X-craft raids on *Tirpitz*, the RN stepped up planning for a new attack to be made before the battleship was again seaworthy—this time led by the Fleet Air Arm (FAA), the aviation wing of the RN. In March 1944, an armada of more than 30 British warships in two formations led by the aircraft carriers HMS *Furious* and HMS *Victorious* embarked from Scotland. Their primary task was to protect Convoy JW 58—a convoy of 49 merchant ships carrying supplies to Murmansk in Russia. But that task also provided vital cover from German intelligence for the attack code-named Operation Tungsten.

Aboard *Furious* and *Victorious* were 42 Barracuda torpedo and dive bombers formed in two strike forces from the FAA's bomber squadrons and the squadrons of 52 Wing RAF, supported by 40 fighter aircraft. The 163 FAA airmen in the attacking units included two Australians and twenty-eight New Zealanders. One of the New Zealanders, Lieutenant Jeffery Gledhill DSC, would later swap navies and complete his distinguished career as director of intelligence in the Royal Australian Navy.

On the afternoon of 2 April 1944, with Convoy JW 58 safely through to Russian waters, the two carrier groups converged about 250 miles northwest of Kaa Fjord. The attack on *Tirpitz* was launched just before dawn the next morning as Gledhill, who led one of the flights of Barracudas, would recall:

The aircraft formations flew very low on the sea until the snow-covered mountainous coast of northern Norway was inland. They crossed the peaks surrounding Kaa Fjord, snowfields gleaming in the sun and stretched to the horizon, but here heavy calibre AA [anti-aircraft] fire was bursting near us and the great battleship of 122 guns came into view. Fighters were sent down to strafe and the Barracudas deployed for their attack, rolling into steep dives in rapid succession with AA fire coming from the ship and shore batteries. Smoke was released from canisters round the fjord. Explosions, fires, and clouds of smoke occurred as many bombs hit. Meantime No. 52 Wing of 19 Barracudas and its escorts was launched from the fleet. On arrival over the target, they found the ship almost obscured by smoke, nevertheless they carried out their attack and then headed for the coast and out to sea to their carriers.[16]

Two Australian fighter pilots in the thick of the attack were Sub-Lieutenant Fred Sherborne from East Fremantle in Western Australia and Sub-Lieutenant Walter 'Jimmy' Bowles. Sherborne had trained as a pilot after serving two years as an ordinary seaman gunner in the Mediterranean and surviving an Italian torpedo attack on the merchant ship SS *Imperial Star*, which was later scuttled. In August 1944 he would be shot down near Avignon, in the south of France, and hidden by villagers until the area was liberated by Allied forces. New Zealand-born Jimmy Bowles went on to serve in the Korean War, flying fighters from HMAS *Sydney*, and winning both a DSC and a United States Legion of Merit for his gallantry.

The dive-bombing attack on *Tirpitz* was spectacular and the pilots and crews flew back to the aircraft carriers reporting multiple direct hits, explosions and fierce fires—convinced that they had crippled the great ship. Captain Michael Denny, the commander of *Victorious*, immediately signalled Vice Admiral Sir Henry Moore, the Vice Chief of the Naval Staff: 'It is certain that *Tirpitz* is badly hit by first strike.'[17] After a detailed study of the crew debriefings and photographs from the bombers' cameras, Denny concluded that ten bombs from the first wave of aircraft had hit the ship. He then sent a second message to Moore: 'I believe *Tirpitz* now to be useless as a warship.' Final Admiralty reports would credit their aircraft with at least twenty-four hits, with the loss of eight FAA aircraft and nine airmen. German records would credit fifteen hits and two near misses.

Once more, the jubilation was premature. Although the RN's official history would judge the strikes as 'beautifully coordinated and fearlessly executed'[18], many of the hits were ineffective against the thick deck armour of *Tirpitz*. Many pilots dropped their bombs below the specified minimum altitude of 3000 feet to boost their chances of hitting the ship, consequently limiting the chances of their bombs causing serious damage. Two bombs that exploded near the ship blew holes in the hull that caused flooding, but none of the fifteen bombs the Germans conceded had struck the ship penetrated her main deck armour belt and her guns, magazines and machinery were not seriously damaged. But considerable damage had been done to the ship's superstructure and the area between her armoured decks. The starboard aircraft catapult and crane, and both float planes were destroyed. One of the starboard 6-inch gun turrets was knocked out and another on the port side suffered significant damage. The officers' mess and several galleys were wrecked.

Bomb fragments that had hit the ship's funnel caused damage to all of the boiler intakes. While *Tirpitz* was still able to steam within Kaa Fjord, her casualties were heavy: 122 killed and 316 wounded—15 per cent of the crew.

Work on repairing the ship began in early May after equipment and teams of workmen were sent to Kaa Fjord from Germany. All the repairs, along with the addition of new anti-aircraft guns, were completed by mid-July. The Germans also beefed up the defences around Kaa Fjord with extra radar stations, observation posts and smoke generators. Despite quite reasonable doubts about the ability of dive bombers to eliminate *Tirpitz*, another force of 42 Barracudas and 40 fighters attacked her on 17 July, but failed to score any hits as the ship once more was hidden by a smokescreen. Four more raids from aircraft carriers were mounted in August, resulting in only light damage, before the navy decided to cut its losses after concluding the Barracudas would never be able to reach the ship before its smokescreen was successfully activated.

It was time to pass the baton back to the RAF.

Chapter Eight

NORMANDY

In war men have got to become barbarians, because wars are fought to defeat the enemy, and anything goes. If you're not willing to accept that, well you should keep out of it. It's impossible to have a civilised war.

Flight Lieutenant Don Charlwood[1]

The beginning of April 1944 marked the official start of the switch in focus of air operations in Europe from area bombing, designed to degrade Germany's war production and demoralise its people, to preparing the way for the Battle of Normandy and the Allies' return to France. The RAF and the USAAF, now drawn together under a single command, would play a critical role in enabling what would be the greatest amphibious assault in history, an operation vital to bringing an early end to the war.

From March 1944, Bomber Command had begun attacking key infrastructure, destroying railway junctions, bridges and marshalling yards. Now the pace quickened. In the final weeks before June 1944, thousands of aircraft ranged across France and the Low Countries (Netherlands, Belgium and Luxembourg) attacking German airfields and bases, shooting up trains and convoys and making it impossible for the enemy to move troops or supplies during daylight. Further attacks knocked out more than twenty radar stations, eliminating German radar coverage over large areas of the English Channel. Photo-reconnaissance aircraft provided crucial intelligence, mapping German positions and lines of communications.

Bruce Buckham and his crew were in the thick of it. On 5–6 April they took part in a raid by 144 Lancasters that caused extensive damage to three aircraft factories on the outskirts of Toulouse, in south-west France. That operation almost ended in disaster before it had begun. As they were taking off from Waddington, one of the Lancaster's four engines suddenly failed. Reacting instinctively, flight engineer Jock Sinclair immediately feathered the disabled engine and nursed the aircraft safely into the air. Undeterred, Buckham flew on to Toulouse, successfully completed the bombing run and flew home—all on just three engines. Months later, Sinclair's quick thinking that night was finally applauded when he was recommended for the DFC: 'There is little doubt that by his efficiency and skill under conditions when cool and calm thinking was so necessary, this officer contributed to a large extent to the successful completion of this operation.'[2]

The next night, on 6–7 April, Whoa Bessie, her failed engine replaced, joined a force of more than 200 aircraft, including 16 other Lancasters from 463 Squadron, that largely demolished the railway marshalling yards at Juvisy-sur-Orge, about ten miles south of central Paris. That night would leave Buckham with a new perspective on his adversaries in the Luftwaffe.

It was a pretty active night and the searchlights were up. They were firing. There was an aircraft ahead of us that had been hit and some of the boys had bailed out. One in particular, not too far ahead of me, a few miles I guess, was floating down in his parachute and a German fighter came around and riddled him with bullets. After that I guess my attitude to the Germans and the German airmen hardened. Then again, we might have had types that did that too. Perhaps that German pilot had lost his family in bombing raids on Berlin or wherever. You can't tell.

On 20–21 April they attacked the railway yards at La Chapelle, in the north of Paris, with similar results to the Juvisy-sur-Orge raid. On 22–23 April the target was the city of Brunswick (Braunschweig) in Germany and yet again Buckham's crew would have a terrifying brush with oblivion.

The Brunswick raid was a significant moment in the bombing war as it was the first time that 5 Group had employed a new low-level target-marking method over a heavily-defended German city. The initial marking by Mosquitoes from 617 'Dambusters' Squadron was accurate but many of the main force bombers missed the mark due to cloud and poor communications between the various bombing controllers. Moments after dropping their bombs, as they were photographing their results right above the target, Whoa Bessie collided with another Lancaster, which knocked out her starboard outer engine, damaged the starboard inner motor and tore off part of the wing towards the tip, as Bruce Buckham recalled.

He came up underneath me. As this happened, our props on the starboard side sheared off his guns and chewed a pattern through the top of his fuselage and chopped off the top of his tail fins. It was bloody lucky. If I had plunged the stick forward to get out of the way, I'd have gone straight into him as he was coming up.

Moments before the collision, Buckham had seen nothing but sensed another aircraft was perilously close.

A split second before it happened, I had a feeling that there was another plane there and I whipped the throttles off and heaved the stick back at the same time. Of course, she rose up and that was just enough to let him through underneath us. If I had pushed the stick forward, I'd have cannoned into him and we'd have both gone down—two crews and two aircraft. I had no time to work it out, I just did it.

While Buckham's instincts and sharp reflexes had averted a disaster, the pilot was soon confronted with a new crisis. Straight after the collision, Jock Sinclair had quickly feathered the badly damaged outer engine and smothered it in fire-retardant foam while setting the inner engine to idle at about 1000 revs per minute.

So, we started to come home on three engines, but I hadn't gone very far before I had to close the starboard inner motor down as well. Jock adjusted the fuel in the aircraft, pumping between the various tanks, to give us more stability. And so I retrimmed for two-motor flying. It was okay. I could fly it on one if I had to but that's very tricky. With just two engines we lost about 40 or 50 miles per hour in speed, so were slower getting out of there. Luckily, we were not attacked again. If the Germans had known they had a couple of wounded birds up there, they'd have been after us like lightning. But we got home to Waddington okay.

There would be a colourful postscript to the Brunswick collision. Two days after the raid, several members of Buckham's crew were drinking in the bar of the Saracens Head Hotel in Lincoln, a popular aircrew watering hole they dubbed 'the snake pit', not least on account of its offering upstairs rooms for rent on a very short stay basis. Others called it the '5 Group Briefing Room', Most nights the air at Saracens was thick with beer fumes and bravado and loose lips that might well sink airships. It was rumoured that the barmaids knew more about Group operations than most of the senior officers. On this night, the boys overheard the conversation of another crew on the other side of the bar that instantly raised their hackles, as Buckham would recount.

They heard them talking about this prang they had in the air over Brunswick the other night. My guys cocked their ears up and one of the other group said, 'Oh the bastard flew right into us. He was weaving madly.' Well, my fellers took umbrage at that. They walked over and checked out the time and the target and said, 'We've got something to tell you. You were the guys who were weaving. We were flying straight and level finishing the bombing run and taking the bombing frame photos when you came up under our starboard wing and hit us. You bastards wouldn't be alive if it hadn't been for what our skipper did, and probably we wouldn't either. You were weaving and you're bloody lucky that if you hadn't hit us you were going to hit someone else. But you got home, didn't you!' Then someone threw a punch. Well, that was bloody it. It was on! My boys scattered them and then went back to finish their beers.

The targets that night of the forceful displeasure of Buckham's crew were from 61 Squadron RAF, which just a couple of weeks earlier had been relocated to RAF Skellingthorpe, a station on the western outskirts of Lincoln, only a few miles away from Waddington. Soon after the altercation, Buckham received a phone call from his old friend Arthur Doubleday. One of the most celebrated pilots to fly with 460 Squadron and later 467 Squadron, Wing Commander Doubleday, from Coolamon in New South Wales, had only recently taken over as CO of 61 Squadron.

Doubleday: Buck, you've got some pretty rough boys over there.
Buckham: Yes, they are tough aren't they, Arthur? But you tell your fellers just to watch what they say or there might be another round.

And, within the great fraternity of the Australians in Bomber Command, that was the end of the matter.

If their brush with disaster on the Brunswick raid had been an extreme test for Buckham and his crew, their next operation, ten days later, would try their luck even further. The target on the night of 3–4 May was the Panzer Division training camp on the outskirts of Mailly-le-Camp, a commune about 80 miles east of Paris. Built in 1902, the military camp had since the fall of France been used by the Germans to train replacement tank crews for units that had suffered losses in the east. A force of 346 Lancasters, predominantly from 5 Group, was deployed with an advance party of four low-level marker Mosquitoes from 617 Squadron. The Marker Leader was the esteemed Wing Commander Leonard Cheshire, who four months later would be awarded the VC for his repeated gallantry on operations across four years of combat with Bomber Command. His deputy on this night was David Shannon, one of the Australian heroes of the Dambusters Raid. Ahead of the marking, the main force bombers were ordered to orbit at an assembly point 12 miles from the target, at stacked altitudes with just 33 yards separation between each layer of aircraft. Cheshire was unaware that on the same frequency allocated for the raid, the US Armed Services Radio was broadcasting a program of big band swing music for the entertainment of American troops. As he swept in low over the target, an illumination flare provided excellent visibility and Cheshire was able to mark the camp with precision. But when he called in the waiting Lancasters, no one received the message thanks to Benny Goodman and co. As they continued to wait like sitting ducks on a clear night with a full moon, German night fighters scrambled from four nearby airfields and swarmed in for the kill.

The air combat over the assembly point was short but devastating. Sergeant Frank Broughton, the wireless operator aboard a 97 Squadron Lancaster, saw six large explosions nearby and realised aircraft were being blown to pieces all around them. Rear gunner Sergeant Dick Woodruff of 12 Squadron would liken the scene to 'a swarm of gnats on a warm summer evening.'[3]

Woodruff aimed bursts of machine gun fire at the converging Messerschmitt and Junkers attackers, but with little effect. Witnessing from a distance the unfolding mayhem in the assembly area, Cheshire tried to abort the operation. 'I can remember my near despair at finding no way of getting through either to the controller or directly to the aircraft themselves,' he would later recall. 'I was desperately trying to call the whole attack off, and none of the main force could hear me . . . they were not receiving us. I had never seen so many aircraft going down in so short a space of time.'4

Still receiving no order to attack due to the jammed frequency, the deputy main force controller, Canadian Squadron Leader Ned Sparks of 83 Squadron—wrongly assuming that the controller had been shot down and was unable to communicate—finally gave the order to attack the target. Having survived the onslaught over the staging area, Buckham's crew were heading in to bomb the camp when they too were hit—by friendly fire. Another Lancaster flying above them in the congested attack formation unloaded its containers of incendiaries immediately on top of Whoa Bessie, as Buckham would recount.

It was one of my mates up above. It was just too congested. Suddenly, right in front of the windscreen, I could see these incendiaries were falling like rain. We were hit between the trailing edge of the main planes on the port side and the leading edge of the tail planes. A big, ragged section was sliced out of the panels. Some of the incendiaries pierced the number one fuel tank right next to me. They didn't explode because they hadn't fallen far enough to ignite. It was amazing that we were not blown to pieces. It was so quick.

Oh my God. I don't know how the props didn't set anything off. We flew through the lot. There were literally hundreds of them.

After they limped back to Waddington, the ground crew found half a dozen incendiaries floating in the damaged fuel tank. Part of the aircraft's frame and several fuselage panels had to be replaced before they could fly again.

The raid, during which 1500 tons of high explosives were dropped, levelled most of the Mailly-le-Camp training base. A total of 114 barrack buildings and 47 transport sheds were destroyed along with 37 tanks and 65 other vehicles, with 218 soldiers killed and 156 more wounded. But the price of that success was very high, with 42 Lancasters and 294 crew lost, a casualty rate of 11.6 per cent. More than 100 French civilians were also killed, including POWs and forced labourers within the camp as well as people living nearby. It was a dreadful night for 460 Squadron RAAF, which lost five of its 17 Lancasters and 35 crewmen. The night fighter attacks, which had continued over the target and on the route home, also claimed the Lancaster of deputy controller Ned Sparks, who had stayed over the target until the end of the attack. Miraculously, all his crew survived. Two were taken prisoner but Sparks, his flight engineer, bomb aimer, wireless operator and both gunners evaded capture and made it home to England with the help of the French Resistance. Sparks would not be so fortunate when he was again shot down over Germany in August 1944, spending the rest of the war as a POW.

On the night of 10–11 May, just four weeks ahead of D-Day, a massed raid with more than 500 aircraft was mounted against railway marshalling yards at Courtrai (Kortrijk), Dieppe, Ghent, Lens and Lille. The attack on the Lille yards would end in the heaviest setback suffered by the RAAF squadrons in Bomber Command. Waddington provided 31 of the total force of 86 Lancasters that attacked Lille. The bombing was very concentrated and effective but the response by German night fighters was devastating. Each of 463 and 467 squadrons lost one flight commander and two other crews—20 per cent of the RAAF crews sent out. One of those shot down was piloted by a close friend of Bruce Buckham in 463 Squadron. Flying Officer Dudley Ward, from Roseville on Sydney's Upper North Shore, had been with Buckham during their initial flight training in Australia. The two men had travelled together to England and had joined 463 Squadron just a few weeks apart. Two nights before the Lille raid, Ward had won an immediate DFC after limping home from an attack on the Bavarian city of Schweinfurt with just one of his Lancaster's four engines still functioning. Buckham was in awe of the high-wire achievement.

They tossed out everything they could, the wireless, all the guns and the ammunition trays, all the bomb aimer's stuff. There wasn't anything left, just a bare aircraft. Dud then took it down very slowly to about 2000 feet. You couldn't take it down any further. He had already given a mayday [distress signal]. He knew the correct revolution and power boost for the motor, and he trimmed and retrimmed it for straight and level flying. Up to that point, they had been fighting off German fighters, but the mayday had already gone out. He was very late coming back and by the time he looked out in broad daylight he was absolutely boxed in by Spitfires and Hurricanes, it felt like the whole of Fighter Command was there to bring him back in. They got back across the Channel and crashed-landed at Tangmere, which is one of the big stations where the prangs, the damaged aircraft, used to land. It was marvellous what he did.

While Ward's skill and tenacity that night had saved his life and the lives of his crew, the experience shattered his nerves, according to Buckham.

It got to him. Instead of the affable young man he had been, the poor fellow was shell-shocked. He'd sit alone in one of the corners of the anteroom of the mess. He was really down in the dumps. I went over to him a number of times. He said, 'Oh there's no future for this, Buck. We're gone.' I said, 'Oh come on, Dud, snap out of it. You've had your grim do. It'll be better now.'

Despite Ward's obvious distress, he was ordered to join the Lille raid. Buckham was appalled by the decision but did what he could to try to help his friend get through it. The two pilots agreed to keep in contact on a secondary radio channel during the raid in the event that they got into trouble. And there was trouble from the outset.

Lille was one of the first operations deploying a new target-marking technique, in which 'proximity' markers were laid a short distance away from the actual aiming point. The move failed when the explosions and smoke from some of the first bombs dropped obscured the markers. While the Mosquitoes moved back in to re-mark the target, the bombers were instructed to wait in a holding pattern about ten miles away—with lethal consequences. Bruce Buckham was furious. He had been on his final approach to the target when he was ordered to wait.

We were told to circle around there until they re-marked the target. We ended up with scores of bombers milling around in one spot. There was so much delay. I got down there and did one circuit and saw enough to frighten me to death. I thought this was stupid. There was going to be a crash. I said to the crew, 'We're not staying here, let's get back to the target.'

As he flew away from the holding area, Buckham was called by Dud Ward on the secondary radio channel that was available for use between aircraft in emergencies.

He came on the air straight away and confirmed he was still in the holding area. He said, 'Oh God, it's too willing down here. There are planes colliding everywhere and planes being shot down as well.' I told him, 'Get out of there, get out of there straight away and come across and join me near the target.' That was the last I heard.

Moments later, Ward's Lancaster, still with its full bomb load aboard, exploded with tremendous force. The bulk of the wreckage fell on a factory in the south-eastern suburbs of Lille. All seven crew members were killed.

Buckham and his crew would fly on seven more operations before D-Day. One would be particularly memorable not just for its danger but also for the celebrity guest who decided to come along for the ride. Senior officers such as station commanders were expected to fly on raids occasionally to keep in touch with the men under their command and to stay mindful of the demands that they made of them, night after night. Air Vice-Marshal Ralph Cochrane, the commander of 5 Group and arguably the most important figure in Bomber Command after Arthur Harris, might have been excused from this practice given the potential consequences of losing such a key leader at the height of the war. But Cochrane insisted on following the unwritten convention along with the air commodores and group captains under his command. Buckham's crew was flattered that the boss chose them—an implicit recognition that the senior officer's chances of survival were enhanced by going with such a skilful and accomplished crew. But any pleasurable thoughts were soon extinguished after Cochrane stepped aboard Whoa Bessie.

On the night of 22–23 May the target was again Brunswick. The operation would be a spectacular and costly failure. The weather forecast had predicted clear skies over the target but the main force of 225 Lancasters arrived to find heavy cloud coverage. The marker aircraft had been further thwarted by interference with the master bomber's communications. Most of the bombs eventually dropped landed in rural areas around the city and there were no casualties on the ground. Yet thirteen of the Lancaster crews were lost, 5.5 per cent of the force. Whoa Bessie got through unscathed, except for a bruising onboard encounter with their VIP guest, who kept talking in defiance of the crew's strict custom of maintaining silence on operations apart from essential communication, as Buckham would recall.

He wouldn't shut up. From the moment we took off he kept talking, asking questions and demanding answers about where we were and the way we were flying. I'd developed this very irregular weaving pattern so the German night fighters and the flak gunners couldn't pick us up easily. I used to change direction and sometimes height as well every 15 seconds.

About half an hour into the flight, the air vice-marshal became agitated.

Cochrane: Where are we?

Buckham: We must be about five miles starboard of track, but don't worry, we're right.

Cochrane: What are we doing here?

Buckham: Living

Cochrane (a few minutes later): Where are we now?

Buckham: About ten miles port of track.

Cochrane: God, how do you expect to get there?

Buckham: The navigator knows the pattern

Cochrane: Well, I don't. It's most irregular and you are breaking King's regulations.

Soon the crew became fed up and one of them came on the intercom with a piece of spontaneous insolence that might well have ended with a court martial.

Crew member: Can't someone shut that bastard up? If he doesn't shut up, we'll throw him out of the plane.

Cochrane (shouting): Who said that! He's on a charge!
Buckham: Look, we don't speak during ops. And they mean it when they say they will toss you out.
Cochrane: They wouldn't dare!

The confrontation ended abruptly when a German night fighter swept in and opened fire. Buckham threw the Lancaster into a dive to escape. From there on, the air vice-marshal held his tongue and the wayward crew members concentrated on their jobs. Whoa Bessie reached Brunswick on time and bombed with the first wave. After circling to give Cochrane a good look at the target, they flew home without incident and landed on time at Waddington. At the routine post-operation interrogation, Cochrane stood quietly at the back of the room, listening to everything that was said. At the end, he came up behind Buckham and tapped him on the shoulder.

I turned around and he said—he called me by my nickname—he said, 'You know, Buck, if we had more crews like yours, we wouldn't lose so many.'

It was a great compliment from a senior officer who rarely gave them. A few weeks later, it would be followed by the offer of a job that would make Bruce Buckham one of the most celebrated pilots in Bomber Command. Nothing more was ever said about the threatened mutiny aboard Whoa Bessie on the night of the Brunswick raid.

Chapter Nine

D-DAY

What a plan! This vast operation is undoubtedly the most complicated and difficult that has ever occurred.

UK Prime Minister Winston Churchill, June 1944[1]

By dawn on 6 June 1944 the RAF had already sent more than 1300 heavy bombers in the early hours to pound German beach defences along the coast of Normandy. They had dropped more than 5000 tons of bombs—the greatest tonnage dropped on a single night in the war so far. Other crews had flown diversionary operations in an elaborate deception to confuse the Germans about the direction from which the invasion would come. Bombers from 218 and 617 squadrons had flown slowly back and forth over the Channel, dropping strips of metal they code-named 'Window' that would appear on German radar screens like fleets of ships, while other aircraft used electronic devices to jam enemy radar and reinforce the subterfuge. The ruse worked, persuading the Germans to mobilise troops and resources to Boulogne and Le Havre and away from the real landing sites on the beaches of Normandy. For the most spectacular military mobilisation in history, Bruce Buckham and his crew would have a front row seat.

On the eve of the landings, 463 and 467 squadrons were tasked with targeting the coastal batteries of the Germans' 'Atlantic Wall' defences near Saint-Pierre du Mont, a commune in Normandy's Calvados department famed for its fine apple brandy. It would within hours become even more famous as the hinterland of Omaha Beach where, just a few hours later, 34,000 Allied troops would storm ashore in the face of the 12,000-strong German 352nd Infantry Division. A force of fourteen Lancasters was dispatched from 463 Squadron includ-ing the crew of Wing Commander Rollo Kingsford-Smith, then completing his final days as squadron commander. Buckham and his crew joined the operation as their second sortie of the night. Hours earlier, they had been sent to bomb the commune of Isigny-sur-Mer, a few miles south-west of Omaha. The town had been occupied by a unit of Ukrainian troops fighting as part of the Wehrmacht. Buckham recounted the moment.

It was as dark as you could have it—very heavy cloud cover—and I came down through the cloud pretty well right above the target. Jimmy Manning, the bomb aimer, was spot on again, but there wasn't much to see. We bombed the hell out of this place where all the defences were and went back, loaded up again, and came back to Saint-Pierre du Mont. But Isigny didn't get a mention.

Inexplicably, the sortie would not appear in the squadron Opera-tions Record Book for 5–6 June 1944, and it was not recorded in Buckham's logbook. On the return flight to Normandy, they lifted off from Waddington at 0235 hours—9 minutes behind Kingsford-Smith and a few minutes behind two other 463 Squadron Lancasters. The heavy cloud they had earlier experienced over Isigny-sur-Mer had begun to ease and they had a smooth run to the target. 'Bombing looked good,' the pilot would report back.

That was something of an understatement. Another of the 463 Squadron pilots, Flight Lieutenant Bill Purdy, would describe the scene as they homed in on a battery of five big naval guns on the coast: 'We dropped tons of bombs on an area less than a city block and we just wiped out the whole place. We took half the cliff, the gun emplacements and everything else away.'[2] Later, writing in the Operations Record Book, 463 Squadron Adjutant Flight Lieutenant Bill Hodge would gush: 'We can take pride in the fact that, with [the] other squadron of our base, this very large gun position was entirely wiped out, and the results of our bombing, which was staggering, has never been excelled, and paved the way for a successful landing on the beachheads by our troops. The concentration of our bombing was really outstanding.'[3] Soon after they had turned for home, Buckham's crew would be treated to a panorama they would celebrate for a lifetime: the Allied armada on its way to France.

We got about halfway back across the Channel and the cloud began to break up and the sunshine came streaming through as if someone had just pushed a button. All you could see, as far as the eye could see, were boats—battleships, troop ships, barges, you name it—from coast to coast. There were literally thousands of them. Eric at the rear looked down and said, 'Bloody lot of boats underneath us.' Jimmy Manning, up in the nose, said, 'Oh, that's nothing. You should see them from here. They stretch all the way to Dover!' It was a truly remarkable sight.

Their joy at the spectacle would be short-lived as they witnessed at close range another Lancaster being shot down—by a gun crew on one of the United States warships crossing to France.

We were all flying a bit low to have a bloody good look at everything then one of our aircraft flew low over an American cruiser. I was coming up to the port side of the cruiser and was behind the other plane by about 200 yards. Then suddenly they shot him down. Just one burst from one of their anti-aircraft guns, one burst, and bang up went a beautiful Lancaster and crew, and they plummeted straight into the sea and were gone. They didn't have a chance to save themselves. I should have flown around the vessel and taken its number but they probably would have taken a shot at me. I wouldn't have had any qualms about putting a bomb on them to smarten them up!

At the later post-operation debriefing, Buckham vented his anger.

I raised hell when I got back. The Royal Navy ships had been ordered not to mount their guns. They were told that the only aircraft in the air that day were going to be ours—and they were everywhere, fighters galore swarming the sky while the bombers were doing their work. But there were no German aircraft over the Channel that morning. The only aircraft I saw were bombers or Spitfires or Mustangs. A German fighter wasn't within 100 miles of Normandy that day. Those bloody Yanks were so trigger-happy. They must have had their gun crews in battle order as if they were heading off to take on the whole of the German fleet. Whoever was in charge of that gun on that cruiser must have known when he looked up and saw all those aircraft that they were ours—including this one poor unfortunate crew. But one shot and down they went. And as far as I know, the Yanks didn't do anything about it.

Buckham was convinced that the lost crew were from another squadron in 5 Group but he was never able to confirm who they were. Eight RAF bombers were lost on operations on the night of 5–6 June but there is no record of any being victims of 'friendly fire'. Yet the shocking event was no isolated incident. Other aircrew reported being fired on by American warships as they crossed the Channel that morning. And six weeks after D-Day, B-17 Flying Fortress and B-24 Liberator bombers from the US Eighth Air Force killed and wounded hundreds of American troops while carpet-bombing German positions near the city of Saint Lô. General Dwight Eisenhower, the Allied Supreme Commander, was reported to have been so furious at the debacle that he declared he would never again employ strategic bombers on tactical targets.[4]

Soon after D-Day and a short leave, on the night of 23–24 June 1944, Buckham and his crew were sent as part of a force of Lancasters from 5 Group on a raid to Limoges, the city famous for its porcelain, 250 miles south of Paris. It would be a memorable night not least because it was the twentieth and last operation of gunner Johnny Muddle's second tour. Once completed, Muddle would be 'screened'—stood down from operational flying for at least six months, which, in mid-1944, meant his war effectively was over. Their target was the city's railway marshalling yards, which contained substantial quantities of German armaments and ammunition. The attack was a success, destroying a large amount of German matériel, stopping all rail movements through Limoges for a week and producing a spectacular pyrotechnic display, as Buckham recalled.

Flying at 12,000 feet, visibility was so good some ground detail could be observed. Pathfinder flares broke out right on time and target indicators in red and green were spot on, and so was the bombing. We dropped our load of twelve 1000-ton bombs, staying straight and level until frame 6B of the F28 camera had turned over, then the bomb doors were closed. Just at that instant, the whole place blew up. There were terrific explosions and fires in a multiplicity of different colours, with the added colours of flak snaking up towards us. We watched the scene fascinated for some minutes before heading northwards.

But the raid would be remembered most for what unfolded next. It was a perfect night with a huge full moon illuminating the countryside almost like daylight. As they headed home, they flew low over the rolling countryside towards the Cherbourg Peninsula. Suddenly, Muddle called out that he had spotted a train. Buckham peered down out of his port window and there it was, a 'Puffing Billy' steaming along an embankment. Immediately Muddle called out again, 'Let's go and get it, I must get me a train!' Buckham refused, then the entire crew chimed in, 'Aw, come on skipper, let's get the train.' A moment later, Buckham capitulated.

I had a good look around. The force had gone. I said, 'Look, I'll take you down but don't start shooting until I tell you to. And, for God's sake, stop when I tell you to.' I swung Whoa Bessie 180 degrees, descending down to about 70 feet, and came up behind and slightly to starboard of the train, which was travelling along a stretch at the top of the embankment. I put the wheels down and a bit of flap to slow us down and give the boys a bit more of a chance, but we were still doing a bit more speed than the train. I said to them, 'Don't open fire until I tell you to and don't shoot the carriages.' There were a lot of passengers on it. By now we were only about 50 yards away and level with it. I could see the driver and the fireman, it was so clear. They must have wondered what the hell was going on. As I came level with the engine, I gave the order to fire. The boys had the sense to open up a little ahead of the train. It was exciting to see the tracer bullets from the mid-upper turret's two guns and the four from the rear turret streak towards the train, go up to the embankment to the rails and then hit the engine, which blew up. Great plumes of smoke and steam burst skywards as the train came to a dead stop. I called, 'Cease fire!' and everyone gave a great hurrah. Then I said, 'Let's get out of here.'

By now the unscheduled adventure had delayed them by about twenty minutes. Buckham put his wheels up, his flaps away and turned towards the French coast. As they picked up altitude and speed, he warned the crew that they had broken ranks, an offence that could trigger a court martial and a lot of trouble.

Everyone was sworn to absolute secrecy; they had done nothing, seen nothing. But soon there was another surprising event that would further delay their flight. As they approached the coast, south of Brest, they tracked towards an airfield that was not logged in Doc Board's charts.

Suddenly searchlights burst on and so did the flak. There was nothing for it but to go down and shoot the place up, as aircraft were taking off. Johnny and Eric put the searchlights out and shot up the gun emplacements as we flew around it and then dived right down to sea level to get rid of our shadow and kept going. The sea was as smooth as a mirror that night. It was so calm. We headed straight out west to get far enough out that the German fighters wouldn't be able to reach us and, if they did, they wouldn't have enough fuel to get back. We went all the way towards the Atlantic before we turned up north-east to get back to England.

By the time they landed back at Waddington they were an hour behind the rest of the Lancasters that had been to Limoges, but they strolled nonchalantly into the base headquarters as if it were just another night shift. During the post-operation intelligence debriefing, the vow of silence held. Doc Board helpfully gave the map coordinates for the uncharted airfield they had discovered, but nothing else was mentioned. A couple of nights later, Air Commodore Hesketh, the base commander, button-holed Buckham and mentioned that a train had been shot up in France down in the area where he had been bombing and the reports from the French underground were that it was a British bomber. Asked whether he had seen anything, Buckham kept a straight face: 'No sir, I didn't see anything of any consequence.' Four or five days later, Buckham wandered into the officers' mess. Hesketh was sitting in his usual spot in one corner with a pot of beer and his bull terrier by his side. He summoned the young pilot.

Hesketh: Oh Buck, I've got something to tell you. You remember that incident that I told you about?

Buckham: What incident was that, sir?

Hesketh: That incident about the bomber stopping the train.

Buckham: Oh that, yes. Go on.

Hesketh: I thought you'd like to know that at that precise moment there were six escaping airmen fleeing from the Gestapo. They were on the train and that heaven-sent opportunity of the attack enabled them to get off the train and escape into the trees just as the Gestapo were about to capture them. They were picked up by the French underground and I thought you would like to know that they are back in this country now.

Buckham: Isn't that great, sir.

While Buckham maintained a straight face, there was a knowing half-smile on the face of Allan Hesketh.

With Johnny Muddle completing his second and final tour of ops, Buckham needed a new gunner for his crew. The replacement would be a former member of Rollo Kingsford-Smith's crew who needed to fly another ten operations to complete his first tour. Darrell Procter was a 22-year old from Mosman on Sydney's North Shore who had been studying dentistry at Sydney University when he enlisted in March 1942. Procter came with glowing references from Kingsford-Smith—for his skills in the air and on the ground. His former skipper would praise his 'untiring non-stop searching of the skies from the rear gun turret, which played a substantial part in our survival.'[5] Kingsford-Smith would also note that Procter 'had a way with women'—a skill that would stand him in good stead among others in the Buckham crew. At the wedding of Kingsford-Smith's navigator to an English girl, Procter had 'made a hit with the bridesmaids.' He was one of a number of rear gunners who, despite the already frigid conditions in which they worked, had removed the Perspex covering the turret to avoid fogging and give them a clearer view of approaching fighters. With Procter's arrival, Buckham moved Eric Giersch from rear to mid-upper gunner, the more important gunnery position on the Lancaster, with its 360-degree view of incoming attacks.

Once the D-Day landings had been successfully supported, Bomber Command's focus shifted to a new and terrifying menace emerging from the French territory still under German control. Six days after the invasion, the Germans launched the first V-1 rockets against London. The Vergeltungswaffen-1 (Vengeance Weapon-1)—dubbed flying bombs, buzz bombs and doodlebugs by those upon whom they rained—was the forerunner of the modern cruise missile. From 13 June 1944 to 29 March 1945 about 10,000 of the jet-propelled V-1s were launched against London, primarily from the Pas-de-Calais region of northern France and sites along the Dutch coast. While fewer than a quarter hit the target area, they killed more than 6000 people and wounded another 18,000. It would have been a lot worse if not for the success of the RAF in helping to neutralise the threat.

Bruce Buckham and his crew joined the campaign against the V-1 sites on the night of 24–25 June—two nights after their 'shoot the train' escapade. A force of 739 aircraft from across all Groups in Bomber Command were mustered to attack seven rocket sites. A total of 34 Lancasters were sent from 463 and 467 squadrons to target the V-1 storage and launch sites near Prouville in the Somme region. During the pre-operation briefing at Waddington, there was more than the usual apprehension about the risks of bombing raids on heavily defended targets, according to Buckham.

In the run up to D-Day and the days afterwards, Bomber Command were put on low-level bombing—about 4000 feet—and we were getting slaughtered from the ground and in the air. Losses, which had averaged seven per cent, went straight up to 15 per cent and on a few occasions even higher. During that period, we were losing the cream of our fighting forces, lots of the senior crew who were looking forward to being screened [given a six-month break from operations] after a few more trips. So many went missing, including some of our squadron commanders.

During the briefing, one of the pilots asked if there was any chance of getting relief from this alarming situation.

The CO said yes, things would be different this night—'There will be an aircraft out there, just ahead of you as you are going in to bomb.

There will be someone there taking care of the anti-aircraft fire and the searchlights, and you should get a fairer go.' Asked who it was that would do this, he said that the chosen pilot didn't know yet but when he got out to his aircraft there would be an envelope stuck to the control column and that would give him the final instructions.

When Bruce Buckham climbed into the cockpit of Whoa Bessie a little later that evening, that fateful envelope was waiting attached to his control column.

Oh, my godfather, the envelope was for us! So I opened up the seal and had a look at it and I said to Doc, 'Here, this is for you and Jimmy, you go through the detail and make sure you get everything right and then you to tell me what to do and when to do it.'

The Lancaster had been loaded with a dozen crates, each one containing a couple of hundred highly volatile fragmentary bombs. The task of Buckham and his crew was to fly in low over the target area, catch the German ground defence crews by surprise and neutralise them before the main force came in to bomb.

We had a chart with all the exact spots for the V-1s and the time for the bombing to start. We actually got there right on time, or a fraction before it, and the anti-aircraft guns swung into action because they thought we were it. But they soon found out they had an even bigger problem as we started dropping the fragmentaries all over the place. Instead of going in at the designated height of 3000 feet, which didn't seem have a future to it, I went in at ground level—about 200 feet—so they wouldn't have time to get their searchlights on us. I came onto them so quickly they were not able to do a bloody thing about it. As soon as any of the searchlights came up my gunners would put them out and when the batteries opened up, Jimmy Manning would drop a whole container of the fragmentary bombs. And they were brutes, absolute killers. Like super grenades, they were lethal to personnel within a range of about 75 yards. The strategy was to wipe out as many of the ground crews as possible before the bombers came in and that is just what we did. There was no return fire after we dropped them, none at all. All the aircrews reported that it was quite successful and they didn't meet much resistance from the ground defences when they arrived. It was a remarkable thing to do, but it worked. The leadership had some crazy ideas sometimes, but this was a good one.

Buckham was under no illusions about the heightened danger they faced that night. He was flying a powder keg. If hit by flak or attacked by a night fighter, the Lancaster would have had little or no chance, most likely disintegrating in a massive explosion. There would have been no time to bail out and, even if they could have, they were flying too low for parachutes to engage. But the crew had learned to banish fears of their mortality while on operations.

I don't think we worried about how dangerous it was. If something had gone wrong, we wouldn't have known anything about it. It would have been instantaneous.

While Buckham and his crew came home unscathed and triumphant—to the surprise of some of the senior officers who had chosen them to receive the 'lucky' envelope and a task that made them one of the most vulnerable aircraft flying that night—the operations of 24–25 June took another heavy toll on Bomber Command. The efforts of Buckham and his crew might have greatly reduced the threat posed by the German ground defences, but that was only part of the danger for bomber crews. A total of 22 Lancasters were lost—most to German night fighters blessed by the clear, moonlit night. Among those losses were 6 aircraft—3 each from 467 Squadron and 463 Squadron—out of the total of 34 that flew from Waddington. Most notable among the 463 Squadron losses was Wing Commander Donald Roy Donaldson, who just five days earlier had taken over as squadron CO from Rollo Kingsford-Smith. Unlike the other two 463 Squadron pilots—Pilot Officer Jeoffrey Tilbrook and Pilot Officer John Martin—who were both killed along with all but one of their crew members, Donaldson and all of his crew survived after their Lancaster was hit by heavy flak at 12,000 feet, one of their engines caught fire and the rudder controls failed. All seven men managed to bail out safely. Three were taken prisoner but the rest, including Donaldson, evaded capture. After walking for four days to Amiens, he made his way back to England with the help of the Resistance. Soon after the war, Donaldson was appointed personal pilot to the Duke of Gloucester, brother of King George VI, when he became Governor General of Australia. He ferried the great man between England and Australia, earning an AFC and an appointment as a Member of the Royal Victorian Order for his efforts.

As the Allies began to push back the German forces in the aftermath of D-Day, reclaiming territory and neutralising air

D-DAY

defences at least in the coastal hinterland, Bomber Command began to switch to regular daylight operations. Five days after the Prouville raid, 463 and 467 squadrons joined a daylight attack on V-1 sites at Beauvoir, a commune just south of Mont Saint-Michel, the iconic towering abbey on the coast of Normandy. The crews were delighted with the change, as the 467 Squadron Operations Record Book would attest: 'Today was a "Red Letter Day" in the history of this Squadron. It was our first daylight operation and volunteers were numerous. Everyone wanted to go, but only fourteen 467 crews took part.' From 463 Squadron, Buckham's crew was one of twenty that flew. While the crews rejoiced at being spared the terrifying spectacle of pyrotechnics, searchlights and blazing targets that had become a way of life on night raids, the day operations were still dangerous. One of the 467 Squadron crews was shot down. The Lancaster piloted by 20-year-old Flying Officer George Edwards, from Killara on Sydney's Upper North Shore, was hit by flak at 18,000 feet and caught fire. Three of the crew bailed out and were later taken prisoner but Edwards and the remainder of his crew perished. The raid was judged a success by the two squadrons from Waddington with the target well marked, the bombing concentrated and forest around the V-1 site well ablaze as the aircraft turned for home.

Several other aircraft were hit by flak after completing their bombing runs. The most seriously damaged was Whoa Bessie but, yet again, Bruce Buckham managed to nurse the wounded Lancaster home to Waddington.

143

Chapter Ten

PARIS

When I am right, I get angry. Churchill gets angry
when he is wrong. We are angry at each other much
of the time.

French President Charles de Gaulle[1]

The Battle of the Falaise Pocket would be the pivotal event of the Battle of Normandy. Six weeks after D-Day, the German Army was in trouble. The Allies had faced severe resistance following the Normandy landings, but the fierce fighting had exacted a heavy toll on German manpower and resources. To break out of Normandy, the Allied armies planned a concerted operation in several stages. It started on 18 July 1944 with Operation Goodwood, a British and Canadian attack along the eastern battle front around Caen. The Germans responded by throwing most of their armoured reserves into the battle.

Then a five-mile section of the German lines around Saint Lo was carpet-bombed by the Americans on 25 July, allowing US troops to break through, although they sustained significant casualties from friendly fire. Lieutenant General George S. Patton's US Third Army quickly pushed south and then east while British and Canadian troops pushed south. The retreating

Germans formed a pocket around Falaise, Calvados, where they were encircled by Allied forces.

On 14 August the Allies launched Operation Tractable to recapture the commune of Falaise and the nearby towns of Trun and Chambois, and to open the way to Paris. The operation began at 1200 hours when 800 RAF Lancaster and Halifax bombers struck German positions along the front. Bruce Buckham and his crew were given the target of a road junction near Falaise, south of Caen, which a large German armoured column was expected to pass through as they retreated.

Visibility was good as the Lancaster reached the junction and, with bomb doors open, Buckham made his final approach. At the last moment Jimmy Manning, the bomb aimer, called out for a pause, saying he thought he had seen signs of a large number of German tanks heading into the cover of woodlands about three miles further ahead. His skipper obliged.

I had a look and thought I saw the tail end of some tanks moving into the far end of the woods. So we flew further along and I gave permission for Jimmy to drop the bomb load as we flew over the entrance to the woods. Well, he dropped the lot, the whole bloody load, into the woodland. Straight away there were explosions galore and bits and pieces of Tiger tanks flying up into the air. Jimmy was whooping like hell. He was jumping out of his skin. I said, 'Now steady on, I hope they're not American and British tanks!' But he had picked the right ones; they had swastikas all over them. We were told later this had really held up the movement of the German armoured divisions through that area. We turned away after we had taken our photos and headed back towards the coast.

The crew would be sent on several daylight operations across France during the month of August as the Allies advanced and eventually liberated Paris, and President Charles de Gaulle made his triumphant return. After one, they decided to include some unofficial sightseeing on the way home—with dramatic consequences.

I don't know what it was, mainly devilment on my part I suppose, but I said to the boys, 'Nice day, isn't it? Would you like to take a look at Paris?' They said sure, so I said, 'Okay, we'll go and have a look at Paris and then go home.'

As he headed into the great city, Buckham dropped the Lancaster down to just above rooftop height: 'We were low, very low, when we got right in, and I had to pull the plane up a bit to get over the Arc de Triomphe and then scoot down the Champs-Élysées.' The news of Buckham's joy ride would precede him back to Waddington. The French were not amused and the Lancaster's squadron code, JO-F—painted boldly across the bomber's fuselage—would have not have been missed by anyone looking up from the streets of Paris. As soon as Buckham and his crew landed back at the station, they were confronted by a squad of RAF police.

When we stepped out of the plane, we had a wing commander in charge of a squad of service police with their rifles at the ready. He said, 'We've got to take you in charge.' Everyone was standing at attention. I said, 'Where?' He said, 'Well, you'll have to come up to the watch house.' And I said, 'Well, I've got news for you. The first thing that happens after an operation is you go to interrogation. That's where we are going. You may come along with us and, from then on, I'm your man.'

The police squad then piled into the crew coach with Buckham and his men and they all headed over to the administration building to begin the operation debriefing. After the details of the bombing run were concluded, the intelligence officer, Pilot Officer Tony Giles, had a final question.

Giles: Did you see anything unusual, Buck?

Buckham: Oh yeah, I asked the boys if they'd like to have a look at Paris.

Giles: Yes, and I understand you had a bloody good look at it. You upset the applecart.

Buckham: I'm sorry about that.

At that point, the patience of the wing commander reached its limit. 'That's it,' he said. 'You will have to come along with me now.' An indefinite sojourn in the watch house beckoned—and a likely court martial for breaking ranks on operations. Then, suddenly, a voice was raised from the back of the room: 'That's alright wing commander, you can stand down your squad. I'll take charge of this matter now.' It was Air Vice-Marshal Ralph Cochrane. Uncharacteristically, Cochrane appeared to be greatly amused. Buckham heard nothing more of the matter for some weeks until he was buttonholed one evening in the officers' mess by Air Commodore Allan Hesketh, the Waddington base commander.

Hesketh: Buck, you know that flight you did over Paris?

Buckham: Yes, I won't forget that in a hurry.

Hesketh: You know, you were a goner. As soon as you'd done it, we got a message straight back from Paris that aircraft JO-F . . . They didn't have to tell me any more, I knew who it was. Bad. Bad. Bad. But you're okay now.

After Buckham's rescue from the service police by Cochrane, the story of the joy ride had spread far and wide. Cochrane told Sir Arthur Harris, the chief of Bomber Command. Harris then told Sir Winston Churchill who, Hesketh told Buckham, was 'absolutely beside himself with laughter.' Before leaving England to return to France, with the liberation of Paris imminent, de Gaulle was said to have been lobbying Churchill to send a squadron of RAF aircraft to form a fly-past to adorn his homecoming victory parade on 25 August. Churchill flatly refused, curtly pointing out that there was a war still be won and no time or resources to waste on pageantry. According to Buckham, Hesketh told him that when Churchill was informed of the Paris escapade by the Australian crew he had 'laughed like hell, a great big tummy laugh and remarked, "Well, there was the fly-past!"'

By the end of August 1944, Bruce Buckham had completed 40 operations—including the first D-Day run to Isigny-sur-Mer that escaped the official record. This was well more than the usual 'tour' of 30 sorties that completed the combat obligation of most aircrew and ended the Russian roulette for airmen of wondering whether each mission might be their last. For Buckham, it was time for a change, but his war was far from over.

Like most other pilots completing their first tour, Buckham was expected to take a break for six months or so and then return to operations. And like many other pilots and specialist aircrew, Buckham was sent to help train new bomber crews. His orders were to relocate to the OTU at RAF Swinderby, just a few miles south-west of Waddington. Swinderby was the home of No. 1660 Heavy Conversion Unit, which trained crews to fly Lancasters. A shortage of aircraft meant that in September 1944, the courses were still operating with substitute Stirlings, which Buckham had earlier qualified on before converting to Lancasters. The Australian's dread at the prospect of being relegated to the mundane role of a trainer for 'sprog' pilots was compounded when he realised who his new boss would be.

In February 1944, while completing his own Lancaster training at Swinderby, the cocky young pilot had been involved in an incident that, while highly amusing at the time, he now had cause to regret. One day, as he was coming in to land after a training flight, Buckham spotted a shiny black Humber RAF staff car about to cross the end of the runway—taking a short cut to the base administration building via the perimeter track. When it became clear that the car had no intention of giving way to the landing aircraft as required, the pilot eased back on the throttle and gently skimmed the roof of the Humber with his wheels. No damage was done, except to the pride of the VIP passenger, Group Captain Rowland Coats, the CO at Swinderby.

Well, he was absolutely livid and I was up before him in next to no time and he declared that he was going to put me on a charge. He said that I'd seen him and deliberately failed to take evasive action. I said, 'No, I was doing a precautionary landing. I had the whole of my attention attached to putting that aircraft down as close to the end of the runway as I could. I didn't even see you. I didn't even know you were there' . . . I had come in and the front wheels just grazed the roof of his car. He had no right to be there. He broke the rules. But boy, I must admit that I ran it a bit close, although I lifted the tail up so it wouldn't smack the back where he was sitting.[2]

Rowland Coats was still in charge at Swinderby when Bruce Buckham returned to begin his new posting in September 1944.

I packed up and paid my bills at Waddington and went over to Swinderby and sat down in the mess. There was nobody about and then the CO came through the door and walked through the lounge where I was sitting. I stood up to attention and said, 'How do you do sir.' And he said, 'Ah Buckham, you're just the fellow that I have been waiting for.' And I thought to myself, I don't think this will be a very restful place for me to stay. He was definitely still gunning for me over the little incident with his car. I waited for him to get out of sight—I still hadn't seen the mess president to see where my room was—and so I went out to the little Standard, hopped in and drove back to Waddington.

Once back at Waddington, Buckham planned to visit Air Commodore Hesketh to see if he could find another job well away from Swinderby and Group Captain Coats. But first he decided to wander over to the hangars to see who might be about and promptly ran into Air Vice-Marshal Cochrane.

Cochrane: What are you doing here, Buck?

Buckham: I didn't like the posting. I thought I'd come back and see if there was any work I could do here.

Cochrane: Oh, that's very interesting.

Buckham: I'll have a look around for my crew.

Cochrane: It's alright, they are all here, they haven't been posted yet. Would you like to do a second tour of ops?

Buckham: Oh, yes sir.

Cochrane: Well, it will be a bit different to the last one you did. I'll tell you what I want you to do. You take your crew out tonight and buy them a few drinks. See if they'll carry on and do a second tour of ops with you.

That night Buckham rounded up the crew and took them to the Horse and Groom, another of their regular pubs in Lincoln.

There I was, filling them up with beer and they were filling me up with beer and I'm trying to talk them into a second tour and they were trying to talk me into taking them on a second tour! If ever there was a put-up job, dear oh dear. Cochrane had set the whole thing up. He had earlier told the boys that he wouldn't be surprised if their skipper turned up and had urged them to try to talk me into doing a second tour. And so the deal was done. We were in.

Cochrane had a firm plan of what he wanted one of his most trusted and experienced crews to do—and it would make them one of the most celebrated Australian crews in Bomber Command. Their new role was to take over specialised flights carrying additional crew from the RAF Film Production Unit (FPU) on key bombing raids—a task that had been performed with distinction through most of 1944 by Flight Lieutenant Freddie Merrill from Port Augusta, South Australia. They would fly only when Cochrane requested and Buckham would report directly to him.

The FPU had been formed in August 1941 and by February 1942 had established its headquarters at Pinewood Studios, west of London, attracting men and women with experience in the pre-war British film industry. By 1943, three operational FPUs were covering United Kingdom–based operations, the Mediterranean theatre and the war with Japan. A fourth unit was formed in April 1944 to cover D-Day operations. The units produced a steady output of short films and newsreels that were either straight records of airborne operations, using footage shot by their cinematographers, or more narrative films. Their work was valuable not only for monitoring the effectiveness of operations and to assist training but also, when released publicly, to boost civilian morale as the war continued. Every Lancaster carried a vertical F24 camera, up near the nose on the pilot's side, which automatically took photos at the moment of bombing to check the accuracy of targeting. Now Buckham's aircraft also carried two 16 mm cinecameras. One was set on a frame in the bomb aimer's compartment at the front of the plane. The second camera could be mounted either at the front end of the bomb bay or by the side door.

The first operation for Buckham and his crew in their new role was a daylight run on 5 September 1944. A force of

60 Lancasters from 5 Group was sent to bomb gun positions outside the port city of Brest in Brittany, where the German garrison was still holding out against the Allied advance. The raid was a success, no aircraft were lost and there was even time for a little sightseeing at the end.

It was a lovely day and after we did our bombing I turned around and flew up and down the waterfront opposite all the luxury buildings. The girls were out on the verandas in their flimsies. They were no further away from us than just across the street. They were all waving and we opened the windows and we were waving back.

The weather—and the view—would be far less enticing on their next operation.

Chapter Eleven

BAD BLOOD

The Pathfinder idea grew and, although opposed bitterly by some, it eventually came out on top as the only means of saving our bomber offensive. Few people knew . . . that I had sowed the seed of the idea so early in the proceedings.

Air Vice-Marshal Don Bennett[1]

While mostly there was great camaraderie between the squadrons of Bomber Command, and particularly those that shared the same stations, there was plenty of bad blood between rival Groups—from the top down. The most infamous and abiding enmity was between the commander of 5 Group, Air Vice-Marshal Ralph Cochrane, and the Pathfinder Force pioneer Don Bennett, particularly after Bennett was rapidly promoted and given his own command, 8 Group.

The rivalry between the austere Cochrane, who led the most prestigious and accomplished Group within Bomber Command, and the upstart Australian who sought to recruit the best crews to strengthen Pathfinder operations, would infect attitudes between more junior officers and aircrews on either side of the leadership divide. Buckham would be drawn directly into the conflict

155

between Bennett and Cochrane with his new job of flying the aircraft that was filming the results of bombing raids. Those results were pored over by Cochrane and other senior officers to determine how effective the raids and the work of individual crews had been, and to improve the planning of future operations.

Don Bennett got really upset when he found out the nature of the work that I was doing. He thought that we were checking up on Pathfinders. Ultimately, the Air Officer Commanding [Cochrane] said, 'As a matter of fact, Don, your Pathfinders could do a better job marking the target.' Oh God!

One day early in his tour piloting the camera aircraft, Buckham was the target of some vitriolic abuse from a 'high-ranking and very highly decorated bloke' from Pathfinders, another Australian. The officer—whose identity Buckham chose not to reveal even long after the war—had visited Waddington for a leadership meeting and confronted him in the mess.

He came into the bar and someone said, 'Oh that's Bruce Buckham over there.' Apropos of nothing he came around to where I was having a drink and tore into me. He tore strips off me. He was very caustic and he called me all sorts of names—a so-and-so and a so-and-so. He said I didn't know the first thing about flying and then he said something personal that was very rude. He looked as though he was going to push me in the chest. I took a half step back and thought, if this bastard does that, I'll hit him square in the basket, right in the solar plexus and as quickly as he was doubling up he would have a left upper cut. It was on.

At that moment, Air Commodore Hesketh, the base commander and former pugilist, stepped into the ring.

This great big arm came across my chest. It was Hesketh and he just held me back. And straight away he said to this guy, 'You apologise immediately to Mr Buckham. This is absolutely out of order in the officers' mess.' And this guy said, 'No. I will do no such thing.' The base commander was the higher ranked officer and he said, 'You will do so.' And again, this officer refused. Hesketh then told him, 'Drink your beer and get out. You are no longer welcome in this mess, ever, unless you apologise.' He then escorted him to the door. I don't know what went on at the meeting later on that night and the next day, but it wouldn't have been too pleasant.

Don Bennett was widely respected as a pilot and a highly skilled navigator but he had few friends among the senior officers in Bomber Command and there was little warmth in his relationships with those who served under him—a problem that perhaps was not helped by the fact that he neither drank nor smoked, two of the favourite activities of most airmen. Arthur Harris had strongly opposed the formation of Pathfinders. While everyone recognised the need to improve targeting after the woeful record of the early years of the war, Harris and other group commanders shared Ralph Cochrane's view that cherrypicking the best and most experienced crews to form an elite target-marking force would undermine capability and morale within the other Groups in Bomber Command. Harris also found Bennett prickly. While conceding his skill and gallantry as demonstrated when he was 'shot down in flames' over Norway, the

Commander-in-Chief famously observed in his memoirs: 'His consciousness of his own intellectual powers sometimes made him impatient with slower or differently constituted minds, so that some people found him difficult to work with. He could not suffer fools gladly, and by his own high standards there were many fools.'[2] But when Air Chief Marshal Charles Portal, the Chief of the Air Staff, approved the formation of Pathfinders, Harris got behind Bennett and gave him the support he needed. Bennett declined to reciprocate the loyalty. After the war, he would damn his former boss with faint praise and join the public pile-on condemning Harris for the disaster of the Nuremberg raid in March 1944.

I liked him as a person but not professionally, beyond the fact that he did press on. He would not be stopped by politicians and generally speaking he was a very 'press-on' type. But he made some awful, criminal mistakes—the Nuremberg one, of course . . . We lost 97 aircraft simply because he sent them out to be lost. I told him beforehand, so did everybody else tell him. He wouldn't cancel. That was his biggest clanger. He dropped a lot of clangers. But he was the best person Bomber Command could have had.[3]

There would be few such modifiers in Bennett's assessment of Ralph Cochrane, who avoided returning the Bennett vitriol while skilfully manoeuvring to prevent some of his best crews being commandeered by Pathfinders, and retrieving others who had, all the while working hard to develop new techniques of his own to improve targeting and bombing accuracy. Cochrane was simply, according to Don Bennett, 'the worst enemy we could

have had'—perhaps forgetting for a moment the forces of Adolf
Hitler he was employed to defeat.

We had one outright, knife-you-in-the-back antagonist, a very nice
chap but nevertheless the worst enemy we could have had called
Cochrane, who knew nothing at all about flying or navigation or tech-
nical matters but was out to get Pathfinder Force largely to please
the Commander-in-Chief because the C-in-C was opposed to the
idea. He knew the C-in-C would not himself do anything, shall we
say dirty, therefore Cochrane did things like instructing his squadron
commanders to report instantly to him if mistakes were made by
Pathfinders. Well, normal channels would have been quite adequate,
but he wanted to get his knife in us and would do everything he could
to stop us. And he was very successful. He almost ruined Pathfinder
Force with his dirty tricks.[4]

Don Bennett claimed to be and is widely credited as the architect
of the target-marking techniques at the heart of the Pathfinder
operations, an achievement that would persuade some historians
to regard him as one of the greatest Australian military leaders
of World War II. But the man he chose as his personal navigator would claim sensationally that the idea was actually stolen
from him.

At the start of the war, Bennett, who had left the RAF in
1935 to join Imperial Airways, was appointed as a civilian to
run the Atlantic Ferry Organisation, which flew thousands
of aircraft manufactured in the United States and Canada to
the United Kingdom. In December 1941 he rejoined the RAF
and was made CO of 77 Squadron, which at the time was flying

the underperforming and outdated Whitley bombers—'the worst aircraft they could find for me.'[5] One of the navigators in the squadron was Sergeant Thomas Henry Albert 'Phil' Eyles, who had survived twenty operations on Whitleys. Bennett was impressed and when after just four months he was transferred to command 10 Squadron, he took Eyles with him as his own navigator. This was quite a compliment from the man who in the late 1930s had written an acclaimed handbook on aircraft navigation used not only by RAF training units but also, liberated Allied POWs would later report, by the Luftwaffe. But while Bennett had been impressed with Eyles, the feeling was not mutual. From the outset, the 34-year-old Englishman found his boss to be aloof, arrogant and narcissistic.

Although he was possibly the world's top navigator at that time, and his book on navigation was probably the top book of its kind, he was, nevertheless a 'sprog' when it came to operational flying, as he had only done civilian flying. For myself, I suppose one should not speak ill of the dead, but I never really liked the man, although I fully appreciated his abilities as a flyer. I didn't like his 'I'm the big man' attitude.[6]

Eyles would relate an incident illustrating Bennett's poor relationships with aircrew, which occurred when they were delayed in Scotland once.

We had been up at Lossiemouth for two or three days, waiting for the right weather, and I think that it must have got to Bennett, because we had been waiting at dispersal for some little time, and he had the 'squirts' come on him, and he had to use the Elsan pan in the plane.

160

Now, I've never known of anyone using it . . . in fact, I didn't even know there was one in the plane to tell you the truth . . . but it seems that he used it and apparently there was no toilet paper, and he really had a go at the corporal in charge of the ground crew, tore a strip off him and said that he was going to put him on a charge as soon as he returned. Whether he did or not I don't know, but that's the type of man he was.

Eyles' opinion of Bennett deteriorated even further when he discovered that the ideas to improve bombing accuracy that he claims to have first proposed to Bennett were presented by the Australian as his own—and used to propel himself into the top ranks of the RAF. Eyles says he and Bennett had flown together on a raid to attack the port of Saint-Nazaire in France in early 1942.

At the pre-raid briefing we were told to be absolutely sure that we pinpointed the target, because there were concerns that French civilians were being killed and injured by indiscriminate bombing. We had been there the previous night and most of us had returned back to base without having dropped a bomb because of cloud cover. All sorts of ideas were suggested and rejected when I suggested that the first one, to be absolutely sure that they were over the target, should drop a flare, then the others could fly towards it. They all agreed that was a good idea. It so happened that we dropped the flare, which was followed almost simultaneously by another flare! . . . The fact that he [Bennett] called them the Pathfinders was his idea, but the flares, that was my idea. But I don't want any credit for it. It's simply that I'm trying to tell you my estimation of that man.

Soon after the Saint-Nazaire raids, Eyles and Bennett had flown on their ill-fated sortie to attack *Tirpitz* at her berth near Trondheim in Norway. Eyles was one of the three crew members captured by German soldiers soon after they bailed out of the stricken aircraft. He knew nothing of Bennett's escape into Sweden—and subsequent career advancement—until, much later, word reached the POW camp where he was being held.

Can you imagine my surprise, when a group of newly shot down airmen arrived at the camp gates, and in answer to the question, 'What squadron are you from?' some said that they were from the Pathfinders Squadron, which was Bennett's idea!

In the late 1950s, Don Bennett published an autobiography recounting his wartime exploits. It was not well received by Phil Eyles, particularly in its account of the crash in Norway.

I recall getting Bennett's book . . . from the public library and naturally read first his account of the attack. One gets the impression that he was the only one in the bloody plane. The way he describes the raid, he did everything, except for the last minute when it was Colgan [flight engineer] who made sure everything was okay. According to Bennett, he himself even dropped the bombs! . . . after reading that, I didn't trouble to read any more of the book . . . one shouldn't speak ill of the dead, but he's a right bullshitter.

Eyles was not the only one of Bennett's wartime contemporaries to take issue with his memoirs. An unflattering account of his relationship with one of the most highly decorated and flamboyant characters in Bomber Command would end up in acrimonious proceedings before the High Court in London.

William Ernest 'Bill' Staton was a hero of both world wars and a larger-than-life figure in physique and personality. A big and boisterous man known variously as 'Bull' and 'King Kong', he sported a prominent scar on his head, acquired when he was hit with a chair at a rowdy mess party. During World War I, Staton was decorated three times in the space of just over six months on his way to shooting down a total of 26 German aircraft over the Western Front. Early in World War II, he would twice win the DSO for leading many precarious early bombing raids. He commanded the first British air raid on Berlin on the night of 1–2 October 1939 when four Whitleys from 10 Squadron battled through severe weather to drop a cargo of propaganda leaflets on the German capital. He would also star in the classic wartime documentary drama *Target for Tonight*, which won an honorary Academy Award in 1942.

During his early operations with Bomber Command, Staton realised how woeful the RAF's bombing accuracy was and he became an early advocate of the idea of using flares and Very lights to mark targets. Like Phil Eyles, he thought these methods should be adopted across Bomber Command; but also like Eyles, he would be unable to progress his ideas after being detained by the enemy. Sent to the Far East a few months before the fall of Singapore, Staton was assigned as the senior air staff officer in Java. In March 1942, after the Battle of Java, he was captured and would spend the rest of the war as a pestiferous prisoner of the Japanese.

None of this, it seems, impressed Don Bennett, stickler for discipline. The two men first met when Bennett was still a civilian stationed in Montreal, running the operations for ferrying new aircraft across to the UK. In his memoir *Pathfinder*, Bennett would describe having to be 'very firm' with Staton.

He had arrived over there with a few other Air Force officers for one trip with the Atlantic Ferry, and as such he had come under my control. Most of the RAF officers who came to do a trip with us were relatively junior, but Bill Staton had arrived as a group captain and had apparently felt it beneath his dignity to associate with civilians. He apparently ignored a number of the administrative requirements of the Atlantic Ferry, and I therefore had to ask him to report to my office. He came to my office in the centre of Montreal in shorts. Without much ado I told him to get out and come back properly dressed. He was a little troublesome and eventually I had to make it quite clear that either he complied with our disciplinary require-ments, or I would put him straight back on a ship for England. He eventually complied and all was well.[7]

When the two men next met, the tables would be turned. After rejoining the RAF, Bennett was appointed a wing commander and CO of 77 Squadron. His new squadron was based at RAF Leeming in North Yorkshire where the station commander was none another than Group Captain Bill Staton.

When I reported to his office at Leeming it was clear . . . he had not forgotten the episode [in Montreal]. He gave me his usual welcom-ing speech, which I gather he gave to all squadron commanders or other relatively senior officers who reported to the station. In brief, it was, 'I am the only cock that crows on this muck-heap and so, my boy, you remember that.' I assured him that I would remember, and in due course he realised that I was quite aware of Air Force discipline and that there would be no trouble from me. I must say, I was very glad when in a very short period after my arrival at Leeming he was posted overseas.[8]

Staton was infuriated by the book and sued Bennett for defamation in 1960, claiming substantial damages. By that time, Staton had retired from the RAF as an air vice-marshal and had further enhanced his formidable reputation by captaining the British shooting team at the 1948 and 1952 Olympic Games. When a new paperback edition of Bennett's book was printed in 1960, the offending passages and all references to Staton by name had been removed.

The book would also provoke a renewed dust-up with Ralph Cochrane. In a letter to the publisher, Frederick Muller Limited, Cochrane claimed that a series of criticisms of his leadership were both wrong and libellous in that they questioned his fitness to manage bomber operations. The criticisms included Bennett's claims that higher aircrew losses were a result of Cochrane's decision (made when director of flying training) to remove the second pilot on heavy bombers, his role in sending crews on a deadly raid to Berlin and his alleged support for dangerous low-level target marking at 50 feet (in fact, the marking had been done between 500 and 1000 feet). Cochrane cited multiple sources to thoroughly discredit Bennett's assertions. In response to his publisher, Bennett agreed to the removal of all the offending passages in the subsequent edition of the book—but insisted he stood by his claims and agreed to the changes only because Cochrane was a friend and he valued their friendship. As Cochrane's biographer Richard Mead would observe: 'At least in the letter he spelt Ralph's surname correctly, having failed to do so throughout the book! As to the suggestion of friendship, this had not been readily visible at any time since 1943.'⁹ The changes were duly made in the 1960 edition, including fixing the spelling of Cochrane's name. But, as Mead reported, 'When the book was republished in 1983, six years after Ralph's death, it reverted to the text of the first edition, bringing back not only all those sections which had previously been excluded, but also the misspelling of Ralph's name.' A friend indeed.

The British establishment would deliver its own verdict on the difficult Australian. At the end of the war, Bennett was the only Group commander in Bomber Command not to be knighted for his services, which unquestionably were far more substantial than those of many of his peers. And it would undoubtedly have infuriated Bennett that his nemesis, Ralph Cochrane, ended up with two knighthoods—Knight Grand Cross of the Order of the British Empire and Knight Commander of the Order of the Bath—as well as retiring eventually from the RAF as an air chief marshal.

Chapter Twelve

RUSSIA

Lashed to the floor were two shining steel monsters.
They were like sharks, slim, streamlined and with
sharp noses. 'Bombs,' Cheshire said, almost in awe.
'Wallis's Tallboys.'

Paul Brickhill, *The Dam Busters*[1]

After the repeated failures of the FAA dive-bomber operations, the focus of the campaign to sink *Tirpitz* once more shifted back to Bomber Command. While getting close enough to strike the ship in the northernmost waters of Norway was now a greater challenge than ever, it was also clear that a more powerful weapon was needed to pierce the ship's armour-plated decks and deliver a knock-out blow. In the celebrated Dambuster raids that destroyed Germany's Möhne and Eder dams in May 1943, an ingenious new bomb that bounced across the water to breach the dam walls had been developed by the brilliant aircraft designer and engineer Barnes Wallis. Wallis was subsequently tasked with developing an earlier proposal for a 10-ton 'earthquake bomb' that would burrow beneath a target before exploding underground with devastating effect. Ralph Cochrane's initial interest had been in using the super bomb to attack fortified canal and river targets in Germany.

At a meeting at the Air Ministry in June 1943 it was resolved to modify those plans to build a 12,000-pound bomb that could be dropped from 20,000 feet from a Lancaster. The new bomb would be dubbed the Tallboy, reputedly in honour of its inventor, whose height was six feet and one inch. If beauty could be ascribed to a munition designed to wreak such devastation on its recipients, then the Tallboy certainly qualified. Unlike previous bombs constructed of relatively crude steel casings, it was precision engineered from molybdenum steel to be both strong and light enough to encase 5000 pounds of Torpex explosive (an explosive 50 per cent more powerful than TNT). It was 21 feet long and tapered to a fine point. Its creator would enthuse: 'I gave this bomb perfect aerodynamic shape and arranged the fins so that they would impart to it an increasingly rapid spin. As the bomb attained a high velocity, it actually passed through the speed of sound and penetrated the ground to a depth of 100 feet.'[2] It was also designed to fit neatly into the bomb bay of the Lancaster.

The first Tallboys were deployed by 617 'Dambusters' Squadron two days after D-Day against the Saumur railway tunnel in France, 125 miles south of the Normandy beachhead—a raid led by Wing Commander Leonard Cheshire VC. Other successful raids against targets including German V-weapon sites proved the potential of the new bomb. Plans to build several hundred Tallboys were quickly revised following an order from the Air Ministry for 2000 to be built, half of them in the United States.

In early September 1944, Cheshire's replacement as CO of 617 Squadron, Wing Commander James Brian 'Willie' Tait, was called to a top-secret meeting with Ralph Cochrane. The air vice-marshal began with a blunt declaration: 'Tait, you're going to sink the *Tirpitz*.' Tait, two of whose predecessors as 617 CO—Guy Gibson and Cheshire—had won the VC, was a legendary figure in Bomber Command in his own right. He had already won the DSO three times and the DFC for his exceptional gallantry and skill as a bomber pilot. By the end of the war, he would be the only airman to be awarded the DSO four times, as well as being awarded the DFC twice, while completing an extraordinary 101 combat operations. A quietly spoken and seemingly shy man, he was renowned for his determination and stubbornness. Cochrane would later say of him: 'I got to know that when he put on what I called his "mule face", there was no point in continuing the argument.'[3] Another squadron member would describe Tait 'looking like a hawk that had landed for a drink as he stood at the bar, slightly aside from the group, with a tankard in hand, listening without speaking. If he did open his mouth, it was to puff on his pipe or, occasionally, to make a dry but perceptive and meaningful comment.'[4]

Bruce Buckham was instructed by Cochrane to work closely with Tait, who was based at RAF Woodhall Spa, about twenty miles east of Waddington. Buckham would share the respect of many others: 'I believe Willie lost some of his family in the London Blitz, so you can imagine how he felt. He was absolutely fearless and showed no emotion whatsoever. He would go out on raids at any time.' In the spring of 1944, Tait had served as base operations officer at RAF Waddington. He was discouraged from flying on operations but ignored the disapproval of his superiors. In his first six weeks at Waddington, he flew on nine raids with 'sprog' crews from the two Australian squadrons, as Buckham recalled. 'If a crew was missing their pilot, he'd go out to the crew hut as they were about to put all their gear away and say, "Stay where you are, I'll take you tonight." And some nights he didn't even have a parachute with him.'

Most of all, Tait was an exceptional pilot as well a natural leader. Born in Manchester, he had been taken to an air show by his father at the age of twelve and came away determined to fly. He won a scholarship to RAF Cranwell and graduated as a pilot in 1936. His first wartime operation was to bomb Oslo aerodrome in an antiquated Whitley in April 1940. Over the next four years, he flew many death-defying missions, attacking targets in Germany, joining the first raids on Italy after crossing the Alps in a thunderstorm to bomb Turin, dropping paratroopers into southern Italy and flying on all three of the thousand-bomber raids over Germany in the spring of 1942. But his meeting with Ralph Cochrane would reveal the most important mission of his illustrious career.

Kaa Fjord lay 2100 miles from Lossiemouth in Scotland, the northernmost RAF base in the British Isles. A Lancaster modified to carry a Tallboy and a full load of fuel could manage the distance needed but not the flight home. The decision was therefore made to mount a new raid on *Tirpitz* by staging through northern Russia with Lancasters from 617 and 9 squadrons. After extensive consultations with the Russians, it was resolved that the attacking force would use a remote air base at Yagodnik, on the Dvina River south of Archangel. The initial plan was that the strike force would land at Yagodnik to refuel after the bombing run before flying home, but at the eleventh hour it was decided to reverse the plan and launch the attack from Yagodnik. A weather reconnaissance Mosquito was to fly ahead of the main force to Russia as well as two 511 Squadron Liberators carrying ground crew, spare parts, a medical officer and the officer appointed to command what was now christened Operation Paravane, Group Captain C.C. McMullen.

Colin Campbell McMullen was station commander at RAF Bardney in Lincolnshire, the home base of 9 Squadron. Born in Sydney, McMullen had graduated in veterinary science at Sydney University before moving to England in 1931 to join the RAF as a trainee pilot. In January 1937, he was made CO of the newly reformed 79 Squadron, which was soon equipped with Hawker Hurricane fighters. At the end of 1941, he moved to 109 Squadron, which had taken over the role of the RAF's Wireless Intelligence Department. The department's main task had been to identify German radio beams and to develop methods to jam them, in addition to developing wireless and radar navigation aids for Bomber Command. It was Colin McMullen who later encouraged Don Bennett to adopt the Mosquito as the most effective method of deploying the newly developed Oboe target-finding device with his Pathfinder squadrons. His work was recognised with the award of the AFC. McMullen had extensive contact with Bruce Buckham while preparing the flight plan for the *Tirpitz* raid. As Buckham recalled:

We were involved in the flight planning. We went down to Woodhall Spa and Willie Tait met us and we went into a pre-operation briefing. That's where I met Barnes Wallis. Going into the foyer part of this briefing room they had this beautiful big bomb, the Tallboy, 12,000 pounds—it was so highly machined you could have shaved [in the reflection]—standing upside down on its fins. It fitted very neatly into the bomb bays of the Lancaster.[5]

In addition to the Tallboys, some of the aircraft deployed in the operation were to carry another experimental weapon, the 500-pound 'Johnny Walker'. This was a mine, dropped with a parachute, that was designed to sink to a depth of about 60 feet before rising to explode against the hull of the battleship. If the mine failed to find the target, it would sink again and then 'walk' several yards to another position before rising—a process that would continue until the target was hit or the mine's compressed hydrogen fuel canister was exhausted. And if that concept sounded impossibly complicated, it was. Flight Lieutenant Tony Iveson, of 617 Squadron, was one of many pilots to deride the Johnny Walkers: 'They were supposed to fall into the fjord, reach the bottom and jump about in the hope that in one of their jumps they would strike the underside of the *Tirpitz*. I cannot think of anything more stupid than the JWs we carried that day.'[6]

Just after 1900 hours on 11 September 1944, eighteen Lancasters took off from Bardney led by Wing Commander Jim Bazin, the 9 Squadron CO who had scored multiple 'kills' as a Hawker Hurricane fighter pilot during the Battle of Britain. At the same time, another nineteen Lancasters from 617 Squadron departed Woodhall Spa led by Willie Tait. A single Lancaster lifted off from Waddington—Bruce Buckham and his crew from 463 Squadron carrying the vital film reconnaissance equipment, two camera operators, two war correspondents and almost

3000 gallons of fuel. The camera operators were from the RAF's 1 FPU based at the illustrious Pinewood film studios at Iver Heath in Buckinghamshire. They were Flight Lieutenant John Loftus, a Royal Canadian Air Force (RCAF) officer, and Flying Officer Hugh Rogers RAF.

The correspondents were Guy Byam of the BBC and W.E. West of Associated Press. Byam had served as an officer with the Royal Naval Volunteer Reserve and was one of only 68 survivors of the crew of HMS *Jervis Bay*, sunk in the North Atlantic in November 1940. *Jervis Bay*, a merchant cruiser, had been the sole escort for a convoy of 37 ships bound for England from Nova Scotia when the convoy was stalked by the German battleship *Admiral Scheer*. Despite being massively outgunned by the German raider, *Jervis Bay*'s Captain Edward Fegen resolved to engage her head-on. As the citation for Fegen's posthumous VC would recount: 'He at once drew clear of the convoy, made straight for the enemy and brought his ship between the raider and her prey so that they might scatter and escape. Crippled, in flames, unable to reply, for nearly an hour the *Jervis Bay* held the German's fire. So she went down, but of the merchantmen all but four or five were saved.'[7] Guy Byam lost an eye after being forced to swim through oil and burning debris before he was rescued. Discharged from the navy due to his disability, he joined the BBC as a sub-editor with the French Service before being appointed to the broadcaster's war reporting unit. On D-Day, he had jumped with British para-troopers into occupied France and later was present at the Battle of Arnhem. His luck would run out in February 1945 when he was shot down and killed while accompanying a US Eighth Air Force crew on a daylight raid on Berlin.

While the departures for Yagodnik went like clockwork and the aircraft were not challenged on the 12-hour flight to Russia, via Sweden and Finland, their arrival almost ended in disaster for many of the crews. Despite forecasts of good weather, the force encountered thick cloud as they crossed into Scandinavian air space and conditions worsened as they approached Yagodnik, as Buckham recalled:

We flew from Kinloss and Lossiemouth in Scotland up the North Sea and across Sweden. Unfortunately, a couple of fellows strayed offline and came to grief there. But the main force carried on and most of us arrived in very, very bad weather. We were told by the Russians that it would be quite clear—ten-tenths clear—in fact, it was ten-tenths the other way, low cloud and raining pretty much all the way down to the deck. We flew like a string of ducks right around the foreshore to Archangel and then down the Dvina River towards Yagodnik where we were to land.[8]

Only 26 of the 38 Lancasters were able to locate the Yagodnik air strip and land there. The rest, many short of fuel, were forced to land at other airfields or crash-landed in open spaces. The challenge of flying in such bad weather was compounded by the fact that the RAF's only available map of the Archangel area had very little detail—even important landmarks such as large towns and railway lines were missing. The area was described as 'a waste of marsh with great pine forests and innumerable small lakes'[9], which would be extremely confusing even if the navigators knew the country well, let alone when the aircraft were forced to fly just above the treetops in driving rain.

To make things worse, the crews had been given the wrong call sign for the Yagodnik ground station—8BP not 8VP—due to a mistranslation of Russian. Group Captain McMullen would later marvel that no one was killed or injured and thought that but for the exceptional skills of the crews, half the force might easily have been lost.

Among those who narrowly escaped disaster was the crew of Flying Officer Ian Ross, one of the Australian pilots with 617 Squadron. Ross, who was born in Camperdown in Victoria's Western District, spent almost three hours searching in vain for the Yagodnik strip before running perilously low on fuel and deciding he had no choice but to make a forced landing.

Finally, I selected a long stretch of wooden road running SSE–NNW and void of telegraph poles for a distance of about 1100 yards. Cloud base was at 200 feet in patches and two approaches were made, running in on a heading of 150 degrees. The first one was too far to the right, the second one okay but a lorry load of troops had stopped on it and were gazing up at us. Decided to try on reciprocal, without success. Engineer reported approximately 300 gallons of petrol left so I ordered the crew to crash stations, selected [some] marshy land, selected 20 degrees of flap and approached at 115 mph.[10]

Ross's navigator, Warrant Officer Alf Jackson, recounted what happened next.

On impact the Tallboy left the aircraft and ploughed a furrow about a hundred yards long ahead of us, and when Ian and I got out we faced six Russian soldiers with machine guns, one of whom was kicking the nose of our bomb, and another trying to steal the bombsight. A packet of English cigarettes put things right and we were taken to an 'Intourist Hotel' till Mr Tait found out where we were.[11]

Ross had come down near the port township of Molotovsk, more than 30 miles from Yagodnik. The rough landing wrecked the undercarriage and Lancaster EE131 was a write-off.

As he approached what he thought was the Yagodnik area, Willie Tait descended to 500 feet but still could see nothing but greyness. At 400 feet he glimpsed trees 'like ghosts through the drifts and some of the strain lifted from the little huddle in the cockpit. They had been sitting there 10 hours, silent in the glow of the instruments.'[12] At 300 feet they were still flitting in and out of cloud with drizzle blurring the windscreen. The estimated time for their arrival had passed. They were lost and running low on fuel. Tait turned south after Flying Officer Walter Daniel, his Canadian bomb aimer, suddenly shouted that he could see a river through a break in the cloud. Tait descended further, breaking into clear area and immediately spotting an airfield with a Lancaster landing and two others circling. Five minutes later they were on the ground at Yagodnik.

Some of the other planes came down at Kegostrov, an island 12 miles upstream from Archangel and about 20 miles west of Yagodnik. As Flying Officer Raymond 'Butch' Harris of 9 Squadron followed Squadron Leader Drew Wyness of 617 Squadron down to the Kegostrov strip, a horse careered across the runway just as they were about to touch down. As he took violent evasive action, the undercarriage of Wyness's

Lancaster collapsed. Harris was then forced down, nose first, into an adjoining potato field. Both aircraft were effectively written off.

Bruce Buckham was among those who lost their way due to the almost zero visibility and also came down at Kegostrov.

We couldn't find Yagodnik and so came back to the mouth of the river and landed on a little island aerodrome—they were flying things smaller than Tiger Moths—but we got these monster Lancasters down with their Tallboys onto the ground. Some of the aircraft didn't pull up soon enough. When I landed there were noses pointing out of buildings and tails sticking up in the air . . . When the weather cleared, I was the first to have to take off—literally at the end of the run towards these buildings. I bounced the aircraft up into the air by moving the control column forwards and backwards and getting a big enough bounce to, at the appropriate time, turn it on its side and fly sideways out through the buildings. All I could hear from the ground—we were linked by radio telephony—was 'Oh shit, oh Christ, have we got to do that?' and I said, 'Yes, that's the only way you can get off.' And so, we went on down to Yagodnik.[13]

There were similarly chaotic scenes when Buckham finally reached Yagodnik, which had only a single rough runway constructed of sand and arctic turf that was made more treacherous by snow and ice. By that stage, six Lancasters had careered off the runway into the marshes that surrounded the airfield. In the end, only 27 Lancasters from the original force would be made serviceable to take part in the *Tirpitz* raid, many hastily repaired with parts cannibalised from some of the wrecked aircraft.

In the days that remained until those aircraft were ready, the crews were subjected to the dubious pleasures of Russian frontier hospitality. Most of the officers and senior NCOs among the 325 RAF personnel were billeted in the presumed luxury of a paddle steamer, the *Ivan Kalyev*, moored on the banks of the Dvina River and adorned with a banner: 'Welcome to the glorious flyers of the RAF'. The rest of the crew and the ground staff were accommodated in a series of dugout barracks, half-submerged in the ground with their roofs covered in earth, ranged along the northern boundary of the airfield. The barracks were infested with insects and vermin that an urgent fumigation failed to fully eradicate. Conditions aboard the *Ivan Kalyev* were not much better, as Bruce Buckham attested.

We arrived in Yagodnik mid-morning and the first thing they did was give us a bite to eat and bedded us down on the *Ivan Kalyev*. They said it was the best accommodation up there, but it made the *Altmark* [German POW transport ship] look like the *Queen Mary*. It was used for transporting political prisoners. The accommodation was rows and rows of bunks with straw palliasses. We were tired and buggered anyway, so we went to sleep and didn't wake up until the next morning. But it wasn't the nicest waking. Most of the fellows had been bitten by bugs and infested with lice. Lots of them had bites around their eyeballs and they were all swollen up. For some reason they didn't bite me, but my clothing was infested. I rustled around and found the medical officer who'd flown up on one of the Liberators and he set up a centre outside. Everyone had to strip off their clothes completely and we were hosed down, fumigated, and our clothes were fumigated and then we

TOP LEFT: Gwen Buckham, who had never heard of *Tirpitz* until the BBC announced that her husband had helped sink the battleship. (Buckham family)

TOP RIGHT: Bruce Buckham, who found the love of his life after their eyes met across the aisle at church. (Buckham family)

BOTTOM: Buckham in the cockpit of an Avro Lancaster bomber: 'I was egotistical enough to feel that the Lancaster had been specially built for me to fly.' (Australian War Memorial, UK1218)

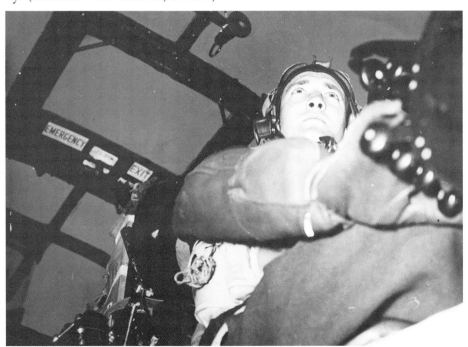

TOP LEFT: Eric Giersch, Buckham's rear gunner, room mate and best friend. (Carey Buls)

TOP RIGHT: William 'Jock' Sinclair, the Scottish flight engineer adopted by an all-Australian crew. (Buckham family)

BOTTOM: Buckham and crew at a pre-operation briefing at RAF Waddington. From left: Eric Giersch, Jock Sinclair, Jimmy Manning (bomb aimer), Buckham, Johnny Holden (wireless operator) Robert "Doc" Board (navigator) and Johnny Muddle (mid-upper gunner). (Australian War memorial, UK1211)

Buckham and crew return from an operation over Germany in April 1944. From left: Holden, Board, Giersch, Sinclair, Muddle (above), Buckham and Manning. (Australian War Memorial, UK1213)

Lancaster ME701, 'Whoa Bessie'. Bruce Buckham's aircraft would survive 33 combat operations only to be destroyed in a maintenance accident at Waddington. (Heritage Centre, RAF Waddington)

Jock Sinclair and Eric Giersch test their oxygen masks, April 1944.
(Australian War Memorial, UK1216)

Buckham during a pre-operation briefing at Waddington. (Buckham family)

Buckham aboard 'Whoa Bessie': a milk bottle to record every operation flown. (Buckham family)

Jimmy Manning in his bomb sight station in the nose of the Lancaster. (Australian War Memorial, UK1214)

Eric Giersch in his rear gun turret: like many gunners, he ditched the perspex screen to get a clearer view of incoming German fighters—and suffered frostbite. (Australian War Memorial, UK1219)

Prime Minister Winston Churchill and Ralph Cochrane, Air Officer Commanding 5 Group, Bomber Command, who sent Buckham's crew on a lone raid to Berlin from which they were not expected to return. (RAF Upavon Records)

Wing Commander Rollo Kingsford-Smith (seated), Commanding Officer of 463 Squadron RAAF and nephew of aviation pioneer Sir Charles Kingsford-Smith, with squadron adjutant Flight Lieutenant Bill Hodge. (Buckham family)

Wing Commander William 'Billy' Brill, the fabled Australian pilot who took Buckham's crew on their first combat operation. (Australian War Memorial, SUK12497)

Bomber Command chief Sir Arthur Harris with the King and Queen at his headquarters at High Wycombe, Buckinghamshire. (National Archives, UK)

In the control tower at RAF Waddington. Front left is Station Commander Group Captain David Bonham-Carter. Billy Brill stands at the back to the left of the screen. (Martin Willoughby)

Ground crew celebrate Lancaster 'S' Sugar surviving 100 raids. Base Commander Air Commodore Allan Hesketh (front right) looks on as Ted Willoughby decorates a bomb. (Australian War Memorial, SUK12226)

In like Flynn: 'Doc' Board turns on the charm with a WAAF officer (centre) in the Waddington officers' mess. (Australian War Memorial, UK2209)

Kriegsmarine Schiffe (KMS) *Admiral von Tirpitz*, at the time the biggest and deadliest battleship ever built, at the outbreak of World War II. (Public domain)

Adolf Hitler at the Wilhelmshaven Dockyard for the launch of *Tirpitz* in April 1939. (Heinrich Hoffman)

Flight Lieutenant George 'Dusty' Miller RAAF (facing camera) in custody aboard the German cruiser *Prinz Eugen* after being shot down near Trondheim, Norway, during the Halifax raids against *Tirpitz* in early 1942. (Linzee Duncan)

LEFT: Air Vice-Marshal Don Bennett, the Australian pilot shot down over Norway who escaped and made it home to form the legendary Pathfinder squadrons. (Australian War Memorial, SUK12632)

RIGHT: Luftwaffe fighter ace Adolf Galland (right) with Reich Marshal Hermann Göring in 1941. Bruce Buckham's crew were almost added to Galland's record of 104 'kills'. (Library of Congress)

Lieutenant Henty Henty-Creer, the gallant Australian Navy commander denied a posthumous Victoria Cross. (Wikimedia Commons)

Henty-Creer and colleagues, including the crew of his mini submarine X5, all of whom perished during their audacious attack on *Tirpitz* in September 1943. (Imperial War Museum, A19637)

Sub Lieutenant K.C.J. Robinson at the controls of one of the X-craft subs. (Wikimedia Commons)

An X-craft sub training near Rothsay, Scotland, in April 1944. (Imperial War Museum A22899)

The 12,000-pound 'Tallboy' bomb: the secret weapon that finally sank *Tirpitz*. (Imperial War Museum, CH15363)

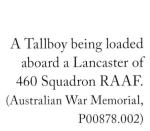

A Tallboy being loaded aboard a Lancaster of 460 Squadron RAAF. (Australian War Memorial, P00878.002)

Lancasters prepare to bomb *Tirpitz* in Kaa Fjord in September 1944, before the smokescreen swept in to conceal the battleship. (Imperial War Museum, C4873)

Bruce Buckham and his pilot's logbook—with the final *Tirpitz* raid he recorded in red ink. (Russell Shakespeare)

The camera crew aboard Buckham's Lancaster captures the critical moments of the final *Tirpitz* attack. (Australian War Memorial, SUK13388,133909)

Dead in the water: the wreck of *Tirpitz* capsized in the shallow waters of Tromso Fjord, November 1944. (Imperial War Museum, CL2830)

LEFT: Bruce Buckham speaks at a London press conference the day after he returned from the raid carrying the first confirmation that *Tirpitz* had finally been sunk. (Australian War Memorial, SUK13405)

RIGHT: *The Sydney Morning Herald* front page of 15 November, 1944. (Buckham family)

From left: Eric Giersch and Bruce Buckham with other officers from the *Tirpitz* raid—Flying Officer Denis Nolan, Squadron Leader A.G. 'Bill' Williams, Flying Officer Walter 'Danny' Daniel and Wing Commander J.B. 'Willie' Tait, CO of 617 Squadron, who led the final attack. (Australian War Memorial, SUK13401)

Willie Tait (left) celebrates the *Tirpitz* sinking with Air Vice-Marshal Ralph Cochrane outside the 617 Squadron mess at RAF Woodhall Spa, Lincolnshire. Bruce Buckham received the Distinguished Service Order for his part in the raid, Tait an extraordinary third bar to his. (IBCC Digital Archive)

Tait (left) inspects the wreck of *Tirpitz* at the end of the war with Flight Lieutenant Kenneth Hesketh of the RAAF Historical Section. (Australian War Memorial, P09148.002)

Bruce Buckham DSO DFC in Brisbane in 2004 with his medals up: 'I wear them in honour of the boys who did not come back . . . They were the real heroes.' (Russell Shakespeare)

got dressed again and the whole ship was fumigated. Some hours later we got back on board. So that was the best accommodation available!

Like Buckham, Willie Tait was not bitten at all, which inspired one of his junior officers to quip that 'clearly even Commie bugs respect rank.' Later, during their second day in Yagodnik, Buckham and his crew were given a sobering lesson that while they might be guests of their Russian allies, they were not permitted to go anywhere without express permission. After deciding to wander across to the airfield to inspect their plane, they were stopped abruptly by bursts of gunfire: 'They didn't yell out to us to stop, they just opened fire on us. I yelled out to everyone to get down and we crawled forwards. The bloody Russians came over and were still pointing their guns at us before we explained we were Australians. It was a close call.' The next day, an impromptu soccer match was scheduled by the hosts, who took their sport very seriously.

We didn't have any football gear with us, so we had to play in our flying gear. The opposition trotted out and they were a team of Mongols. They were all seven-feet tall and all had stainless-steel teeth and not a blade of hair—all bald, big and brawny—so they bowled us over like nine pins. I think they won nine–nil. We spent most of the afternoon standing to attention listening to the Russian national anthem. After each goal was scored, they played the anthem. And of course, we were punch-drunk with the number of times they bumped us and sent us hurtling into the turf.

The visitors soon got their revenge, in a different kind of competitive sport.

They did entertain us on vodka. Now it's not the vodka that we know in this country. It was thick syrupy stuff like paraffin. And I must say this, we didn't perform too well and got quite sloshed. However, the following night we entertained them on our drinks . . . They were doing quite creditably until we started mixing whisky with brandy and gin and everything—they were real Molotov cocktails we were handing to these guys and they were, 'Skol! Down the hatch!' Anyway, we stepped over them and went to bed later that night.[14]

Another night the visitors were invited to see a film. The feature turned out to be a gruesome documentary detailing atrocities committed by German forces as they invaded Russia. The footage was graphic and deeply shocking. After watching for about half an hour, Buckham and others decided to leave: 'We'd had enough because it wasn't nice seeing people raped, others garrotted, strung up to lamp posts and so on. We got up to walk out and were very smartly jostled back with Tommy guns pointed at us. So we had to sit down again and take it.' Fortunately, the next day the men were recalled to the fetid underground cinema illuminated by oil lamps for the final briefing before the launch of Operation Paravane.

The attack began, finally, on the morning of 15 September 1944 after the photo-reconnaissance Mosquito returned at 0400 to report clear conditions in the target area. The plan was for the two squadrons to hit *Tirpitz* simultaneously. Force A, the twenty Lancasters armed with Tallboys, were to bomb from between 14,000 and 18,000 feet in four waves of bombers flying five abreast—each wave separated by a few hundred yards. Force B, the six Lancasters carrying the Johnny Walkers, were to fly in a formation of pairs, dropping the mines from between 10,000 and 12,000 feet. Bruce Buckham took off from Yagodnik at 0848 hours with his full crew, the two camera operators and correspondents Byam and West. 'All aircraft set course behind the leader (Tait) dead on time,' he reported.[15] The stream flew below 1000 feet to the Finnish border, startling a herd of reindeer, before climbing to bombing height for the final leg of the journey to Kaa Fjord. But as they reached the target area it was clear that the Germans were alert to the impending attack, as Buckham recounted.

The fjord was practically full of smoke from smoke floats on the tops of the fjord, around the banks and on the water and all around the ship as well. I went in pretty low. The other boys went in from their normal bombing height of 13,000 to 18,000 feet because the Tallboy reaches a terminal velocity of 693 miles an hour from 13,000 . . . I dropped the eight Johnny Walker magnetic bombs that I had, the idea being to drop them inside the nets . . . I think we must have done something because the cross Ts on the main mast were just visible as we did our run. They hadn't quite disappeared and Jimmy Manning the bomb aimer was able to do an accurate run. But we didn't really hear what had happened.[16]

The smokescreen had completed enveloped *Tirpitz* as the rest of the bombers made their run, forcing the bomb aimers to target their Tallboys where they thought the battleship lay, or at the flashes from the ship's guns visible through the smoke. Several bombers failed to release on the first run and were forced to make a second run, helped by the fact that the smoke that hid the ship also hid the attacking force from the batteries of anti-aircraft guns below. In the end, only one of the big bombs hit *Tirpitz*, but it was a severe blow. The Tallboy hit the foredeck on the starboard side, passing through the bow and the forward gun turret before detonating. The explosion blew out a large area of bow plating below the waterline, causing extensive flooding. There was also damage to the radio masts and the fire-control system but only eight crew members were injured. Once again, *Tirpitz* had survived a potentially fatal blow, but her days were now numbered.

After the attack, the Lancasters returned to Yagodnik to regroup before their flights home, which were staggered over the following couple of weeks. Only one aircraft came straight home and that would be a journey more perilous than the raid itself. Bruce Buckham was ordered to fly back with his precious film and photographic records 'out towards the North Pole' beyond the range of any German fighters before turning south towards the British Isles—battling through two fierce storm fronts on the way.

We flew on down across the North Sea through the most atrocious weather I have ever experienced. It was unbelievable, rough as billy-oh and very, very cold. There was nowhere to fly as we headed south, apart from a space between the tops of the angry sea and the bottom of these ice-laden clouds. We were not far above the water,

20 feet at most and that was for the best part of six hours, I guess. Occasionally the tops of the waves were whipped off by the gale force winds and went all over the aircraft. It was a most horrifying experience to have to battle the aircraft all the way. Sometimes we were almost plunged down into the water by the down draughts. Next you could be tossed up, or thrown on your side. I was wrestling the whole time and correcting. We averaged about 60 miles per hour instead of about 220 for hour after hour getting through that lot. During that time, Doc took drifts off the sea from smoke floats to estimate how much we were being blown off course. It was the only navigational aid we had.

The weather began to improve as they approached the Shetland Islands, but then thick cloud started to form just as they broke radio silence. Buckham was immediately advised that fog had blanketed the entire British Isles—there was no flying and all RAF stations were closed to landings.

Flying at a ground speed of only 60 miles an hour I had to use more revs and power than I would normally. I started with a plus-four boost and 2400 revs but when the weather worsened and we were being tossed around like a moth in a gale, I went up to 2650 revs and plus-six or -eight boost. I had plenty of boost—I was damned well going to keep those motors going—but it chewed up a hell of a lot of petrol. Yet I still had about 500 gallons left. They didn't ask me what the fuel status was and I didn't offer it. Otherwise, they would have sent me out to North Africa and I'd had enough of flying at that stage. I told them I was going to land at base.

Despite being warned that there was a 15,000-feet bank of thick cloud hanging over Lincolnshire, Buckham insisted that he was going home to Waddington. He knew the area better than anywhere else but a beam approach landing with zero visibility would test to the limit the skills of an exhausted crew.

I didn't think about it at all. It just occurred to me that I'd done all this instrument flying. I'd done an excellent beam approach training course and got a high rating. I had absolute faith in instrument flying and also in my ability to apply that to this particular situation. But none of our people had ever been required to do it in a Lancaster before. It was a pretty tricky thing to do and it was also pitch black and late at night. I had to really rev myself up to land in those conditions. It was the same thing for Doc and Johnny Holden, the wireless operator. They were all on red alert and there was absolute silence in the aircraft. I had the two cameramen and the two war correspondents—that's eleven people that I had to get safely home.

As they came in over Waddington, thick cloud still enveloped the area, but they soon picked up the signal transmitted by the beacon mounted on the airfield controller's wagon at the end of the runway and prepared to make a blind landing.

Doc put me over the wagon when I was at about 50 feet. You could see the pundit, the beacon that sent out WD for Waddington, and I did a rate one turn climbing away and, as we came round, I was getting down again and I was practically back to zero on the altimeter and the wagon was there, the beacon was there, you could see it, and I just cut the throttle. She floated on and we couldn't see a thing in front of us as we came straight down onto the runway. I have never heard such sighs of relief when the wheels touched. I put the landing lights on, and I still couldn't see anything, just a big white sheet. They had to send one of the crew buses out to lead us to the control tower.

According to Doc Board's log, the Lancaster had been in the air for fourteen and a half hours, but with the time differential between Archangel and England, it was actually another hour in the air. It was the longest continuous flight ever made by a Lancaster, a record that would never be broken. Throughout that gruelling journey, Bruce Buckham was the sole pilot and never left the controls.

I had to fly the thing myself the whole time with no relief because, would you believe it, they were modifying the automatic pilots and in that aircraft it was unserviceable. I couldn't use it and the weather was so bad I couldn't give it to anybody else to fly. The next question I'm usually asked is what did you do about toilet? The answer to that was the crew very kindly kept the tops of the smoke floats that we were tossing out. I eased myself up into the seat and I used one of these things and opened the window chute and the suction was so much that all you had to do was go like that and this liquid came out and went straight down the chute and out. The only trouble was that on the second trial I spilt it and it went down and spilled all over the bomb aimer and he was not pleased. And that's where that expression comes from—although Guy Gibson was the one to introduce it—being pissed on from a great height!

Buckham had failed to tell his crew, although flight engineer Jock Sinclair would certainly have known, that he still had enough fuel in the Lancaster's special reserve tank to divert to an airfield in southern France or North Africa where the skies were clear. But the pilot had had more than enough: 'I was at the end of my reserves, and I just wanted to get us down and out of it.'

Once back inside the Waddington station headquarters, Buckham was 'surrounded by gold braid'—high-ranking air force and naval officers. As his was the first aircraft to return from Operation Paravane, the commanders were desperate for news of how the raid had unfolded. As he was stripping off his flying gear to cool off, one of the most senior officers was 'aghast' to notice that above the breast pocket of Buckham's tunic was just a single ribbon for the 1939–45 Star—a service medal awarded to all crew—and not the white and purple colours of the DFC. 'Is that all he's got?!' the officer declared. It was indeed long overdue, but a DFC award for Buckham had already been approved but not promulgated. And it would not be long before he was also awarded the DSO—the second highest award for gallantry after the VC.

The two war correspondents joined the crew at the usual post-operation briefing soon after they had landed. 'They were very interested in the way we presented our story, and they did voice the opinion that I knew how to fly,' Buckham recounted. 'They were very thankful to be back on terra firma.'

When Willie Tait finally made it home to 617 Squadron's station, Woodhall Spa, Ralph Cochrane ruefully remarked to him how close Operation Paravane had come to destroying the battleship. 'Another minute's sight and you'd have got her. I was afraid those smoke pots might baulk you.'[16]

Chapter Thirteen

HURRICANE

To demonstrate to the enemy in Germany generally the overwhelming superiority of the Allied Air
Forces . . . the maximum effort . . . against objectives
in the densely populated Ruhr.

Air Ministry Directive, 13 October 1944[1]

Despite the exhausting ordeal they had just endured, Buckham
and his crew were cut no slack by the relentless taskmasters at
Bomber Command. The day after they got back from the Norway
raid, they were instructed to join the force supporting Operation
Market Garden—the audacious airborne operation to drop para-
troopers at Arnhem and Nijmegen in the Netherlands, seize the
Rhine River bridges and open the way for the Allied armies to
advance into northern Germany. A force of 200 Lancasters and
23 Mosquitoes was sent to bomb airfields and defences in the
area ahead of the mass airlift of troops. But Buckham dug his
heels in.

The day I got back from Russia I was told to dress up and go to Arnhem.
I said, 'I'm not going. I have stood the crew down and they need a
rest. We've just had a very tough old spin and it's been a bit rough

up in Russia for three weeks.' Unfortunately, I didn't look to see who the poor, unfortunate wretch was who took my alternate aircraft out, but they didn't come back.

While Buckham's refusal to fly on the ill-fated Arnhem mission was grudgingly accepted by his superiors, he was back at work four days later. On 20 September a force of 646 aircraft was sent to attack German positions around Calais. This was the first of a series of raids in preparation for the attack by the 3rd Canadian Infantry Division on the German garrison that had laid siege to the port city after the Allied breakout from Normandy. Calais had been declared a fortress by the Germans but when pressed, it soon surrendered.

Joining the crew on the Calais run was an Australian veteran of the FPU. Alongside Flight Lieutenant John Loftus, the Canadian who had been with Buckham on the *Tirpitz* mission to Russia, was Flight Sergeant Robert Buckland, a former naval reserve officer from Bellevue Hill in Sydney. Bob Buckland had trained as an air gunner but was recruited to the FPU soon after arriving in England from Australia in 1943. By the time he joined Buckham's crew with his 35 mm Bell & Howell cinecamera, Buckland had flown on many operations with 467 Squadron before being transferred to 463 Squadron. On D-Day he had flown seven missions with Freddie Merrill—the special camera crew's previous pilot—and been fired on by jittery Allied forces while crossing the English Channel. And Buckland had, just a few days earlier, while Buckham and his men rested, filmed the Arnhem airlift with another crew. But Buckland's biggest adventures still lay ahead, within the five further operations he would fly with Bruce Buckham.

After a short leave break, the crew's next target would be the Dutch port city of Flushing (as the British called Vlissingen). Control of the 60-mile-long Western Scheldt estuary, which connects Antwerp to the North Sea, had become vital to enable the Allies to open new supply routes ahead of the final advance against Germany. Since the breakout from Normandy by British and American troops in August, German forces had stubbornly clung to the French and Belgian ports near the English Channel. Breaking that hold and, particularly, retaking the huge port of Antwerp had become an urgent priority of the Allied 21st Army Group commanded by Field Marshal Bernard Montgomery.

The Battle of the Scheldt would be one of the biggest and most intense military operations on Dutch soil during the war. In the opening stages, on 11 October, Bomber Command attacked German defences on the northern and southern shores where the Scheldt estuary opens to the North Sea and where all shipping must pass to reach Antwerp. Flushing is located on the former island of Walcheren, on the northern bank. The town of Breskens sits on the southern shoreline. A force of 180 Lancasters and Mosquitoes from 1 and 8 groups, Bomber Command, targeted the Fort Frederik Hendrik battery at Breskens while 115 Lancasters from 5 Group attacked the guns near Flushing. Another 63 aircraft were sent on an unsuccessful attempt to breach the sea walls at Veere on the north coast of Walcheren. The attacks on Flushing and Breskens began well, but heavy smoke and dust over the targets forced more than half of the Breskens force to abandon the raid. Two large explosions were seen over the target at Flushing. As usual, Buckham's Lancaster bombed along with the main force at Flushing, then ranged low over the area to enable his camera crew to capture the outcome. As they were preparing to finish up and head home, Buckham saw two Lancasters hit by flak, and at least one appeared to be going down.

It was a daylight raid, clear as a bell, and we could see the gun emplacements. We didn't have to look hard as they were shooting at us! They gave their positions away and we wiped them out—very big gun emplacements. After we had bombed, I saw one or two Lancasters in trouble and I knew it was our boys. I was very close to them. They were out in front of me, probably 100 yards at the most. Instinctively, I followed one of them as they were going down to see what happened and to count the parachutes. Only six parachutes came out so one of the crew was still inside when the aircraft crashed and caught fire.

Buckham thought the ill-fated Lancaster was piloted by Flying Officer Cy Borsht, from Queensland, one of Buckham's best friends in 463 Squadron. But he had misread the Lancaster's markings. Borsht's luck would hold, though not for long. Only one Lancaster was lost on the Flushing raid and it was not from either 463 or 467 squadrons—all of whose aircraft made it safely home to Waddington that day. But Buckham's decision to follow the wounded 'kite' down—with Loftus and Buckland continuing to film the dramatic moments—would land him in very hot water.

About an hour after we got back to base, they called me up and said I was in trouble. I had broken ranks and done the wrong thing. I was told I hadn't been sent out there to film our own people being shot down. They were really shitty. They said my job was bombing and filming the attack and I had no business doing anything else.

A panel of senior officers was formed to question Buckham and decide whether or not there would be a formal court martial. While being questioned by the panel, Buckham stood his ground.

I told them that as far as I was concerned, what I did was filming part of the attack. I said, 'If you gentlemen think we go out there and don't get hurt, we don't bleed and we don't get killed, you've got another think coming.' Then someone said, 'Buckham, you can't speak like that.' I then told them they should use the footage we had shot to good purpose. I said, 'I understand this country is doing its best to encourage the sale of war bonds and you should show this in the newsreels and advertisements. You'll get a strong response. Show them the bombing but also show them some of our boys being shot down. It's the reality of what we do.' Eventually I think they did what I suggested, and it had a powerful impact.

While a number of senior officers remained unhappy with Buckham's conduct, there was no court martial, and no disciplinary action was taken against him. Not for the first time, Buckham had a powerful ally at court in Air Commodore Allan Hesketh, the Waddington base commander. When told what had happened at the panel hearing, according to Buckham, Hesketh replied: 'Bloody good, Buck. Bloody good!'

While Buckham had indeed been mistaken about the identity of the Lancaster that had been shot down, Cy Borsht's number would come up just weeks later when 463 Squadron was again sent to attack targets at Flushing. On 23 October, a force of 112 Lancasters was dispatched from 5 Group to hit the German batteries. Visibility was poor, the bombing was scattered and four aircraft were lost—two from 463 Squadron, including Cy Borsht's Lancaster. The moment they broke cloud at about 4000 feet, the German Bofors guns opened fire and the aircraft was hit almost instantly. Two engines and the bomb bay caught fire and the English flight engineer, Eric Leigh, was severely wounded by another shell. Borsht gave the order to abandon the aircraft. He was the last to jump after dragging Leigh out through the bomb aimer's hatch. All of the crew survived the jump—except for Leigh, whose body was later retrieved from the river, his parachute unopened. Borsht and four other crew members were quickly taken prisoner while their navigator, Snow O'Connell, was hidden by a Dutch farmer until Canadian troops liberated the area two weeks later. Borsht and the other surviving crew were sent 'on a free eight months' vacation in deepest Germany.'[2] Bruce Buckham would speak of his Jewish friend's good fortune in being captured late in the war rather than earlier: 'Even though he got interrogated, from there on they seemed to be on the move all the time as the war was closing in on Germany. He was lucky to get away with not being taken in by the Gestapo and dispensed with.'

On 13 October, only two days after Buckham filmed the doomed Lancaster over Flushing, Arthur Harris and his American counterpart Lieutenant General James H. Doolittle received a directive to mount a 24-hour bombing operation to demonstrate to the Germans the overwhelming superiority of the RAF and the US air forces and 'cause mass panic and disorganisation in the Ruhr, disrupt frontline communications and demonstrate the futility of resistance.'[2] The next day, Buckham's crew was sent to join the bombing, the largest airborne operation of the war flown by Bomber Command. Codenamed Operation Hurricane, it might well have succeeded in demonstrating that the Allies now had overwhelming superiority in the skies over Western Europe, but the costs—to both sides—were staggering.

Through the day of 14 October, more than 1000 Bomber Command aircraft—Lancasters, Halifaxes and Mosquitoes—were dispatched to Duisburg, escorted by RAF fighters. They dropped more than 3600 tons of high explosive and 830 tons of incendiaries. At the same time, more than 1200 American heavy bombers, escorted by 749 fighters, hit targets in and around Cologne. A second wave of RAF raids on Duisburg during the night of 14–15 October dropped a further 4000 tons of high explosive and 500 tons of incendiaries. Some of the RAF crews, including Buckham's, flew on both day and night raids. That night, the RAF also attacked Brunswick. In just 24 hours, Bomber Command had flown 2589 sorties and dropped more than 10,000 tons of bombs. They lost fourteen aircraft—almost 100 aircrew. The Americans lost five of their heavy bombers.

The attacks were devastating for those below. More than 2500 civilians died in Duisburg alone. The city centre of Brunswick was destroyed and more than 500 civilians died. The toll in Brunswick might have been far higher if not for the heroic efforts of fire crews who, four hours after the raid, reached the first of eight large public shelters that had been cut off 'in a sea of fire'. All but 200 of an estimated 23,000 people trapped in the shelters were saved.[3]

The daylight raid on Duisburg would be one of the most terrifying that Buckham and his crew had faced.

We took off from Waddington about 0830 hours. There were hundreds of aircraft. In all my operations over Europe, I had never seen such perfect flying conditions. The sky was absolutely cloudless and the temperature and wind conditions were close to perfect. We were directly behind the controller with the rest of the bombers behind us. Not long after we crossed into Germany, all hell broke loose. Anti-aircraft fire was coming at us from a fortified front stretching about ten miles wide and four miles deep. This massive barrage was ranging flak between 18,000 and 22,000 feet and it looked like there was no way you could get through it. The sky was just black with explosives bursting all the time. It was a shocker. Someone must have informed the Germans we were coming.

As they approached the maelstrom, Buckham and flight engineer Jock Sinclair were joined beside the cockpit by several other members of the crew.

They were absolutely nonplussed by the barrage of flak. So I just said to them, 'We're going though,' and I just flew straight through it following the controller. There was no point in weaving. If I'd veered one way or the other, I'd have probably been shot down. There was an overwhelming pall of cordite from all the firing. It felt like if we'd stayed there any longer, we would have suffocated. Both our aircraft and the controller's Lancaster took some flak. One piece lodged in my chest. Fortunately, I was wearing special chamois flying gloves and I grabbed it and threw it out of the window.

After passing largely unscathed through the barrage, Buckham joined the controller's aircraft near the target, but few of the other aircraft had an appetite for playing Russian roulette.

The two of us flew up and down, up and down, and tried to encourage the boys to come through. We told them that if they did the barrage would ease off as soon as they started dropping their bombs. Four or five attempted to get through but they got shot down. The rest of the bombers abandoned the attack, with half exiting via the south and the other half by the north.

Instead of heading home with the rest of the bombers, Buckham and his crew turned north-east, flying deeper into Germany on a highly secret mission for which their presence in the Duisburg attack may have been no more than a smokescreen. The lone raiders were not told what their target was before or after the raid and it remains shrouded in mystery to this day.

We had been instructed to leave the main force after filming the bombing at Duisburg and to head to a position near the Dortmund-Ems Canal. It was a factory well over a mile long and half a mile wide. Cochrane's instructions to me were not to go below 18,000 feet under any circumstances. He did not say why. I lined up on the target at 19,100 feet, giving us some money in the bank. I told my bomber

Jimmy Manning that we were at altitude 19,100 feet at 180 miles per hour. We had 16 thousand-pounders in our bomb bay. We dropped our entire payload, the first one hitting the back door, the last one at the front door.

Soon after Buckham threw the Lancaster into a steep dive 'to gain speed to over 400 mph and get the hell out of there,' it was clear that this was no routine target.

Suddenly the aircraft was hit by enormous shockwaves in these beautifully stable air conditions. It caught us miles away from the target and the crew could not believe their eyes. A mushroom cloud billowed to a height of about 12,000 feet. The target was completely obliterated. We blew it off the face of the earth, just one aircraft.

Months later, after witnessing footage of the mushroom clouds that accompanied the destruction of Hiroshima and Nagasaki in Japan, Buckham would suspect that his target was a key site in Germany's fledgling nuclear weapons program. While the consensus among historians is that Germany was nowhere near having the resources or capability to build an effective atomic bomb by the end of the war, German historian Rainer Karlsch in his controversial 2005 book *Hitler's Bomb* claimed to have uncovered evidence that the Nazis had developed and tested a 'nuclear weapon' by early 1945—if only a so-called dirty bomb, a radiological weapon combining radioactive material with conventional explosives, rather than a standard nuclear weapon.

But on his return from the raid that day, Buckham's efforts to find out more about the factory complex he had bombed were brushed aside by Ralph Cochrane. And, yet again, the 'unofficial' factory attack did not appear in the 463 Squadron Operations Record Book for that day, nor in Bruce Buckham's logbook. The air vice-marshal was, according to Buckham, 'mad as hell' at the failure of most of the aircraft from 5 Group to press on to the Duisburg target and bomb as ordered. Accusations of lack of moral fibre—the air force code for cowardice—were being muttered against those pilots who had turned away in the face of the German flak barrage.

Cochrane: We'll bloody well have to go back there again tonight! But what about your target, Buckham?
Buckham: I did as I was told, I bombed the thing and got the hell out of it straight away. I didn't come down below 18,000 feet and here I am.
Cochrane: Good.
Buckham: Now I will be able to go on leave.
Cochrane: No, you won't. You're going back to Brunswick tonight.

Within an hour, after a quick meal and the routine debriefing interrogation, Buckham and his crew were back in the air and heading for Brunswick. Mercifully, they did not face the same intense flak that had greeted their arrival at Duisburg a few hours earlier and the operation went relatively smoothly. The results would quickly restore Ralph Cochrane's good humour. The diversions and fighter support operations provided to the bomber stream were so successful that only one Lancaster was lost. The widespread destruction of the city—which Bomber Command had failed to deliver on three previous mass raids—was now achieved. And, according to Buckham, the photography on the raid was also a triumph.

The night photography was excellent. They were very happy with the quality, which was up to that point the best night photography they had ever had. Apart from bombing at the right height, I came down pretty low, well under 10,000 feet, to take more photographs. The marking had been done very well. It was spot on. So the Hermann Göring Steelworks really copped it from us that night.

When they finally landed back at Waddington from Brunswick at about 0400 hours the next morning, Buckham and his crew had been in the air for a total of almost 18 of the previous 20 hours. Over subsequent days, Buckham tried hard to find out what his mystery target had been after diverting from Duisburg, but his superiors refused to tell him. There would be no such reticence about what was to follow just two weeks later, the most important operation of their war.

Chapter Fourteen

TROMSØ

We climbed up to bombing height and we spotted
it 20 to 30 miles away. It was so gin clear and
I remember saying to my bomb aimer, 'By God
Mac, she's had it today.'

Flying Officer Fred Watts, 617 Squadron[1]

Tirpitz had been seriously damaged in the attack of 15 September 1944. It would not be revealed to the Allies until after the war, but at a conference of the German naval staff on 23 September attended by Grand Admiral Karl Dönitz, Supreme Commander of the Kriegsmarine (German navy), it was estimated that it would take nine months to make the battleship fully operational again. Dönitz resolved that she should be put into semi-retirement—no longer considered for action at sea but moored further south in Norway and used as a floating battery to deter invasion. His secret review declared: 'After successfully defending herself against many heavy air attacks, the battleship *Tirpitz* has now sustained a bomb hit, but by holding out in the operational area the ship will continue to tie down enemy forces and by her presence to confound the enemy's intentions.'[2]

201

At midday on 15 October, *Tirpitz* slowly emerged from Kaa Fjord protected by a flotilla of almost fifty ships and flanked by two ocean-going tugs in case her damaged bow gave way. Five hours later, after creeping south-west along the coast at rarely more than three knots, the wounded 'Beast' anchored off the island of Håkøya, west of the fishing port of Tromsø. The following day, no longer able to move under her own power, she was towed closer to Tromsø. Here the battleship was protected by a double net anti-torpedo screen and a formidable array of anti-aircraft barrages and flak ships. But there were two fatal flaws in *Tirpitz*'s new defences. The rapid smokescreen generators that had saved her in Kaa Fjord were now much less effective. She was no longer berthed in a narrow fjord surrounded by steep protective hills that would hold the smokescreen but on more open water subject to dispersing winds. And, crucially, *Tirpitz* now lay 200 miles closer to Britain.

As soon as the battleship's relocation was confirmed, Bomber Command began preparing for a fresh attack, codenamed Operation Obviate. Unlike Kaa Fjord, Tromsø was just within Lancaster range—an estimated 2252-mile round trip that could be managed with extra fuel loads. The one-way flights to Yagodnik in September had proved an endurance test for the aircraft and their crews. The round trip to Tromsø posed fresh and equally daunting challenges. To enable them to carry their extra two-ton fuel load, the Lancasters had to be substantially modified. More powerful Rolls-Royce Merlin 24 (1640 horsepower) engines were fitted in place of the standard Merlin 22s. The mid-upper gun turrets were removed, as were the front guns and ammunition and 3000 rounds of ammunition from the rear turret—making the aircraft far more vulnerable in the event of an enemy fighter attack. Also jettisoned were the protective armour plates positioned behind the pilots' seats and all bottled oxygen—which meant the crews would have to fly most of the way at lower altitudes to avoid the need for oxygen. The modifications reduced substantially the weight of the bombers and enabled them to carry overload tanks with hundreds of gallons of extra fuel. All of the aircraft would this time carry Tallboys, the Johnny Walker mines having fallen out of favour after assessments that they had performed poorly during the September raid.

Operation Obviate was scheduled for the final week of October, the exact date depending on weather conditions. The 5 Group Operation Order noted that the battleship had suffered 'severe damage' in the September raid and was unfit for seagoing operations but declared: 'So long as the *Tirpitz* remains afloat it continues to be a threat to our sea communications with Russia.'[3] Once more, the task would fall to 617 and 9 squadrons, each scrambling eighteen crews, and again under the leadership of the two squadron commanders, Willie Tait and James Bazin. And once more Bruce Buckham and his 463 Squadron crew would carry the film unit. Six of the other Lancasters were also piloted by Australians—Flying Officer Arthur Kell DFC, Flying Officer Daniel Carey and Flying Officer John Sayers DFC of 617 Squadron, along with Flying Officer John Dunne DFC, Flying Officer Alexander Williams, Flying Officer Kevin Arndell and Flying Officer Alec Jones of 9 Squadron. All were skilled and experienced pilots who had faced life-and-death challenges during extended tours of operations with Bomber Command. But few had a more colourful resume than Flying Officer Williams, during and after the war.

Alexander Francis Phillip 'Kit' Williams was born in Ballarat, Victoria, and enlisted in the RAAF in June 1942. After arriving in England and being commissioned on the recommendation of Rollo Kingsford Smith in July 1944, he was assigned to 9 Squadron and soon attached to the 8th United States Army Air Force in southern Italy, taking part in 29 operations aboard the American B-17 Flying Fortress bombers and returning to RAF Bardney and Lancasters just days before the *Tirpitz* raid. Following the war, Williams would spend two years with the British Commonwealth Occupation Forces in Japan before heading to Malaya 'for some excitement'.[4] Remaining an officer in the RAAF reserves, he worked in a range of shadowy security and intelligence jobs while indulging his passion for hunting. His life of intrigue and adventure would inspire the Melbourne *Argus* newspaper article, 'HE KILLS FOR PAY AND PLAY'. It described him as a 'young flier who stalks armed bandits in the Malayan jungles during working hours and hunts wild tigers and elephants for recreation', known throughout Malaya as 'the Little White Tiger' for his exploits. But notoriety had its price. The insurgents placed a large bounty on Williams' head and he was severely wounded and lost most of his possessions when his house was blown up on New Year's Day, 1955.

With no need for a mid-upper gunner due to the stripped-down armaments for the *Tirpitz* raid, the regular crew of seven in each Lancaster was reduced to six. The 'bombed-up' Lancasters proceeded to the RAF bases at Lossiemouth, Kinloss and Milltown in Scotland to await further orders. After a reconnaissance

Mosquito reported favourable weather in the Tromsø area, the operation was set for the early hours of 29 October.

Soon after 0100 hours that day the Lancasters took off from the bases in Scotland. Weather conditions were good across the North Sea. After crossing the Norwegian coast hours later, the aircraft turned inland towards Sweden, seeking to keep the mountains between them and the German radar stations near Tromsø. As they finally approached the target, they could see the ship clearly but at the same moment they also saw huge drifts of cloud moving in from the sea. The wind had suddenly changed direction.

A minute from the bomb release point, the leading aircraft could still see *Tirpitz* but with just 30 seconds to go cloud enveloped the ship. Walter Daniel, Tait's bomb aimer, kept his bomb sight on the position where he had last seen the ship and moments later, as flak burst through the cloud near them, called 'Bombs gone!' As four or five other Lancasters bombed positions where they estimated *Tirpitz* was moored, Tait saw flashes of bombs exploding in the water near the ship. Other crews circled back in the hope of getting a clear sight of the target but in vain.

Australian Daniel 'Bill' Carey's aircraft had been hit by flak on the first run. His starboard outer engine was knocked out and petrol was streaming out of a ruptured tank. Despite the damage, Carey turned back for another run but was still thwarted by the cloud. He went round again and again until, on his sixth run, his bomb aimer released their Tallboy in frustration, knowing there was only the faintest hope of a hit. As the Lancaster dived down to 1000 feet and turned for home, they passed over a small island. A single gunner opened fire from below, knocking out a second engine and piercing another fuel tank. Moments later, the hydraulics ruptured and the bomb doors and undercarriage flopped down. Now flying with just two engines on full power and with his engineer warning there was no longer enough fuel to get back to Scotland, Carey turned back towards Tromsø and threaded his way through a mountain pass. Half an hour later, the remaining engines dangerously overheating, the Lancaster crash-landed in a bog near the township of Porjus and all the crew climbed out. They had made it to the safety of neutral Sweden. Carey's courage and tenacity would be rewarded with the DFC.

While the Carey crew had been wrestling with its crisis, Alec Jones was battling his own. Born in Leeds, Jones had migrated to Australia before the war and had been farming at Tolga on the Atherton Tablelands in Queensland when he enlisted in the RAAF in November 1941. Just as his bomb load released over *Tirpitz*, his aircraft was hit by flak and Jones was temporarily blinded by particles of flying glass. In intense pain and unable to see, he kept the Lancaster flying level while his English bomb aimer, Flying Officer Ronald Blunsdon, took over the controls. Blunsdon had no pilot training but managed to nurse the plane all the way home before handing the pilot's seat back to Jones. As the citations for their subsequent DFCs explained: 'Although in much pain, he never relinquished his captaincy. When base was reached, he took over the controls and the able directions from his air bomber enabled him to judge his approach and he effected a safe landing.'

When they landed back in Scotland, the rest of the crews were greeted with the dispiriting news that *Tirpitz* had suffered no further damage in the raid. After refuelling, Tait headed straight on to 617 Squadron's station at Woodhall Spa. A message was waiting for him from Ralph Cochrane: 'Congratulations on your splendid flight and perseverance. Luck won't always favour the *Tirpitz*. One day you'll get her.'[5] That day was fast approaching.

~

Tirpitz had narrowly survived destruction twice in the space of just a few weeks, and the odds were swinging inexorably in favour of Bomber Command. But time was running out. The already small window of daylight in which the Lancasters could operate was about to slam shut. By 26 November continuous winter darkness would descend over northern Scandinavia. Cochrane was determined not to miss that deadline.

However, after the failure of Operation Obviate, a new and alarming challenge confronted the crews of 5 Group. Intelligence reports confirmed that between 20 and 30 German fighters had been moved to the Bardufoss airfield, about 30 miles from Tromsø. Without their mid-upper guns and with reduced fire-power from their remaining rear guns, the Lancasters would be highly vulnerable in the event that the Bardufoss fighters were scrambled before they had bombed. Instead of the triumph of finally sinking *Tirpitz*, the RAF might well be facing a slaughter of its own. But Ralph Cochrane was determined that the job must be done, whatever the dangers.

A new operation, a new code name: Catechism. At first, the raid was scheduled for 5 November. The day before, all the aircraft once more moved to the forward stations in Scotland. That evening a gale warning was issued and all the crews were stood down. On 6 November they again were ordered to stand by but, yet again, the weather intervened. Finally, just after midnight on 12 November, a reconnaissance Mosquito landed back at Lossiemouth and reported that while weather conditions over Tromsø were poor, there were signs of improvement. Barely two hours later, the flocks of Lancasters, most of them two tons overweight with extra fuel and their Tallboy bomb loads, lumbered into the air from the bases at Lossiemouth, Kinloss and Milltown. Once more there would be six Australian pilots joining the raid along with another ten Australian flight crew. As well as Bruce Buckham and two other pilots who had taken part in the previous Tromsø raid—John Sayers and Arthur Kell—there were two additional Australian captains from 617 Squadron, Queenslander Flight Lieutenant William 'Bunny' Lee and Flying Officer Ian Ross, who had survived a forced landing on his way to Yagodnik in September.

Anticipating the propaganda coup that news of the elimination of *Tirpitz* would have to demoralise the Germans and boost British morale, Bruce Buckham's aircraft was again carrying the two cinecameramen from the FPU. It was the same pair who had been with him to Russia—RCAF Flight Lieutenant John Loftus and RAF Flying Officer Hugh Rogers. 'Lofty' Loftus had enlisted in the RCAF in 1937 as a photographer and by 1944 was an officer with the FPU. The *Tirpitz* raids were among 22 operations that he would take part in with Bomber Command. But, unlike the rest of the crews he flew with, Loftus never wore a 'flying badge' on his tunic—the pilot's wings or the half wing brevets of the navigators, engineers, bomb aimers and gunners. The authorities deemed the short course he had taken in gunnery as insufficient to earn a badge. In February 1945, Loftus would be shot down and taken prisoner during an attack on the Mittelland Canal in central Germany. He had been flying with the crew of 463 Squadron CO Wing Commander Bill Forbes, who was killed. The episode would help Loftus earn the DFC. After the war, he would be an oddity among Canadian veterans, a brave DFC winner with no brevet to indicate how he had won the medal.

Special modifications had been made to Buckham's Lancaster for the camera team. The front gun turret had been removed and a mounted 35 mm Bell & Howell EYEMO KF-2 cinecamera fitted in the space. Other modifications had been made in the middle of the aircraft for a second camera to film vertically and from a starboard side angle, as Hugh Rogers would explain.

The opened panel at the rear of the bomb bay gave a vertical sighting and the second sight was on the door edge to the starboard side of the fuselage, the top half of which opened at the time of filming, hence [I] required an electrical heated inner suit. I learned that the temperature at my station was minus 19 degrees Centigrade [Celsius] and it confirmed my view that I had drawn the short straw. To sustain our long flight, we did not have a Tallboy loaded but there was a large red fuel tank fitted in the space above the bomb bay. It contained about 80 tons [sic] of fuel, which I rested on during the flight.[6]

Rogers had joined Buckham's crew at a final briefing at Lossie-mouth, shortly before take-off.

[We were] in a badly lit, barnlike room with Wing Commander Tait giving his last remarks to the nineteen pilots of 617 Squadron. We were all standing in a group around Tait . . . he emphasised the importance of the prescribed course, which had been designed to avoid detection by the enemy. Over the North Sea, the course was to be 1500 feet, and this was to be maintained until the Norwegian coast was approached.[7]

The weather would claim several aircraft in the force before they even left Scotland. Severe icing meant that 9 Squadron commander Jim Bazin and his crew could not get off the ground, as Flying Officer Roy Harvey, Squadron Leader Bill Williams' navigator, would recount.

Wing Commander Bazin's aircraft could not be made ready in time. The weather was atrocious, and the ground crews had the task of cleaning frost off the wings on a bitterly cold night. As the aircraft was so overweight with additional fuel and the Tallboy it would have been suicidal to have attempted to do so . . . As it was, I seem to recall having to call out the air speed well above the normal for the take-off before Bill finally managed to break the ground friction by 'bouncing' the aircraft off. I suppose it was suicidal anyway.[8]

Soon after they were airborne, Williams, now leading the 9 Squadron force, would be given more bad news. With the permission of operation commander Group Captain Colin McMullen, Bazin broke radio silence to inform Williams that a total of seven of their Lancasters had been defeated by the icing and were out of action.

Buckham and his crew were delayed by almost an hour by the icing of their aircraft but quickly made up time to rejoin the stream. After turning out over Moray Firth, the 617 Squadron Lancasters set course north-east for the Norwegian Sea at 1500 feet as directed. After reaching 46 degrees north, they turned eastwards towards the Norwegian coast, maintaining their low level. After crossing the coast and climbing rapidly to clear the mountains, the aircraft crossed into Sweden and then headed north, hugging the border to the rendezvous point—Akkajaure, a large reservoir 150 miles south-southwest of Tromsø. The lake was obscured by cloud but still recognisable to the converging crews. About half an hour later, as the force approached Tromsø, Willie Tait marvelled at the spectacle.

The sun was resting on the horizon, so the snow-covered mountains were turned pink in its light. The sky was cloudless, the air calm and the aircraft rode easily without a bump to disturb the bomb aimer's sights. We sighted the *Tirpitz* from a range of at least 20 miles, lying squat and black among her torpedo nets, like a spider in a web; silhouetted against the glittering blue and green waters of the fjord and surrounded by the beautiful hills. Down below everything was quite still. The whole scene—water, mountains and sky—blazed in the cold brilliance of the arctic dawn.[9]

As Tait led the bomber stream in with about five miles still to go, *Tirpitz*'s main guns opened fire, their shells bursting 20 seconds later in front of and below the attackers. The air was filled with puffs of smoke as the guns positioned along the shore joined the fusillade. But none of the aircraft deviated from the formation. Bruce Buckham moved into position to begin filming the bombing.

Tait was the first to release his Tallboy, from 13,000 feet, at 0841 hours GMT. One minute later, five other Lancasters released their bombs, including the crew of Bunny Lee, who would recount during the later operational debriefings that *Tirpitz* was obscured by smoke just after his bomb was released: 'Our bomb went straight down into the centre of the smoke. All bombing we saw appeared very well concentrated and firing from the ship ceased after the first bombs went down.'[10] At 0843 another wave of five 617 Squadron Lancasters bombed, including Arthur Kell: 'We bombed along the length of the ship turning to starboard and running in on the bows. Our bomb, which registered a hit or a very near miss, fell in the centre of the smoke coming up from just in front of the superstructure.' John Sayers was the last of the 617 Squadron pilots to bomb at 0845: 'We followed our bomb down nearly to the ship when it was lost in smoke. It was either a hit on the bows or a very near miss.' As the 9 Squadron aircraft followed closely in the wake of the 617 Squadron Lancasters, the fate of *Tirpitz* was sealed. The crews could not believe their good luck—the weather had held, the smokescreen pots had not been activated and, most crucially, the German fighter squadron at Bardufoss had failed to scramble in time to intercept the attackers before they had bombed.

Three Tallboys were later confirmed to have made direct hits on *Tirpitz*. The first, dropped by Willie Tait, struck amidships on the port side of the funnel. The other two pierced the armour-plated deck beside the Anton and Caesar main gun turrets. There were several other near misses that caused additional damage to the port side of the hull. Just 10 minutes after the last of the Tallboys had been dropped, a massive blast blew the Caesar turret clear from its mountings, probably the result of an explosion in an ammunition storage bay.

As the last bombers from 9 Squadron completed their runs and dived towards sea level to begin the flight home, it was still not certain that *Tirpitz* was finished. The last to depart was Bruce Buckham's Lancaster. After flying for 30 minutes 'over it, around it and all about', Buckham decided to call it a day. *Tirpitz* was still afloat under a giant mushroom cloud of smoke that plumed several thousand feet into the air, although fire had broken out behind the funnel and there were signs that she was starting to list. As Buckham flew out towards the mouth of the fjord, rear gunner Eric Giersch called out over the intercom, 'I think she's turning over, skipper.' Buckham turned to port to take a look and then immediately headed back towards the ship, flying just 50 feet above the water. As they got close, *Tirpitz* 'ever so slowly, and gracefully' heeled over to port and capsized—the moment captured for history by the forward camera operator, Flight Lieutenant John Loftus.

On the water, Armageddon had arrived. Captain-Lieutenant Alfred Fassbender was *Tirpitz*'s first flak officer and the most senior crew member to survive the attack. In a later detailed account of what unfolded, he recorded that 'a stick of bombs' had fallen inside the battleship's net enclosure.[11] There were two direct hits on the port side, one on the aircraft catapult and one abreast of B turret. Seconds later, *Tirpitz* began listing to port. As the first bombs hit, damage control parties were ordered to correct the trim by flooding. At about 0945, the list increased to 30 to 40 degrees and Captain Robert Weber, the former executive officer who had taken over command of the ship just eight days earlier, ordered the evacuation of the lower decks. Less than five minutes later, the list increased to 60 to 70 degrees, then the 700-ton Caesar turret exploded and arced upwards, then plunged into the water. Soon after that, *Tirpitz* capsized, trapping hundreds of men beneath the upturned hull.[12] Scores of men who had made it up onto the deck hung precariously onto the hull until the first rescue boats arrived after about fifteen minutes. Hundreds more struggled through the icy waters to reach the shore. An estimated 1700 crew were aboard *Tirpitz* on the morning of 12 November, about 700 others having been transferred to shore-based work since the relocation to Tromsø. Within two hours, 596 men had made it ashore or been rescued from the water. A desperate struggle unfolded as teams tried to free those trapped in air pockets inside the wreck, a task hampered by the lack of acetylene torches to cut through the thick steel plates. Over the next two days, just 87 men were recovered before it was estimated that the last oxygen had expired. The final death toll was reckoned to be 971—including Captain Weber and almost all of his officers, many of whom were trapped inside the armoured control room where he had gathered them to direct the defence of the ship. Captain-Lieutenant Fassbender would be awarded the German Cross in Gold for his bravery during the desperate final moments of *Tirpitz*.

All but one of the Lancasters would make it safely home. As they were making their bombing run with the rest of the 9 Squadron aircraft, Flying Officer David Coster's Lancaster was hit by flak and lost an engine. The RNZAF pilot completed the run but soon after dropping his Tallboy began to lose power in a second engine. Realising his damaged aircraft would not make it home, Coster decided to head towards Sweden. As he flew south-west from Tromsø, he was intercepted by a German Me 109 fighter that made two passes from behind. As the rear gunner engaged the Messerschmitt, Coster plunged his aircraft into a corkscrew dive to escape. No sooner had he levelled out than a second fighter appeared. 'I saw another Me 109 coming straight at me,' Coster's flight engineer, Sergeant Jim Pinning, recounted. 'It made just one pass from starboard but didn't press his attack, possibly because he thought we were a dead duck.'[13] As they approached what they thought was the Swedish border, Coster sent a radio message in the hope of locating an airstrip but suddenly lost all power in his second engine and was forced to crash-land in a field. All the crew climbed out of the wreckage unharmed. Still unsure where they were, they hurriedly began burning maps and documents before a farmer arrived to tell them they had landed near the Swedish town of Vännäsberget—news that drew loud cheers and hugging among the airmen.[14]

The crew had been especially fortunate as it was later confirmed that one of the two German fighters that chased them had been flown by Major Heinrich Ehrler, the Luftwaffe CO at Bardufoss and an ace who had already shot down 199 Allied aircraft during the war. Ehrler's distinguished record would do nothing to save him from the fury of the German High Command at the failure of his fighter squadron to defend *Tirpitz*, which was largely due to a series of communications blunders. Within weeks, Ehrler and six other officers were court-martialled, and he was sentenced to three years' imprisonment and demoted. However, the sentence would not stand. In the desperate final months of the war, Ehrler was recalled to active service, shooting down another nine Allied aircraft before he died in an air battle near Berlin in April 1945.

By the time they returned to Waddington, Buckham and his crew had been flying for 14 hours and 19 minutes. But there would be a further drama before they were safely down. As they crossed the North Sea on their way home, the crew had felt and heard a tremendous crash. It was only as they prepared to land that they saw their starboard main wheel hanging down, the engine nacelle panels flapping loose and a gaping hole in the wing.

A later investigation would reveal that a flak shell had passed through the undercarriage bay, travelled between the Number 1 and Number 2 fuel tanks and gone out through the wing without exploding. Buckham was forced to land on one wheel.[15]

Buckham's crew were the last of the raiders home, but because they had lingered over the target long after the other bombers had departed Norway, they carried the first confirmation that *Tirpitz* had been sunk—and the spectacular film evidence to prove it. Even so, their reception was rather an anticlimax. The regular debriefing was attended by Air Vice-Marshal Cochrane. When he asked Buckham how the raid had gone, the Australian replied: 'Well, we will not have to go back after this one. *Tirpitz* is finished.' Despite the dramatic news, Cochrane maintained his usual taciturn composure, much to Buckham's surprise.

Nobody said very much in the debriefing and I said to the crew, 'Christ, they are a peculiar lot.' I said, 'Let's go and sink the bloody *Tirpitz* again.' So we went into the bar and we really enjoyed having a session there and going over the action of sinking the thing—seeing the thing blow up. Our description of it when we were in our cups was far more vivid. Anyway, when I woke up in the morning and I was feeling rather piqued, the steward said to me, 'Oh, Mr Buckham, you'd better hurry up and get dressed and have breakfast, there's a car waiting for you.' I said, 'What the hell's going on now?' He said, 'You've got to go to London.' Eric was snoring away in the bed, so I went over and shook him and said, 'Come on, get up. You're coming with me.'

The Bomber Command leadership had decided to delay the announcement of the sinking of *Tirpitz* to give themselves time to review the footage of the attack and the crew debriefings before conveying the dramatic news to Prime Minister Winston Churchill who, in turn, briefed King George VI. They also wanted time to maximise the impact of their stunning strike against the Germans in the newspapers and on radio—in the United Kingdom and around the world. The RAF Humber limousine sent by Air Vice-Marshal Cochrane conveyed Bruce Buckham and Eric Giersch into central London for a press conference at the Ministry of Information and a round of interviews with the BBC. Back in Australia, Gwen Buckham received a phone call from an uncle who worked at an air force base in Sydney. Until that time, Gwen had no idea what her husband was doing in England, apart from serving as a pilot with a Bomber Command squadron. They had not spoken since Bruce left Australia two years earlier. They wrote regularly to each other, but Bruce would not and could not talk about his day job. As Gwen Buckham recounted:

My uncle had heard on the radio that the Lancasters had bombed the *Tirpitz* and some of the planes were missing. He rang to tell me to listen to the six o'clock news. He didn't know what Bruce was doing but just knew that he flew Lancasters. I said, 'What's the *Tirpitz*?' I didn't even know that! He said, 'It's the battleship, you nong, the German battleship.' Then I really began to get worried. I rang my mother and father and then we all tuned in at six o'clock. They announced that it was London calling from the BBC and then told about the raid on the *Tirpitz*. They didn't mention about anybody not getting back so that was good. After they talked about what had happened, the announcer said, 'I am now interviewing one of the pilots who took part in the raid—Flight Lieutenant Bruce Buckham.' I nearly fell off my seat. I couldn't believe it. He sounded fine, tired of course, but he was alive, which was absolutely wonderful. That was the first time I had heard his voice since the time he had left for Europe.[16]

There was another false alarm for Gwen Buckham a short time later, when a telegram arrived at the family home in the Sydney suburb of Penshurst.

The thing that really worried you was a telegram because if that arrived you would know that things were not good. And I got a telegram. The telegram boy came down the street and my father was in the garden at the time. The boy had a telegram for me, and I just froze. Dad said, 'Give it to me, I'll open it.' He stood there and read it aloud, 'Congratulations are extended to you by the Minister for Air and the Air Board on the award of the Distinguished Service Order to your husband Flight Lieutenant B.A. Buckham in further recognition of his gallant service.' Then a great feeling of relief and rejoicing came over us. Most of all, it again meant that he was alive. I immediately rang Bruce's father who was very, very relieved. If I had known Bruce as well as I know him now, I would not have had any doubt that he would come back, no doubt whatsoever.

When the news finally broke of the *Tirpitz* sinking, it made headlines around the world. The dramatic pictures adorned front pages of the Fleet Street press and the newspapers back in Australia. The *Sydney Morning Herald* of 15 November 1944 splashed with: '800 OF CREW LOST WITH *TIRPITZ*: Last Nazi Battleship Destroyed.' Accompanying the story was a photo of a younger Bruce Buckham in RAAF uniform, helpfully supplied by Gwen Buckham. As well as providing still photographs, the 700 feet of spectacular film footage shot by John Loftus and Hugh Rogers would feature in newsreels screened in cinemas around the English-speaking world.

After their long round of press conferences and radio interviews in London was done, Bruce Buckham and Eric Giersch headed off to a lavish celebratory dinner at the Savoy Hotel with Willie Tait and his crew, and Tait's fiancée, Flight Officer Betty Plumer, an officer in the WAAF. 'We were looked after like lords,' Buckham would say, 'I have no idea who shouted, but it wasn't me.' After the dinner, extremely well fed and watered, the two Australians stumbled out onto the Strand to suddenly realise that it was too late to return to Waddington and no arrangements had been made for their accommodation in London. After trying unsuccessfully to find a room at several hotels, they were even turned away after dropping into a police station to ask whether they could bunk down in a cell for the night. Eventually, they wandered past the Park Lane Hotel, opposite Green Park on Piccadilly, as Buckham recounted.

We went through the blackout curtains into a dimly-lit foyer. Way up at the end was a night porter at his desk reading a newspaper. I asked if they had a room and he said, 'No. We are booked out.' I said, 'Oh, we are giggered, we couldn't get accommodation anywhere and we are stranded. Could we just bunk down here until the morning? We won't make a mess or any noise. We just need a bit of rest and we'll be gone first thing in the morning.' Just then we all looked down at his newspaper and there was this big photo of me talking to the press with my hands up and you could see Eric sitting at the side. The porter looked at this and then he looked at me and he pointed at the paper. I said, 'Oh yes, my name is Buckham and this is Mr Giersch.' Then straight away he said, 'Look, you go on upstairs to room six on the first floor. Give yourself a good bath or shower and by the time you have done that there will be a nice meal waiting for you.' Well, they did better than that, there were a few bottles of cold beer sent to the room.

In the morning, when the Australians went to check out and pay their bill, they were told there was no charge. The clerk told Buckham: 'The management were delighted to look after you last night and, also, when you and Mr Giersch come to London, there is always a room for you here. I've never met any heroes, and Australians at that.' When the RAF car arrived to drive them back to Waddington, the hotel's owner personally fare-welled them. The hotel would become a regular stopover during the men's visits to London for the remainder of the war.

Ralph Cochrane, the architect of *Tirpitz*'s ultimate demise, was typically understated in his response to the triumph, at least in public. At his regular morning meeting the day after the raid, the 5 Group staff officers attending had anticipated 'a break in the iron exterior'.[17] But, after taking his seat and glancing at his notes, the air vice-marshal began, 'Last night's raid. Successful. *Tirpitz* sunk. Now about tonight's operation . . .' But, as he and everyone in the room knew, the success had cemented Cochrane's reputation as one of the most outstanding RAF leaders of the war. It would help propel him on a post-war career that would see him promoted to air chief marshal and twice knighted.

Soon after Buckham and Giersch's triumphant return to Waddington, there were more headlines back in Australia—this time about the crew themselves. As Gwen Buckham had been advised, Flight Lieutenant Bruce Buckham was awarded the DSO—the highest gallantry award for an officer after the VC. Doc Board was awarded a bar to his DFC. By the end of the war, every other member of the crew would wear the DFC, in each case with their service on the *Tirpitz* raids acknowledged in the award citation. The citation to Buckham's DSO said it all: 'Since the award of the Distinguished Flying Cross, Flight Lieutenant Buckham has participated in many photographic sorties and has continued to display a high standard of operational efficiency. His work has involved remaining in the target area throughout the attack to secure photographs. He has taken part in all three attacks on the battleship *Tirpitz*, on each occasion descending far below normal altitude to obtain excellent photographs. He is an outstandingly capable captain of aircraft, resourceful and courageous to a very high degree.'[18] For his outstanding leadership on the final raids, Willie Tait was recommended for the VC by Ralph Cochrane with the backing of Arthur Harris. In his recommendation, Cochrane hailed 'a great leader who in danger is unperturbed and at all times pits a stubborn will against the enemy's heaviest defences.'[19] Inexplicably, the nomination was refused by the inter-service committee that approved high level awards, denying Tait a richly deserved honour that two of his predecessors commanding 617 Squadron, Guy Gibson and Leonard Cheshire, had been granted. But despite this, his record would stand equally alongside theirs.

Chapter Fifteen

GALLAND

Only the spirit of attack borne in a brave heart will bring success to any fighter aircraft, no matter how highly developed it may be.

Lieutenant general Adolf Galland[1]

By the end of 1944, Germany's defeat was seen as only a matter of time, and a matter of months at that. While the pace of the Allied advance had slowed in the weeks from September, Hitler's grand counteroffensive to push the Allied forces back from German home soil—the Battle of the Bulge—would soon be revealed effectively as the Nazis' last stand. In mid-December, General Dwight Eisenhower, the Allied Supreme Commander, had 48 divisions positioned across a 600-mile front between the North Sea and Switzerland, from where there would be no turning back. The battle launched on 16 December in the wooded hill country of the Ardennes would see some of the most intense ground combat of the war and the Allies suffer 75,000 casualties, but the Germans would lose 125,000 men and the hope of ever being able to turn the tide.

For Bomber Command, the focus continued to be on disrupting the ability of the German Army to fight, and to move and supply their forces. But there would be an increasing number of raids in which the strategic imperative was at best questionable and the cost in civilian casualties unconscionable. The attack on Heilbronn on the night of 4–5 December was a shocking case in point. The small city in south-west Germany, with many grand buildings dating to the 1500s, was of little importance to the German war effort beyond the fact that it stood on the main north–south railway line. Yet a force of 282 Lancasters and 10 Mosquitoes was sent from 5 Group that night to drop more than 1200 tons of bombs that within a matter of minutes destroyed more than 80 per cent of the city's built-up area, wrecked large areas of the surrounding boroughs and killed more than 7000 people, including 1000 children aged under ten years. The exact number of victims was impossible to determine because many corpses were burned beyond recognition. Due to the number of incendiary bombs dropped there was an intense firestorm that burned throughout the night and the city was impossible to enter for days. At the first signs of the attack, many people rushed to bomb shelters in the central area of the city, which were soon engulfed in flames. All those sheltering were either burned to death or asphyxiated before the shelters collapsed. Many who attempted to flee the city were also incinerated on the roads.

On their first operation since the sinking of *Tirpitz*, Bruce Buckham and his crew were given a marathon assignment to film attacks on four separate locations through the night of 4–5 December. The first was Heilbronn, and this was to be followed by targets at Frankfurt, Dortmund and the nearby mining and steel production centre of Bochum. While they had been witness to many horrifying spectacles over the preceding month,

Heilbronn was another that would live long in their memories, as Buckham would recount.

They used a vector bombing system that night. Every aircraft had its own separate bombing heading and delays so that the finished product on the cameras looked like an orange being cut up into quarters and then those quarters filling up progressively in order with fires. It was a terrible sight.

While terror reigned on the ground, the odds were not entirely stacked in favour of the attackers. Twelve Lancasters were shot down by flak from two anti-aircraft batteries near the city and a squadron of fourteen German Junkers Ju 88 night fighters. Once they had finished the filming at Heilbronn and evaded the night fighters, Buckham headed north to join his next scheduled operation near Frankfurt. And there they almost met their match.

The operation was almost finished when I got there but I flew up and down filming. While I'd given the fighters the slip at Heilbronn, there was one that caught up with me at Frankfurt. I was flying up one side of the target. They had done a very successful job. One of the main streets was all lit with fires. They had really messed it up. Then I saw a Me 109 fighter flying up the other side of the target going the other way, so we kept an eye on him. On one occasion, he changed direction and so I thought, I will too. I went the same way he did and he thought he'd missed me—always aim to be in the dark part of the sky if you want to be a little bit safer. Then he came around the other side, where he thought he would meet me. Instead, I was behind him again. Anyway, this was getting a bit out of hand, so I then took off to Dortmund.

When they reached Dortmund, the raid had finished. As they prepared to move on to their final assignment at Bochum, another fighter came onto them. This time it was a twin-engine Me 210. Only long after the operation would they discover that it was the same tenacious pilot, who had landed and quickly switched aircraft after tailing them from Frankfurt.

Suddenly we were under attack as he fired off his cannon and machine guns at us. He sent off two rockets at us that very narrowly missed. Those rockets frightened the hell out of me. I felt like I could have put my hand through the Perspex and touched one of them, they were so close. He was within metres of hitting us. The gunners had been giving me directions and the bloody rockets seemed to be following us. They saw them coming and I saw them going. These things happened so quickly. I then dived to pick up speed and evade him and decided to skip the job at Bochum as we were probably too late anyway. But he was very persistent. He followed us all the way to the coast. After crossing the Zuider Zee, I dropped right down low to just above the sea level as that gave me a bit of extra speed, and he followed us down. He must have thought he done us some damage and was following us to confirm the 'kill'. He came about halfway across the Channel. But the firing had stopped. I think he must have run out of ammunition.

As the pursuit continued, Buckham realised that while his priority was to escape, he did have a chance to kill the pilot, who wanted to do just that to him and his crew.

If a fighter came within 400 yards of the Lancaster, we could hit him. Our guns were synchronised—mid-upper and rear—and we could encircle our aircraft with a rain of protective fire. The German pilot knew this. He'd get to 410 yards and back off. He'd come from another direction and get to 415 and back off. He'd even come to 405. I said to the gunners, 'This guy knows what he is doing.' Johnny Holden, the wireless operator, was tracking him on the screen. I said to the boys on the guns, 'As soon as Johnny says 400 yards, give him the lot. Don't ask for permission, just fire. Shoot him.'

But that moment did not come before the Messerschmitt, now surely running close to the limit of its fuel range, gave up the chase and the Lancaster headed safely home to Waddington. As soon as the danger had passed, Buckham realised that he had been in a position to down the fighter and had blinked. Much later he would concede that his decision might have been driven by a subconscious respect for a fellow pilot who, while an enemy, was clearly as resolute and determined an airman as he was.

I realised that I could have jammed the throttles off, put a bit of flap down and jerked the plane's speed back, which would have brought him within range and given the gunners a go, but I didn't. I don't think I'd have been very happy if we'd shot him down and killed him. I didn't feel like it. It wouldn't have made me happy at all. I guess I respected his persistence. And I was more concerned with completing our escape, which we did.

Two days later, Buckham was stopped in the mess at Wadding-ton by Pilot Officer Tony Giles, the squadron intelligence officer.

'Buck, you're famous,' said Giles. 'We've got the German intelligence. It was Galland who chased you out across the Channel.'

Adolf Galland was no less than one of the most successful, celebrated and decorated fighter pilots in the Luftwaffe. The son of an estate manager from Westerholt in Lower Saxony, Galland had cut his teeth as a pilot during the Spanish Civil War, leading a squadron that took part in the infamous bombing of Guernica. His reputation was sealed during the Battle of Britain when he was Germany's highest scoring fighter ace with 57 'kills' against the RAF. In November 1942, at the age of 30, he became Germany's youngest general, soon after being awarded the Knight's Cross of the Iron Cross with Oak Leaves, Swords and Diamonds, one of the highest honours for gallantry in the German armed forces. When he was appointed commander of the German Fighter Force, Galland was forbidden to fly on combat operations but he continued to do so from time to time in defiance of his superiors. After repeatedly arguing to Hitler and Luftwaffe commander Hermann Göring that the air force needed to switch to a more defensive strategy as the war turned against Germany, Galland was sacked from his command and briefly placed under house arrest before being sent back to combat duties. By the end of the war, he had flown a staggering 705 combat missions, been shot down four times—including twice on one day—and had claimed at least 104 British and American aircraft. In short, he was the last enemy fighter pilot you would want chasing you out across the English Channel. Buckham was chastened by the news.

I realised that I should have slowed the plane up and got him within the 400-yard range and told the gunners to fire everything. It was a bit hazy, but their fingers were very itchy. But I had no idea who it was until Tony Giles told me. But I don't think it would have given me any satisfaction to have shot down their number one pilot, none at all. If we had brought him down in the Channel, Doc would have notified the position and we'd have immediately had that information through to the air-sea rescue people and our speedboat fellers would have gone out and picked him up. If that had happened, I'd have been the first one to go over and pay my respects to him.

There would be an opportunity to do just that—but not for another 30 years.

～

The heroic feats of the Dambusters—the crews from 617 Squadron RAF who audaciously attacked and breached the Möhne and Eder dams of the Ruhr valley in May 1943—would rightly become the most celebrated raid in the history of Bomber Command. Almost forgotten in the history of the war is the fact that in December 1944 there was another series of dam raids also involving the Lancasters of 617 Squadron.

In late November, as the United States Army fought its way through the Hürtgen Forest into Germany in some of the heaviest and mostly costly fighting of the war, there were growing fears that the great dams on the Roer River, which cuts through the region, might be used to trigger a devastating flood to halt the American advance. Near the headwaters of the Roer are seven dams, the largest two being the Urft and the Schwammenauel. Completed in 1905, the Urft Dam was at the time the biggest in Europe with its 190-foot high and 741-foot wide wall containing a capacity of 52 gigalitres of water. Further downstream, the Schwammenauel Dam, built in the 1930s, contained a reservoir with almost double the capacity of the Urft. The US commanders, including General Eisenhower, urged the RAF to repeat the success of the 1943 Dambusters Raid and breach the two big dams. Arthur Harris resisted, regarding the task as unlikely to succeed and a wasteful diversion of his resources. The bouncing bombs used so effectively against the Ruhr dams were not a practicable option this time, and there were serious doubts about the ability of even the new Tallboys to effectively breach the Roer dams. In the end, though, the Americans got their way.

The first attack was delayed by bad weather but finally went ahead on 4 December 1944 with a force of 27 Lancasters and 3 Mosquitoes from 8 Group. They succeeded in blasting a four-metre section off the top of the Urft Dam, but failed to breach it. The next day 56 Lancasters from 3 Group flew to the Schwammenauel Dam, but only two aircraft were able to release their bombs due to thick cloud.

The Urft was again targeted on 8 December by 205 Lancasters from 5 Group. This time the raid was led by Wing Commander Willie Tait and 19 bombers from 617 Squadron armed with Tallboys. And this time Bruce Buckham and his film crew were there to bomb and to record the results. They arrived over the Urft Dam to find seven-tenths cloud cover but good visibility of the spillway, as the 463 Squadron Operations Record Book would record.

Bombing seen was erratic, probably due to the bombing run being hampered by cloud conditions. One Tallboy bomb only seen. This overshot and went into the water. Arrived target at 1114 hours when, there being a reasonable gap in the cloud, we bombed. We then orbited and waited for the 617 attack. 617 Squadron orbited for about ten minutes waiting for an improvement in the cloud conditions but at the end of this time Wing Commander Tait ordered force to return without bombing.[2]

All 15 of the other Lancasters from 463 Squadron on the raid were also unable to bomb, the Squadron Record Book noting 'No target attacked' for each of the crews. In the end only a few aircraft in the bombing stream managed to get their bombs away. In the crowded sky over the target one of the Lancasters from 630 Squadron, piloted by Flight Lieutenant Rendel Lewis, collided with another Lancaster—which would stay airborne— losing his tail fin and rudder before plunging steeply into the waters of the dam. Lewis, 29, was a barrister who had been a navigation instructor at RAF College Cranwell. His navigator, Flight Sergeant Kenneth Lenton, who was just eighteen years old, died alongside him in the crash. Only two of the crew escaped by parachute and only one of them, rear gunner Sergeant Joseph Morgan, survived to be taken prisoner.

There was better luck for the RAF three days later when 5 Group sent 233 Lancasters and 8 Group sent 5 Mosquitoes to again attack the Urft Dam. Once more, the aircraft from 617 and 9 squadrons were armed with Tallboys. Willie Tait again led the 617 Squadron aircraft, taking off from Woodhall Spa soon after midday. Flight Lieutenant Dennis Oram DFC from 617 Squadron—another veteran of the final *Tirpitz* raids—dropped the first Tallboy at 1519 hours and others were soon bursting around the dam. Flight Lieutenant Laurence 'Benny' Goodman's rear gunner saw their bomb burst near the centre of the spillway. Ten minutes later, Tait's bomb aimer released their Tallboy and it hit the middle of the structure. There was little flak and all of 617's aircraft returned safely, although another of the Lancasters on the raid was lost. While the dam was not breached, it was sufficiently damaged that the Germans were forced to lower the water level, diminishing the threat to the Allied ground forces of a potential flood. The next day, the Supreme Headquarters Allied Expeditionary Force halted such tactical operations by heavy bombers because they were diverting effort from strategic targets. It was the end of the era of the Dambusters. A month later, it would be the end of operations for Bruce Buckham and his crew.

After an extended break over Christmas and New Year, Buckham's crew were mustered on the night of 22–23 January 1945 to join a force of 150 aircraft sent on an area bombing attack to the industrial city of Gelsenkirchen, near Essen. Once more, heavy cloud cover hampered operations, but it would be reported that 'moderate' damage was done to residential and industrial areas.[3] After returning safely, the crew would reveal in their debriefing more than a hint of growing frustration with the tactics of Bomber Command, as the squadron Operations Record Book recorded.

Cloud prevented accurate bombing, but as the attack was not intended to be intense concentration, the object of the attack was achieved because bombing was evenly spread. Through breaks in the clouds, streets could be seen blazing. It seemed pointless routeing such a large force through the most heavily defended area of the Ruhr.

The crew were so pleased to be back at Waddington after what had been a particularly cold operation, and long—six and a half hours—that the significance of the moment was forgotten by some of them, as John Holden would recall.

We were told that we were grounded. That came as a bit of a shock to us, as we thought we had a couple more trips to do to complete our second tour of operations . . . When we were told by our commanding officer, Wing Commander Bill Forbes, it took a long time to penetrate until he said . . . 'Now finish your breakfast boys, and I'll buy you a round of drinks.' Well, that's 7 a.m. in the morning! You don't normally start drinking until everything is over but on this occasion we were grounded by that command to go to the bar to have a drink![4]

Chapter Sixteen

LAST DRINKS

Throughout the day the boys were looking for land—good old Aussie, but at dusk it had not shown up. At 13 past 6, the skipper tannoyed that the light at South Head had been seen . . . and a wild cheer echoed.

Flying Officer Cliff Halsall, 460 Squadron RAAF[1]

A few months before the *Tirpitz* raids, Bruce Buckham had travelled down to London to spend a few days unwinding on leave. A chance social encounter would draw him into the shadowy world of wartime espionage—and an extraordinary job offer.

On this visit, Buckham booked a room at the Regent Palace Hotel, in Glasshouse Street, close to Piccadilly Circus. Since the start of the war, the hotel had been a popular destination for airmen in search of female company, particularly Canadians, as the BBC series *Finest Hour* would recall: 'Since the Canadians had invaded London [the Regent Palace] had become known as the Canadian Riding School, but Canadians were not the only boys to get riding lessons there . . . Pilots were glamorous in London and there were single women in the downstairs bar of the Riding School who . . . did not take much charming by a man wearing wings.'[2] On his first night in London, Buckham steered clear of the marauding Canadians and headed instead to a nearby dance hall to while away the evening. After one dance with a pretty young woman, he was invited for another and by the end of the evening she asked whether he would be kind enough to walk her home.

She told me that she lived in a pretty tough old part of London, so I agreed to walk her back. On the way, she asked me in for coffee, which I refused. She'd asked me a few questions about flying and the nature of what we were doing, the type of planes we were flying, what we were carrying and the actual operations. I thought there was something there that didn't quite ring true. I felt uncomfortable, even though I didn't tell her the truth. I was pulling her leg with a lot of the things I was saying. She just said she was interested in flying. I strung her along and then said goodnight. On my way back to the hotel I started to have more serious misgivings. I thought there was something quite wrong about it all.

The next day Buckham decided to contact the police and give them details of what had happened with the strange woman. He heard nothing more and thought no more about it until a few months later when he received a VIP visitor at Waddington.

A bloke in mufti [civilian clothes] came to the headquarters at the station and asked to see me. He told me who he was and that he worked for MI5. He then said, 'We thought you'd like to know that the person you told the London police about, we put her under surveillance, and it turned out that she was a double agent for the

Russians and the Germans. We had been looking for that person for quite some time, so thank you very much. You did us a good turn.' She was a Russian, but she spoke impeccable English.

At the end of his second tour of operations, in early 1945, Buckham made another trip to London. This time his leave pass noted that he was planning to make a farewell visit to relatives in Devon but instead he headed back to the Park Lane Hotel opposite Green Park where he and Eric Giersch had been made so welcome after the final *Tirpitz* raid. Late in the evening, as he was about to head up to his room to sleep, he was greeted by a man sitting in the lobby with his wife and another, younger woman who he would later discover was the man's secretary.

This guy who I had never met before just called out to me, 'How's Husky?' I turned around and said to him, 'Who the hell is Husky?' He then informed me that Husky was the base commander at Waddington, my friend Air Commodore Hesketh, and that was the nickname he had been given when Hesketh was the inter-service heavyweight boxing champion. When I sat down to talk with this fellow it was clear our meeting was no accident. They knew everything that I had done since I left Waddington, everything on the train and where I had been in London during the day. I said, 'You amaze me, I didn't put this address down on my leave pass. I was on my way to Devon.' He said, 'That doesn't matter, we knew where you were.'

The man's name was Douglas Channel and he, too, worked for MI5. And it was soon clear that Channel had engineered the encounter with Buckham with a particular purpose. He put a proposal for the Australian to continue flying as a special pilot transporting British VIPs. He would be trained to fly Mosquitoes and would be promoted to group captain—three ranks higher than his current rank of flight lieutenant. Buckham was tempted, particularly by the idea of converting to Mosquitoes—'a beautiful aircraft, I would dearly have loved that.' But one question would bring the conversation to an abrupt end.

Channel: You'll be flying the boss around everywhere.
Buckham: Who's the boss?
Channel: Mr Churchill.
Buckham: Cripes! So who's the navigator going to be?
Channel: You'll have the best navigator in the air force, a wing commander, an English navigator.
Buckham: Oh, you've just lost me. There's only one really good navigator and that's my navigator, Doc Board.
Channel: No, you can't have him, we've got other plans for him.

Buckham then offered his apologies and went up to bed. Back at Waddington the next evening, he went to the officers' mess for a pre-dinner drink and spotted Air Commodore Hesketh seated not far from the bar. He decided to have some fun.

I went up and got myself a glass of beer from Duncan McColl, the chief steward, and out of the corner of my mouth I said, 'How are you tonight, Husky?' You'd have thought he'd been stung. He jumped up and tore across the room. He went straight past me and around the corner and grabbed a couple of these poor, unfortunate young officers by the scruff of the neck, shook them and demanded,

'Who said that!?' They thought he'd gone bloody mad; he'd had a fit or something. They just didn't know what he was talking about. They said, 'We didn't say anything, we were just talking, sir.' He persisted, 'Are you sure? Are you sure?' Then he went back and sat down in the corner with his great pot of beer and the bull terrier sitting alongside him.

Buckham then turned to face Hesketh and confessed to being the culprit.

'It was I, sir.' Then Hesketh said, 'Oh Buck, you'd better come over here, I want to talk to you. Where have you been?' I told him exactly what had happened down in London. He asked what I wanted to do, and I said, 'Well, I will do whatever is wanted of me, but I'm entitled to go home. I've got my points. I've done my two tours of ops and I want to go home and see my wife and my family and see how things are because I've got no idea what's happened in Australia since I left.' He said, 'Well, if you really want that, we'll see what we can do.'

There was another, compelling reason for Buckham's decision to draw his war service in England to an end. The pressures of two intensive tours of operations had finally exacted their toll and he suffered what he would describe as a mental breakdown.

I cracked, I snapped. I got very sick before I got on the ship. I was so damn sick I couldn't even sleep. I was having nightmares. I couldn't even drink a decent drop. I couldn't keep food down. I was thrashing around in the room at night. Eric was in the room with me. After a week he said, 'I'll get you a portagaff.' I didn't know what it was—stout and a bit of lemonade. I told him I'd probably only throw it up. Anyway, he started me on half a glass. After a few days I started to sleep a bit better and I started to take on food without losing it. And, by the time we were ready to go, I was up to a full glass of stout every night. It was building me up beautifully.

The air force determined that Buckham was suffering 'war fatigue' and wanted to send him to a retreat in Scotland to rest and recuperate.

They told me they would send me up to Scotland for six months and I would be well looked after. But I said the war wouldn't last another six months. I said, 'No, I'm not going there, I won't do it.' I told them I could rest on the way home. I want to see my wife and family and I insisted on being allowed to go home. I don't know whether it was wise to take things into my own hands like that, but I was determined. I thought that if I agreed to go to Scotland I probably wouldn't have got home in May 1945. It might have been May 1946!

Buckham had talked to the rest of his crew about his decision and asked what their plans were. Eric Giersch, Doc Board, Jimmy Manning and Darrell Procter then all decided to join him on the journey home. John Holden was the only Australian to stay behind and he had a good reason to break ranks with the rest of his crew. One day, after returning from an operation, the crew were climbing into the transport truck when Holden heard the 'sweet voice' of Dorothy, the WAAF driver, saying, 'Come in the cabin with me, John. I want to talk to you.' It would be, Holden later recalled, 'the first occasion I really had a clear-cut conversation with my wife . . . it blossomed from there.' The couple were married in June 1945 and Holden would remain deployed at Waddington until he and Dorothy returned to Australia in January 1946.[3]

One of the many farewell parties in the mess at Waddington would be to celebrate the award of Buckham's DSO. A notice was posted on the wall of the mess announcing that, 'on the occasion of Buck's recent appointment, a barrel is on the house.'

What they didn't say was that the other 18-gallon keg was on Buck. I had to pay! Everyone is very convivial the night you get a gong. They crept up on me surreptitiously and, after a big struggle, they managed to get my pants off and they put them up on the flagpole outside. All the WAAF officers were laughing like hell when I stood up from behind the piano. One of the lads then turned around to them and said, 'What are you girls laughing at—you're next!' And they all got up and fled in a hurry. What a night! I don't remember much of it.

A short time later, Buckham and most of his crew were aboard the luxury liner SS *Nieuw Amsterdam*, the pride of the Holland America Line, heading home to Australia. As they were crossing the Mediterranean, Buckham would learn, just as Douglas Channel had hinted, that Doc Board had also been offered a prestigious new job—and had refused it for the same reason Buckham had declined the offer to become a pilot to VIPs.

In late 1944 the RAF had launched a project to tackle problems associated with flight navigation accuracy in the polar regions. The Empire Air Navigation School at RAF Shawbury in Shropshire had grown from a training centre for air force navigators into a centre for research into the problems, methods and tools of aerial navigation. A Lancaster christened 'Aries' was modified and fitted out to undertake the first comprehensive airborne investigation of the polar regions to test new navigation techniques, evaluate navigation systems, conduct a magnetic survey, obtain radar mapping and meteorological data and photograph Arctic topography. Two days after VE Day (the end of the war in Europe), Aries would embark on the first flight to both the geographic and magnetic north poles. It would be the ultimate joy ride for air navigators but one of Australia's best had declined an invitation to be part of it, as Buckham explained.

We were halfway across the Mediterranean and up on the sun deck one day and someone asked Doc what he was going to do next. Then he told us that he'd been teased with a very nice proposition, and he didn't know whether he'd done the right thing in turning it down. When we asked what the job was, he said he had been chosen to be the chief navigator on the Aries flight and offered a promotion to wing commander rank. I asked him why he didn't take it. Doc said he'd had enough of flying but there was another reason. He said, 'When I asked them who was going to be the skipper, they said I would have a top pilot, a group captain . . . but I told them they must be joking, there was only one bloke that I would fly with, and particularly on long trips like that, and that was Bruce Buckham.' So that was it. Our loyalty was there. We had both stuck, one to another. That really grabbed at my heartstrings.

As *Nieuw Amsterdam* crossed the Indian Ocean the Australians would celebrate VE Day, on 8 May. After the King's message was broadcast across the ship, the order was given to 'splice the mainbrace'—the naval tradition to celebrate a momentous event by breaking out the rum. And so they did, despite the reluctance of the American in charge of the vessel to indulge his boisterous passengers. Excessive quantities of rum and Coke were consumed and the 'horseplay' with the Wrens (Women's Royal Naval Service) officers reached exuberant heights. During a brief stopover in Perth, the men gorged themselves on fruit, which had been a rare luxury during the years in England. There were gasps when *Nieuw Amsterdam* finally steamed through the Heads and into Sydney Harbour. After a bus ride back to Bradfield Park, where his journey to war had begun, Buckham was at last reunited with his wife and family.

While Buckham was exhausted and had been ready to come home, he had not yet resolved that his war was over. His 'secret agenda' was to go back to flying in Australia. He planned to meet up with his friend and mentor Bill Brill, who had preceded him back home and was now CO of the RAAF training station at Tocumwal in southern New South Wales. Buckham's intention was to do a conversion course onto the American-built Liberator bombers and go back on operations in the Pacific, where it was still envisaged that an invasion of the Japanese mainland would be necessary to end the war. But his plans were thwarted—by the man who had been perhaps his greatest ally in Bomber Command. Soon after his return to Sydney, Buckham had applied for the conversion course, but he heard nothing back.

I'd waited and waited and waited for something to happen and I thought, 'Well, I'd better make some enquiries about this.' So, after lunch one day the postings officer at the RAAF's No. 2 Embarkation Depot at Bradfield Park asked me to go down to his office. He said, 'I'm sorry Bruce, I can't post you because you've got an endorsement on your papers.' I said, 'What endorsement?' He said, 'It's alright, it's green.' If it's red or black, it's a bad mark against you. He passed the folder over to me. The notation on the front had been signed and dated: 'Under no circumstances is Flight Lieutenant Bruce Buckham, DSO, DFC, to be flown on active service again, signed A. Hesketh, Base Commander, 53 Base, RAF Waddington.' And that was it. I was grounded.

Far from being a vote of no confidence in Buckham, the base commander who had wept after sending him off on that lone raid to Berlin in January 1944, convinced that he would not survive, had quietly resolved that one of his best pilots had done more than his share and should not be exposed to further danger. By now it was late June 1945 and within weeks the Japanese surrender would bring the war in the Pacific to an end. Even without Allan Hesketh's order, Buckham had run out of time to resume flying operations. It was time to return to civilian life, but a family friend in the RAAF administration in Sydney recommended that he postpone his discharge just a little longer.

He urged me to stay in for another week, which was all I needed to become a substantive squadron leader, but I said, 'Give us the papers, I'm fed up.' I was due for a promotion. I'd well and truly served my time as a flight lieutenant. Mind you, they could have given me the promotion at any time when I was at Waddington, but they didn't. In the end, I was probably the longest-serving flight lieutenant in the air force. I probably should have stayed a few more days and got that promotion because it would have meant a few more pounds. But I'd had enough. They'd fiddled with me quite enough and I hadn't fiddled with them, although I probably had! Gwennie and I had a talk when I went home that night, and I told her I'd had enough and I would take my discharge. And that's what I did.

Considering his outstanding flying record, Buckham's slow advancement through the officer ranks was inexplicable. He was not formally promoted to flight lieutenant until a week after the final *Tirpitz* raids. By that time he had held the rank of flying officer for more than eighteen months and towards the end of his first tour he had briefly commanded one of the two flights of 463 Squadron—a role normally filled by a squadron leader. Buckham was puzzled by the slow promotions but insisted he didn't care. 'I didn't think about promotions and I didn't think about decorations, or recognition and reward,' he would say. 'Promotion might have helped me, particularly when I became a flight commander, but I think the boys respected my authority even though I still hadn't been made up to flight lieutenant.' His service with the RAAF—one of the most illustrious in World War II—ended on 27 July 1945. Just ten days later, the first atomic bomb was detonated over Hiroshima and a week after that Emperor Hirohito announced the Japanese surrender.

Chapter Seventeen

HOME

I never spoke about the war. I never wanted to speak about it. I didn't even want to think about it for well over 30 years. What could I say to those who were not there?

Flight Lieutenant Bruce Buckham

A few days after his arrival back in Sydney on 23 May 1945, Bruce Buckham was strolling through Martin Place in the heart of the city with Gwen. For once, he was out of uniform, wearing the new suit issued to returning servicemen. As they walked arm in arm, a young woman darted up to them.

When she was almost opposite us, she suddenly lent over and put something in my top pocket. It was that quick, and then she dashed off. It was a white feather! I had an instant fit of rage. I could have gone after her, she was in her twenties, but Gwennie stopped me and said, 'Don't be foolish, don't be foolish. She doesn't know anything about you. Just take that stupid thing out.' I said, 'No, I will wear it around all day.' After a little while she took it out of my pocket and threw it away. 'I won't have that,' she said.

Buckham was not alone in being falsely branded a coward. Peter Isaacson, who was a pilot with 460 Squadron RAAF and 156 Squadron, Pathfinder Force, before flying the first Lancaster back to Australia in late 1943, was also targeted with a white feather. He had been walking down Collins Street in Melbourne in civilian clothes—not long after having famously flown his Lanc under Sydney Harbour Bridge. His foolish assailant might have been shocked to know that the 23-year-old had won the DFC, the AFC and the DFM for outstanding gallantry while putting his life on the line for his country. Wing Commander Arthur Doubleday, a fabled flight commander with 467 Squadron, said some of his Australian crew 'got white feathers from people at home saying . . . you should come home, this is where the real war is.'[1]

The returning heroes of Bomber Command did not always receive a hero's welcome. Many civilians and other servicemen were resentful of the airmen who had fought on the other side of the world while Australia came perilously close to being invaded by the Japanese. The fall of Singapore, the capture of the Australian Army's 8th Division and the death and misery that followed for tens of thousands of prisoners of war was still a raw wound in the memory of the nation. Some thought the glamorous fighter and bomber boys had had it relatively easy, ignorant of the fact that aircrew fighting in Europe had served in the deadliest occupation of any Australian servicemen in World War II.

There was also widespread resentment within the RAAF itself towards those returning from Britain. Peter Isaacson would be treated 'very, very coldly' when he was posted to the RAAF station at East Sale, in Victoria: 'They didn't like the people who had served in Europe, because they had far more experience and some of us had gongs of course and that was a question of jealousy. They were very jealous and treated you very coldly—it was difficult to make friends with them.'[2]

Back at BHP, some colleagues were quick to try to cut their tall poppy down to size. Buckham was treated with disdain and even hostility by a number of colleagues and superiors as he struggled to settle back into the mundane world of office work. Inevitably, the war had changed him. He had enlisted in 1941 as a 23-year-old junior clerk with little life experience. Four years later, he had come home from war as a highly decorated bomber pilot and captain of aircraft who had experienced more and been challenged more than most men are in their entire lifetimes. And he carried the mostly suppressed trauma of the many harrowing things he had seen and done. He was restless, irritable and had a short fuse. 'It was a tremendous change and I struggled to adjust,' he would say. 'I was out of step with the local thinking, and I got myself into quite a lot of trouble disagreeing with people.'

Coming home also forced Buckham to confront the loss of his beloved elder brother John, who had fought with the 2/30th Battalion in Malaya, been taken prisoner after the fall of Singapore and died on the Thai-Burma Railway. In January 1944, Buckham had written home to Gwen after hearing the news that John's fiancée had received a prison camp card saying he 'was okay' when it was sent the previous February. 'According to the latest reports, the Japs have been carrying out the vilest atrocities on the Allies in their hands. Sometimes I fear for his safety. Well, the day of reckoning draws ever closer and I shall do my utmost to be in it when the time comes.'[3] His fears were well founded. At the time he was writing, John had already been dead for almost four months, having succumbed in October 1943 to the effects of malnutrition and malaria. The loss sharpened Buckham's anger towards trade unionists who had taken strike action during the war and refused to load ships with supplies vital to the war effort. One day, while drinking with a group of workers from the BHP steelworks at a hotel in Elizabeth Street in Sydney, Buckham confronted a group of wharfies and 'quite rightly told them what bastards I thought they were for refusing to load supplies for our troops in New Guinea.' Fortunately, his drinking companions dragged him out of the pub 'before the fists started flying.'

Buckham found it difficult to discuss his war experiences, even among family and friends. 'When he first came back, he didn't want to talk about what happened in the war,' Gwen would say. 'He just wanted to forget about it. I didn't care. I was just pleased that he got back in one piece when so many of the boys didn't get back.'[4] Buckham himself would say:

The hardest question to answer when you got home was what it was like over there. You can't say too much. I'd be asked in the street or at home in a social atmosphere. All you could say was, 'Oh, it was pretty rugged.' I'd let it go at that. I'd seen enough warfare. I'd certainly seen too many people shot down, planes going down in flames, planes burning on the ground. Look at the Nuremberg raid, that should never have happened. If I had talked about a lot of the things that happened, people wouldn't have believed me. I found it hard to believe myself.

Three months after he arrived back in Australia, the Japanese surrender ended the war in the Pacific. On VJ (victory over Japan) Day—15 August 1945—cities around Australia erupted with spontaneous celebrations, but other emotions consumed Bruce Buckham.

Sydney went mad but I simply packed up my papers at the office of BHP in Sydney and walked up through all the ticker tape and went home to Penshurst. I went down to the Presbyterian church and then went home to Gwen's place where we were living at the time. And when Pop Pennell came and offered me a beer, I said, 'No thanks. I'll just pay my respects quietly.' Now, come Anzac Day every year, I don't go to those reunions and clubs and pubs. I just come home quietly and have a drink. That does me. And there is also my brother to have a toast to. He was very precious to me.

Buckham's reluctance to talk about the war changed in 1975 when he returned to Europe to join the events marking the 30th anniversary of VE (victory in Europe) Day. About 45 former members of 463 and 467 squadrons were on the trip. The Australian 463–467 Squadron Association, which Buckham and Rollo Kingsford-Smith had helped establish soon after the war, had 'put a touring side together' to visit both Germany and Britain. While in Munich, the visitors were invited to a dinner by the German Night Fighters' Association. There Buckham finally came face to face with Adolf Galland, the German fighter ace who in 1944 had almost added Buckham's crew to his long list of 'kills'. In the spirit of post-war friendship and reconciliation,

Buckham presented Galland with a rare and valuable 1930 Australian penny.

He just looked very steadily into my eye and smiled. We only exchanged a few brief words, but it was a special moment. He knew all about me after that first Berlin raid in early '44, when I was an hour late and bombed the big city alone. They knew all about that. Galland and I were scheduled to do a television interview together in Munich. Unfortunately, something happened at his property back in Spain and he had to leave early, so we never got to go on air and show the public what good fellers we were.

Soon after the war, Buckham had been told by Bill McMahon, a former member of Bill Brill's crew, that the Germans had been looking forward to capturing him. McMahon had been shot down after a raid on the railway marshalling yards at Siegen in Germany in February 1945. The entire crew survived the crash, but the pilot, Flight Lieutenant James Livingstone, was murdered by the German SS (Schutzstaffel, the Nazi special police) after being captured. McMahon and the rest of the crew spent the final months of the war as POWs. When McMahon later met Buckham one day in Taree, in New South Wales, he told him, 'You're lucky you didn't get shot down or you would have got a very unpleasant welcome. They were waiting for you to "drop in". You and Billy Brill headed their blacklist of pilots.' Other airmen who had been captured told Buckham that during their initial interrogation, the Germans would unnerve their captives by discussing other pilots and their crews in great detail—including him.

While in Germany, Buckham visited some of the many war cemeteries—'the dreadful rows and rows of graves where the airmen are, whole crews of boys just nineteen and twenty.' In England he was one of ten former RAAF airmen presented to the Queen at a reception at Windsor Castle. The dignitaries present included Sir Arthur Harris, the former Air Officer Commanding Bomber Command who all those years earlier had ordered Buckham to forget his ideas about joining Pathfinder Force, report to 463 Squadron at Waddington or go home. Back at Waddington there were grand reunions and a demonstration by the last Lancaster still flying in Britain.

Back home, another encounter with a former wartime adversary would rekindle memories of the most dramatic moment of his time with Bomber Command. Shortly after the 25th anniversary of VE Day, the BHP staff magazine published an article about Bruce Buckham's dramatic role in the sinking of *Tirpitz*. By then, Buckham had risen through the ranks to become the company's Queensland state manager. The article was read with particular interest by John Troeger, a leading hand at BHP's Kwinana Nickel Refinery in Western Australia, who had migrated to Australia from Germany in 1958.

As a 22-year-old German navy signaller, John Troeger had begun service aboard *Tirpitz* during her final two years. On the fateful morning of 12 November 1944, Troeger had been sent ashore on courier duty between the ship and Tromsø town. He was returning with a bundle of dispatches when the ship's main guns suddenly opened fire. Through his binoculars he read the signal flags warning of 'attack from the air'. Rushing aboard, he was halfway up the stairs to his battle station on the command bridge when one of the first of the Tallboy bombs dropped by the Allied Lancaster crews hit amidships. The massive explosion threw him into the icy waters of the fjord, as he would recount in the next issue of the BHP magazine.

By this time there were men everywhere in the water. It was bitterly cold, and black smoke was billowing over everything. Then I remember another bomb hitting the waterline alongside. The suction pulled the ship sideways. It stayed there for what seemed a very long time, but water was pouring in through the hole in the side and it suddenly keeled over and slid, bow first, into the harbour sand. That was the end of the *Tirpitz*, exactly as Bruce Buckham described it.[5]

Troeger recalled seeing what must have been Buckham's Lancaster sweeping low over the stricken battleship just after he was pulled from the water by the crew of a German motor torpedo boat.

We were crowded on the deck when a single aircraft came back and circled overhead a couple of times at very low level. I remember saying, 'There you are, they've come back to make sure we are really finished.' It must have been the camera plane ... We spent from ten at night until four next afternoon cutting holes in the two-inch thick nickel-steel keel to free engineers trapped by the water. It was hard work in the wintry conditions but in one case I saw 45 men climb out of a hole we cut.

When the former sailor and the former airman met at Kwinana, soon after the publication of their reminiscences, Troeger said he bore no animosity towards Buckham and the other airmen who sank *Tirpitz*, despite still mourning the loss of so many of his friends and colleagues, 'The war was a long time ago and the Bruce Buckhams and the John Troegers were doing their respective duties.' Bruce Buckham would agree. 'I'm glad you came through,' he said, as they shook hands.

While Buckham's crew were scattered across different parts of Australia after the war, they enjoyed catching up with each other at occasional reunions. 'Our relationships were unchanged,' the former skipper would say. 'We still had that admiration for each other we'd had when we flew together. It didn't need expressing or being put into words. They knew and I knew.' The war they all had miraculously survived would take its toll on some in peacetime.

Doc Board—known to his family as Lin—would have a troubled post-war life, with bouts of alcoholism driven by what his son Peter regarded as undiagnosed post-traumatic stress disorder. Board's first wife, Phyllis, with whom he had three children, would die of cancer in 1979. He would remarry, but died in 1989 after battling poor health for several years. In a tribute for his funeral, his family would write: 'Lin will be remembered . . . as a man whose modesty belied his bravery.' One day, while passing through Wynyard Station in Sydney, Bruce Buckham spotted an impressive group of air force medals, including the DFC and bar, in the window of a coin and medal shop. On closer inspection, he was shocked to see that the medals were Doc Board's. His former navigator had applied for the medals long after the war and sold them when short of money. 'The shop wanted more than $4000 for them,' Buckham would recall. 'If I had been rich,

I would have snaffled them up and given them to Peter Board. It was sad to see that happening.'

Within weeks of their homecoming in 1945, Buckham was best man when Eric Giersch married Dorothy Parmenter, a police inspector's daughter, in Wollongong. Tragically, Dorothy would die eighteen months later while giving birth to twins, Wendy and Peter. Giersch, who was by then working as a commercial traveller across New South Wales, could not manage the children alone and they would be raised by Dorothy's parents. He would remarry in 1965 when the twins were in their late teens and die of prostate cancer in 1994.

For John Holden, memories of war would permeate his peace. 'They're always there,' he would say. 'The loss of your companions, that's war, to be expected. But you retain their memory, you can never obliterate that memory . . . you never will.'[6] After returning to his job at the Wheat Board, Holden and his wife Dorothy would settle in Adelaide. Having survived the endless dangers of flying operations with Bomber Command, he would die in a random road accident. One morning in 1998 after leaving Dorothy to order coffees at a local café, he was struck by a car and killed while crossing the street to post a letter.

Jock Sinclair, who married a WAAF while serving in Lincolnshire, returned to Dundee after the war and took a job with the local water board where he would become a senior manager.

Jimmy Manning returned to his job as a clerk with the New South Wales Railways and would later manage two railway stations in the Tamworth area. Darrell Procter went back to Sydney University to complete his dentistry studies.

Bruce Buckham would survive a severe heart attack in the 1960s and a car accident in which he lost an eye to live to the grand age of 92, a father of three, grandfather of nine and great-grandfather of three. At his funeral in Brisbane in August 2011, his coffin was draped with an RAAF flag and the medals that he had proudly worn 'in honour of the boys who did not come back.' There was an air force guard of honour and a piper played a lament.

A meeting in the late 1980s with his former Bomber Command comrade Leonard Cheshire VC had crystallised Buckham's thoughts about the service and sacrifice of so many with whom they had fought in the war.

I will always remember what Cheshire said to me. Those of us who survived should not be regarded as heroes. A lot of us who came back got all the adulation about the place, and all the honours. As far as I am concerned, the heroes are the men who didn't make it back. They signed up to serve their country, they left their families behind, they honoured their pledge and they gave up their lives. They were the real heroes. My thoughts are with all those boys and always will be.

Acknowledgements

This book began almost twenty years ago with a chance encounter on the internet. While researching unrelated information about the RAAF in 2004, I stumbled upon an article about the sinking of the German battleship *Tirpitz* and the astonishing detail that an (almost) all-Australian Lancaster bomber crew had been in the thick of the final raids and had carried the camera crew that captured the action. Further digging revealed that while six of the seven-member crew had since died, the pilot was alive and well in Brisbane.

As the 60th anniversary of the *Tirpitz* sinking was approaching, I persuaded my editors at *The Age* newspaper that this could make a great feature for our *Good Weekend* magazine. But my ambitions were soon delivered an abrupt reality check. Intermediaries questioned my credentials and motives and insisted that Bruce Buckham was a private man who had for many years resisted the blandishments of historians, researchers and pestiferous journalists who sought to invade his retirement.

Somewhat deflated, I draughted a polite and pleading letter, with not much expectation of success. A couple of weeks later, to my surprise, a handwritten note arrived. It confirmed not only that Buckham was up for an interview but also that happy hour began at 5 p.m. at the Buckham residence in the Brisbane suburb of Indooroopilly. Armed with a tape recorder and a bottle of gin, I jumped at the chance.

I'm still not sure what persuaded the old pilot to open his door, his life and his logbooks to me, but I am deeply grateful that he did. It was to be a profound experience that led me on a remarkable journey of discovery and vicarious adventure. It was quickly evident that while the final *Tirpitz* raids were the highlight of Buckham's career with Bomber Command, multiple events during his many combat operations were a compelling window into the challenges faced by all those men who served in the deadliest theatre of World War II. The magazine article soon became the starting point for a book project that led to more than 60 hours of interviews with Buckham and extensive research across four states with family and friends of the seven-member Lancaster bomber crew from 463 Squadron RAAF. All of the quotations from Buckham in this narrative are drawn from those conversations, except where otherwise acknowledged.

I met Buckham many times over the years that followed, and he introduced me to many of those with whom he served, including Cy Borsht and Rollo Kingsford-Smith, who also indulged me with their time and memories. And I was glad to be able to clutch his hand one final time the day before he died, in August 2011, and honoured to be invited by the family to speak at his funeral. At our last meeting I renewed my promise to complete this book and to seek to do justice to his extraordinary story. I regret that it took another decade, due to work and family commitments, to deliver that book. Whether it succeeds in doing justice to the story is for others to decide.

I am grateful to the Buckham family for their immense and unstinting support for this project—and for their patience. My thanks, particularly, to Gwen and Bruce Buckham's surviving children, Lyndal and David, who generously shared family archives and photographs and spent many hours seeking to answer my endless questions when their father was no longer around to do so. My thanks also to Doc Board's son Peter, to the late Dorothy Holden, John Holden's widow, and to Eric Giersch's cousins Jim and Brian and his stepdaughter, Carey Buls, who shared family photos and Eric's reflections on his war service. I am also grateful to Grace Kingsford-Smith, widow of Rollo Kingsford-Smith, and her daughter Sally, for permission to draw material from Rollo's delightful, privately published memoir, *I Wouldn't Have Missed it for Quids*.

Like all contemporary writers of military history, I am indebted to those who passed this way before and whose work enriched mine. I acknowledge the inspiration of Don Charlwood's *No Moon Tonight* and Hank Nelson's *Chased by the Sun*, the two finest accounts of the experience of Australians who served in Bomber Command. Max Hastings' *Bomber Command* is a magisterial history, especially in its reconstruction of the perilous early years before the advent of the Lancaster. Martin Middlebrook and Chris Everitt's *The Bomber Command War Diaries* is the indispensable bible for anyone attempting to navigate the thousands of sorties flown by bomber crews during the war. Nigel Smith's *Tirpitz: The Halifax Raids* is a fine account of the attacks on *Tirpitz* in Trondheim in early 1942. My thanks to Nigel's widow, Patsy, for permission to quote extensively from his unpublished interview with Phil Eyles, Don Bennett's navigator.

Visits to Norway and England in early 2023 produced some valuable new material and spurred the completion of my writing.

In Trondheim, my generous hosts and expert guides were Linzee Duncan and Morten Moe. When she was in her thirties, Linzee began investigating the story of her Scottish grandfather, William Bruce 'Archie' Archibald, a pilot with 35 Squadron RAF who was shot down and killed with all of his crew during one of the Halifax bomber raids against *Tirpitz* in the spring of 1942. That journey of discovery led her to Norway and to Morten, a newsman and authority on the air war in Norway. After 'crewing up' permanently, Linzee and Morten now divide their time between Scotland and Norway. Their house on a hillside in Trondheim has a stunning view across the fjord to the waters where Flight Sergeant W.B. Archibald's Halifax R9496 TL-L went down on the night of 30–31 March 1942. The website Linzee has built in honour of Archie—archieraf. co.uk—is an outstanding archive of material about the ill-fated raids of 1942 and a loving memorial to the 60 aircrew who lost their lives in them.

In Tromsø, I was warmly welcomed by the venerable lawyer and historian Gunnar Nerdrum, who kindly opened the Tromsø Defence Museum on a Sunday afternoon out of season to show the visitor from the other end of the world its splendid collection of *Tirpitz* artefacts. At Storsteinnes, south of Tromsø, historian

Kjetil Åkra was generous with his time and expertise on the Luftwaffe operations in Norway. His book *Tirpitz: Hitler's Last Battleship*, written with John Asmussen, is a trove of details on the many *Tirpitz* raids and on daily life aboard the doomed battleship. A visit to the site beside Håkøya Island where *Tirpitz* was finally sunk was a powerful moment of reflection for me.

Visiting Lincolnshire enabled me to walk the hallowed ground where thousands of the Australians in Bomber Command once served. RAF Waddington, still an operating air force station, has much that is unchanged since the war, including hangars, living quarters and the officers' mess. While the boisterous wartime Saracens Head Hotel on High Street, Lincoln, has been rehabilitated as a bookshop, the Dambusters Inn in nearby Scampton still does a roaring trade in pints and nostalgia. And the grand Lincoln Cathedral still towers magnificently over the plains of 'Bomber County', its tower light a beacon for all those crews that flew on operations from Lincoln, and those who made it home.

The International Bomber Command Centre (IBCC), which straddles another hilltop on the outskirts of Lincoln, is a wonderful memorial and museum, preserving the memories and memorabilia of those who served. My thanks to Dan Ellin of the University of Lincoln, who curates the IBCC collection, for his extensive help and advice with my research. At the RAF Waddington Heritage Centre, I was honoured to be shown around by Chris Ward, the distinguished author of many fine books on RAF history and a walking encyclopaedia of all things Bomber Command.

When Chris Ward suggested that I should make contact with the 463–467 Squadron Association, I shook my head sadly and informed him that the association, which I had been involved with over many years, had been wound up after the passing of the last veterans. I was astonished when he told me that he meant the British 463–467 Squadron Association, which was still flourishing. A call to association secretary Martin Willoughby produced one of the highlights of my visit. He informed me that not only was the association committed to continue honouring the service of the Australians in Bomber Command but it would be hosting Anzac Day ceremonies the following week. I immediately rewrote my travel plans to return the next Tuesday for the morning service in Waddington village, the later ceremony at RAF Waddington and the long lunch at the Dambusters Inn.

Martin Willoughby is the son of Ted Willoughby, a fitter who served with ground crew at Waddington during the war, working closely with the crews of 463 and 467 squadrons. Both father and son deserve honorary Australian citizenship. A few years after the war, Ted Willoughby acquired the abandoned and derelict Lancaster 'S for Sugar', one of only a few bombers to survive more than 100 combat operations—many of them with Australian crews. Over many years, Ted and Martin, in their own time and with their own resources, completely refurbished the storied Lancaster—then handed her over to the Royal Air Force Museum at Hendon, in London. Today Sugar is the star attraction at Hendon, but nowhere is there public acknowledgement of the heroic effort of the Willoughbys to get her there. Martin, who fondly remembered meeting Bruce Buckham as a boy during the RAAF squadrons' anniversary visit to England, was a great help with additional archival sources and photographs.

ACKNOWLEDGEMENTS

Others who assisted with research, advice and hospitality in the United Kingdom include RAF Bottesford historian Vincent Holyoak, 617 Squadron historian Robert Owen, 9 Squadron historian Dicky James, Phil Bonner of Aviation Heritage Lincolnshire, Christopher Mellor-Hill and Dave Russell. Thanks to the British Library for providing access to a first edition of Don Bennett's controversial memoirs. Australian friends Patrick Walters, Denis Reinhardt, Russell Pratt and Simon Clegg were informed and enthusiastic supporters of this book. My profound thanks to Sir Angus Houston, the most distinguished airman of his generation, for agreeing to be the first to read the manuscript, for his invaluable advice on several corrections and for his generous and unsolicited Foreword. Thanks also to my eminent colleague Michael Veitch for his review.

In the quest to bridge the distance of time and fill inevitable gaps of knowledge and detail, general sources such as Wikipedia, government sites and sites dedicated to recording history, have been helpful in the writing of this book.

I would like to acknowledge the support and professionalism of the staff at Allen & Unwin who, as always, have been a pleasure to work with, particularly publisher Elizabeth Weiss and editors Courtney Lick and Jane Fitzpatrick.

And last, but certainly not least, thanks to my wife Asil, son Emre and daughter Serin for continuing to indulge my endless fascination with words and with the history of Australians at war. This book is dedicated to my late father, Colin, who served with the RAAF during World War II, mercifully far from the deadly skies over Europe.

Notes

Full details of published sources can be found
in the Bibliography that follows.

Prologue
1. Australian War Memorial (AWM), S01670, Buckham interview, 1993, with material supplied directly to the author by Buckham.

Chapter One: Enlisting
1. AWM S01670, Buckham interview, 1993
2. D. Charlwood, *No Moon Tonight*, p. 10 (all quotes in this paragraph)
3. H. Nelson, *Chased by the Sun*, p. 16
4. AWM, Buckham interview, 1993
5. G. Buckham interview with author, 2007
6. AWM, Buckham interview, 1993
7. National Archives of Australia, Item ID 5377349, B.A. Buckham RAAF service file
8. G. Buckham interview with author, 2007

Chapter Two: Crewing Up
1. Bomber Command Museum of Canada Archives, <https://www.bombercommandmuseumarchives.ca/s,tasteof22otu.html>
2. UK National Archives, WO 208/3308/705

3. E. Giersch war reminiscences, unpublished Giersch family papers
4. E. Giersch conversation with D. Coutts, Buckham's son-in-law
5. Australian War Memorial (AWM), S00511, Holden interview, 1989
6. A. Harris, *Bomber Offensive*, p. 36

Chapter Three: The Lancaster
1. Letter from A. Harris to R. Dobson, Avro, 6 December 1945—<https://www.lancaster-ed559.co.uk/building-ed559.html>
2. M. Hastings, *Bomber Command*, p. 80
3. R. Reid, *Bomber Command: Australians in World War II*, p. 8
4. R. Kingsford-Smith, privately published memoir
5. D. Fairhead & A. Palmer (directors), *Lancaster* (film), 2022
6. Australian War Memorial (AWM), S00568, Charlwood interview, 1989
7. AWM, Holden interview, 1989

Chapter Four: Waddington
1. M. Veitch, *Heroes of the Skies*, p. 44
2. Kingsford-Smith, privately published memoir (this and following quotes)
3. H. Nelson, *Chased by the Sun*, p. 178
4. M. Middlebrook & C. Everitt, *The Bomber Command War Diaries*, p. 483
5. University of New South Wales Australians at War Film Archive, Charlwood interview, April 2002

Chapter Five: Berlin
1. Kingsford-Smith, privately published memoir
2. Harris, *Bomber Offensive*, pp. 51–2 (this and following quotes)
3. A. Grayling, *Among the Dead Cities*, p. 62
4. M. Hastings, *Chastise: The Dambusters story*, p. 8
5. Middlebrook & Everitt, *The Bomber Command War Diaries*, p. 1

6. Nelson, *Chased by the Sun*, p. 214
7. Middlebrook & Everitt, *The Bomber Command War Diaries*, p. 324
8. *London Gazette*, 14 November 1944
9. Kingsford-Smith, privately published memoir
10. M. Middlebrook, *The Nuremberg Raid: 30–31 March 1944*, p. 85
11. Middlebrook, *The Nuremberg Raid*, p. 179
12. Kingsford-Smith, privately published memoir
13. Middlebrook, *The Nuremberg Raid*, p. 274

Chapter Six: Angels and Demons

1. Fairhead & Palmer, *Lancaster* (film)
2. UK National Archives, AIR 2/6252
3 The UK National Archives, AIR 2/8591, letter S.61141/S.7.C, 28 September 1940
4. C. Kingdon, 'Behind Closed Doors', *Chicago Journal of History*, issue 2, Fall 2013
5. UK National Archives, AIR 49/357
6. R. Overy, *The Bombing War*, pp. 353–354
7. D. Charlwood, *No Moon Tonight*, p. 117
8. P. Eyles unpublished interview with N. Smith, 1989
9. Kingsford-Smith, privately published memoir
10. D. Horsley, *Billy Strachan 1921–1988*, p. 11
11. Kingsford-Smith, privately published memoir

Chapter Seven: The Beast

1. W. Churchill, *The Second World War: Volume IV, The Hinge of Fate*, p. 98
2. UK Public Records Office, PREM 3/191/1
3. Prime Minister's staff note on conversation between Churchill and Pound, 22 January, 1942, UK National Archives, PREM 3/191/1
4. W. Churchill, *The Second World War: Volume III, The Grand Alliance*, p. 272

5. J. Sweetman, *Tirpitz: Hunting the Beast*, p. 4
6. W. Churchill, *The Second World War: Volume IV*, p. 98
7. G. Miller, private papers (author's collection)
8. N. Smith, *Tirpitz: The Halifax Raids*, p. 210
9. E. Flynn, *My Wicked, Wicked Ways*, p. 95
10. D. Bennett, *Pathfinder*, p. 103
11. Imperial War Museum, IWM9378, Bennett interview, 1986
12. UK National Archives, WO 208/3309/741
13. UK National Archives, WO 208/3309/742
14. UK National Archives, WO208/3310/866
15. Imperial War Museum Sound Archives, IWM2440
16. G. Gledhill, 'Battleship Turpitz [sic] – Operation Tungsten', *Slipstream*, vol. 18, no. 3, p. 9
17. P. Bishop, *Target Tirpitz*, pp. 306–307 (this and following quote)
18. H.W. Roskill, *The War at Sea*, p. 276

Chapter Eight: Normandy
1. AWM, Charlwood interview, 1989
2. National Archives of Australia, NAA: A11234, 870/2/P1
3. J. Currie, *Battle Under the Moon*, p. 76
4. RAF Centre for Air Power Studies, L. Cheshire interview, February 1978

Chapter Nine: D-Day
1. W. Churchill, speech to Commons, 6 June 1944, winstonchurchill.org/resources/speeches/1941-45-war-leader/the-invasion-of-france/
2. Fairhead & Palmer, *Lancaster* (film)
3. UK National Archives, AIR27/1921/15
4. nationalinterest.org blog, 14 November 2020
5. Kingsford-Smith, privately published memoir

Chapter Ten: Paris

1. J. Fenby, *The General: Charles de Gaulle and the France He Saved*, p. 132
2. AWM, Buckham interview, 1993, with material supplied directly to the author from Buckham

Chapter Eleven: Bad Blood

1. Bennett, *Pathfinder*, p. 81
2. Harris, *Bomber Offensive*, p. 129
3. Imperial War Museum Sound Archives, IWM 9378, interview, 1986
4. Imperial War Museum Sound Archives, IWM 9378, interview, 1986
5. IWM 9378, interview, 1986
6. Eyles interview with N. Smith, 1989 (this and following quotes)
7. Bennett, *Pathfinder*, p. 91 (first edition)
8. Bennett, *Pathfinder*, p. 91 (first edition)
9. R. Mead, *Dambuster-in-Chief*, p. 247 (and following quote)

Chapter Twelve: Russia

1. P. Brickhill, *The Dam Busters*, p. 186
2. Wallis interview in E. Mirzoeff (director), *Target Tirpitz* (documentary film), 1973
3. Mead, *Dambuster-in-Chief*, p. 195
4. Obituary of J.B. Tait, *Daily Telegraph*, London, 29 August 2016
5. AWM, Buckham interview, 1993
6. T. Iveson & B. Milton, *Lancaster: The biography*, p. 189
7. *The London Gazette*, 22 November 1940
8. AWM, Buckham interview, 1993
9. W.J. Lawrence, *No 5 Bomber Group RAF*, p. 209
10. UK National Archives, AIR 14/1971, C. McMullen Operation Paravane report

11. C. Burgess, *Australia's Dambusters*, p. 103
12. Brickhill, *The Dam Busters*, p. 211
13. AWM, Buckham interview, 1993
14. AWM, Buckham interview, 1993
15. 463 Squadron Operation-Record Book, AIR-27-1922-2, 15 September 1944
16. AWM, Buckham interview, 1993
17. Brickhill, *The Dam Busters*, p. 216

Chapter Thirteen: Hurricane
1. P. Bishop, *Bomber Boys*, p. 334
2. Bishop, *Bomber Boys*, p. 334
3. Middlebrook & Everitt, *The Bomber Command War Diaries*, p. 602

Chapter Fourteen: Tromsø
1. S. Darlow, *Special Op: Bomber*, p. 266
2. Sweetman, *Tirpitz: Hunting the Beast*, p. 121
3. Sweetman, *Tirpitz: Hunting the Beast*, p. 126
4. *The Argus*, 10 April 1950
5. Brickhill, *The Dam Busters*, p. 226
6. International Bomber Command Centre Digital Archive, ARogersH150409
7. International Bomber Command Centre Digital Archive, ARogersH150409
8. S. Flower, *The Dam Busters*, p. 178
9. Darlow, *Special Op: Bomber*, p. 266
10. Sweetman, *Tirpitz: Hunting the Beast*, p. 141 (this and following quotes in paragraph)
11. Sweetman, *Tirpitz: Hunting the Beast*, p. 154
12. Admiralty report, 'Tirpitz: An account of various attacks carried out by the British Armed Forces and their effect upon the German Battleship', vol 2, p. 84

13. Sweetman, *Tirpitz: Hunting the Beast*, p. 159
14. J. Forsgren, *Sinking the Beast: the RAF 1944 Lancaster raids against Tirpitz*, p. 170
15. R. Leach, *An Illustrated History of RAF Waddington*, p. 212
16. G. Buckham interview with author, 2007 (this and following quote)
17. Brickhill, *The Dam Busters*, p. 223
18. *London Gazette*, 23 March 1945
19. Bishop, *Target Tirpitz*, p. 371

Chapter Fifteen: Galland
1. A. Galland, *The First and the Last*, p. 73
2. UK National Archives, AIR 27/1922 (this and following quote)
3. Middlebrook & Everitt, *The Bomber Command War Diaries*, p. 655 (this and following quote)
4. AWM, Holden interview, 1989

Chapter Sixteen: Last Drinks
1. Australian War Memorial (AWM), PR00791, Cliff Halsall diaries and papers
2. T. Clayton & P. Craig, *Finest Hour: The book of the BBC series*, pp. 215–16
3. AWM, Holden interview, 1989

Chapter Seventeen: Home
1. Australian War Memorial (AWM), S00546, Doubleday interview, 1988
2. P. Scully interview, Friends of the Odd Bods Association Inc. website, <friendsofoddbods.com>
3. Letter to G. Buckham, 29 January 1944, Buckham family papers
4. G. Buckham interview with author, 2005
5. *BHP Review*, June 1975
6. AWM, Holden interview, 1989

Bibliography

Books

Asmussen, J. & Åkra, K., *Tirpitz: Hitler's Last Battleship*, Midt-Troms Museum, 2015

Belford, A.C., *Born to Fly*, Angus Belford, 1995

Bennett, D., *Pathfinder*, London: Panther, 1960

Bishop, P., *Bomber Boys*, London: HarperPress, 2007

Bishop, P., *Target Tirpitz*, London: Harper Press, 2012

Blundell, H.M (Nobby), *They Flew From Waddington!: 463–467 Lancaster Squadrons, Royal Australian Air Force*, Tour Committee of 463-467 Squadrons Association NSW, 1975

Brickhill, P., *The Dam Busters*, Pan, 1954

Burgess, C., *Australia's Dambusters*, Australian Military History Publications, 2003

Charlwood, D., *No Moon Tonight*, Goodall, 2004

Churchill, W., *The Second World War*, London: Cassell, 1951

Clayton, T. & Craig, P., *Finest Hour: The book of the BBC TV series*, London: Hodder & Stoughton, 1999

Cooper, A. & Perl, T., *Dispatch from Berlin, 1943*, Sydney: NewSouth Books, 2023

Currie, J., *Battle Under the Moon: The documented account of Mailly-le-Camp 1944*, Wilmslow: AirData Publications, 1995

Darlow, S., *Special Op: Bomber*, Ohio: David & Charles, 2008

Fenby, J., *The General: Charles de Gaulle and the France He Saved*, London: Simon & Schuster, 2010

Forsgren, J., *Sinking the Beast: the RAF 1944 Lancaster raids against Tirpitz*, Fonthill Media, 2014

Flower, S., *The Dam Busters: An operational history of Barnes Wallis' bombs*, Stroud: Amberley Publishing, 2013

Flynn, E., *My Wicked, Wicked Ways*, London: Aurum Press, 2005

Galland, A., *The First and the Last*, Melbourne: Readers Book Club, 1955

Grayling, A., *Among the Dead Cities: The history and moral legacy of the WWII bombing of civilians in Germany and Japan*, New York: Walker Books, 2006

Harris, A., *Bomber Offensive*, London: Collins, 1947

Hastings, M., *Bomber Command*, London: Book Club Associates, 1980

Hastings, M., *Chastise: The Dambusters story 1943*, London: William Collins, 2019

Herington, J., *Air War Against Germany and Italy 1939–43*, Canberra: Australian War Memorial, 1954

Herington, J., *Air Power Over Europe 1944–1945*, Canberra: Australian War Memorial, 1963

Horsley, D., *Billy Strachan 1921–1988*, Caribbean Labour Solidarity, 2019

Isaacson, P., *As I Remember Them: Men and women who shaped a life*, Clifton Hill: Red Dog Books, 2012

Iveson, T. & Milton, B., *Lancaster: The biography*, London: Andre Deutsch, 2009

Johnson, F., *RAAF Over Europe*, London: Eyre & Spottiswoode, 1946

Karlsch, R., *Hitler's Bomb*, Munich: Deutsche Verlags-Anstalt, 2005

Kingsford-Smith, R., 'I Wouldn't Have Missed It for Quids', privately published memoir

Lawrence, W.J., *No 5 Bomber Group RAF*, London: Faber, 1951

Leach, R., *An Illustrated History of RAF Waddington*, Bognor Regis: Woodfield, 2003

Mead, R., *Dambuster-in-Chief: The life of Air Marshal Ralph Cochrane*, Barnsley: Pen & Sword Aviation, 2020

Middlebrook, M., *The Berlin Raids: RAF Bomber Command Winter 1943–44*, London: Penguin Books, 1990

Middlebrook, M., *The Nuremberg Raid: 30–31 March 1944*, London: Cassell, 2000

Middlebrook, M. & Everitt, C., *The Bomber Command War Diaries*, New York: Viking, 1985

Moyes, P., *Bomber Squadrons of the RAF and Their Aircraft*, London: Macdonald, 1964

Nelson, H., *Chased by the Sun: The Australians in Bomber Command in WWII*, Sydney: Allen & Unwin, 2006

Overy, R., *The Bombing War: Europe 1939–1945*, London: Allen Lane, 2013

Probert, H., *Bomber Harris: His life and times*, Barnsley: Greenhill Books, 2003

Reid, R., *Bomber Command: Australians in World War II*, Canberra: Department of Veterans Affairs, 2012

Robson, M., *The Lancaster Bomber Pocket Manual*, London: Conway, 2012

Roskill, S.W., *The War at Sea: Vol III, The Offensive Part 1: 1st June 1943–31st May 1944*, London: HMSO, 1960

Smith, N., *Tirpitz: The Halifax Raids*, Walton-on-Thames: Air Research Publications, 1994

Spick, M., *Avro Lancaster: An illustrated guide shown in over 100 images*, Wigston: Lorenz Books, 2015

Sweetman, J., *Tirpitz: Hunting the Beast*, Stroud: Sutton Publishing, 2000

Veitch, M., *Heroes of the Skies*, London: Penguin, 2015

Ward, C., *5 Group Bomber Command: An operational record*, Barnsley: Pen & Sword Aviation, 2007

Reports, Journals

'Tirpitz: An account of various attacks carried out by the British Armed Forces and their effect upon the German Battleship', vol 2, 1948, accessed on the Royal Australian Navy website: <https://www.navy.gov.au/media-room/publications/wwii-naval-staff-histories> (see 'Account of attacks on the Tirpitz (Vol. 2): Evidence for Detailed Accounts of Damage') / <https://www.navy.gov.au/sites/default/files/documents/Battle_Summary_Tirpitz_Vol_2.pdf>

Gledhill, G.A., 'Battleship Turpitz [sic] – Operation Tungsten', *Slipstream*, Journal of the Fleet Air Arm Association of Australia Inc., vol. 18, no. 3, 2007

Kingdon, C., 'Behind Closed Doors: Revisiting Air Command's "Lack of Moral Fiber and Waverer Disposal Policy" and its "Treatment" of Neurotic Cases, 1941–1945', *Chicago Journal of History*, issue 2, Fall 2013

Films, Documentaries

Fairhead, D. & Palmer, A. (directors), *Lancaster* (film), Trevor Beattie Films, 2022

Mirzoeff, E. (director), *Target Tirpitz* (documentary film), BBC, 1973

Read, N. (director), *Finest Hour* (television series), BBC Television, 1999

Watt, H. (director), *Target for Tonight* (documentary film), Crown Film Unit, 1941

Archives

Australians at War Film Archive, University of New South Wales

Australian War Memorial, Keith Murdoch Sound Archive of Australia in the War of 1939–45, Canberra

Bomber Command Museum of Canada Archives, Nanton

Imperial War Museum Sound Archive, London

International Bomber Command Centre Digital Archive, University of Lincoln

BIBLIOGRAPHY

National Archives of Australia, Sydney
Public Record Office, National Archives, London
Royal Australian Navy, website
The British Library, London
The National Archives, London

Index